Chen Wenling 陈文令

Chen Wenling 陈文令

CHARTA

Design 设计
Fayçal Zaouali

Editorial Coordination 主编
Filomena Moscatelli

Copyediting 英文编辑
Emily Ligniti（English 英文）
中文：艾米丽 李昵缇（Chinese 中文）

Translation 中文翻译
Bruce Doar
中文：布鲁斯 多尔（中文）
Ling Chen Kelley: 刘凌尘（中文）

Copywriting and Press Office 文案与新闻办公室
Silvia Palombi

Promotion and Web 推广与网页
Elisa Legnani

Distribution 发行
Anna Visaggi

Administration 行政
Grazia De Giosa

Warehouse and Outlet 仓储与销售
Roberto Curiale

e-mail: charta@chartaartbooks.it
www.chartaartbooks.it
Cover 封面
Chen wenling （英文）
陈文令（中文）

Photo Credits 图片来源
Shengwu Zou 邹盛武（中文）
Guiming Li 李贵明（中文）
Shanlong Liu 刘善龙（中文）
Xuefeng Cao 曹雪风 （中文）

Edizioni Charta srl
Milano
via della Moscova, 27 - 20121
Tel. +39-026598098/026598200
Fax +39-026598577

CONTENTS 目录

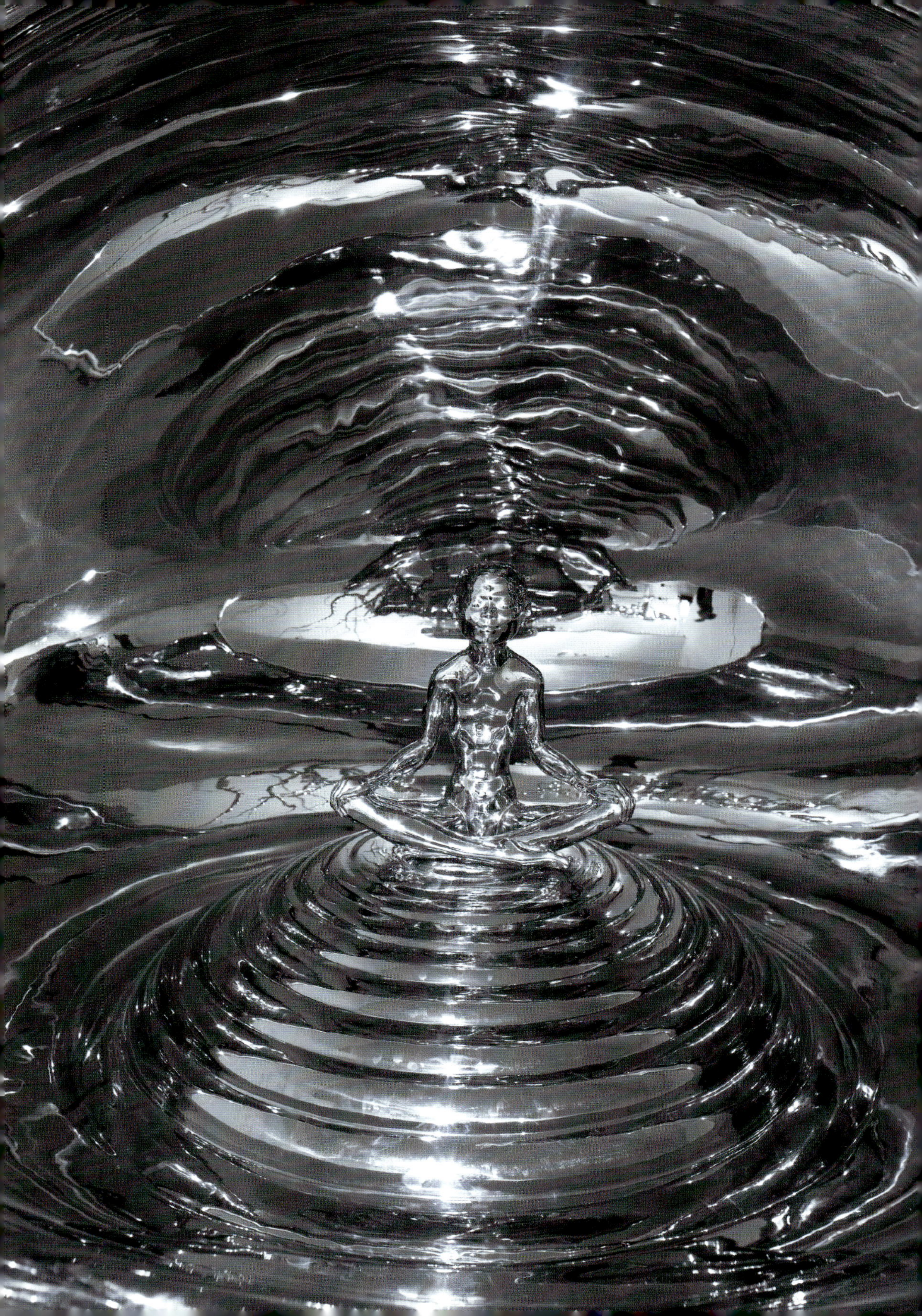

Chen Wenling:
A Well Grounded Form

Fan Di'an

In the Chinese contemporary art world, Chen Wenling is aptly described as one of the prominent new artists who quickly established a distinctive artistic image for himself. Relying on his sustained efforts and exuberant creativity, he successively created several series of works that made him known in the art world, and his participation in a variety of exhibitions and activities caught the public eye. More importantly, his works are imbued with the credibility of his artistic development's inherent logic, and so they have a fresh and original style. In the creation of contemporary art, the unity of conceptual individuality and style is in the first instance a basic measure of artistic maturity and this achievement demonstrates that Chen Wenling has succeeded in constructing his own world.

Many critics have pointed out that Chen Wenling's art has its origins in the real soil of "consumer society," and that is true. For artists of Chen Wenling's generation, the development of the culture of social consumption brought about by China's socio-economic growth and material prosperity has profoundly influenced them, in terms of both visual perception and cultural context, and presented them with the problem of how they incisively convey their own perception of consumer culture and find ways to create narratives and images to express and conceptualize their perceptions. From Chen Wenling's works created over more than a decade, we can see he has retained a firm grip on his sense of focus as he constantly strives in his exploration and refinement of art language to utilize visual images to express precise perceptions. On the subject of "consumer society," all his efforts are expended on how to depict the specific theme of "images of desire" in sculpture, enshrining the characteristics of a social reality in its representation as image.

It can be said that Chen Wenling's art reveals strong characteristics of the new realism. He is sensitive to the socially nurtured hedonism in an age of extremely inflated consumption, and he is invariably looking for ways to express, expose, and critique the language of secular reality, with the result that he has found the key to expression in the "bio-logicality" of his humans and animals. The works firstly express humans in certain ecstatic or joyous states, and these extremely personal states reveal the nature of material desire, that can also be seen as the artistic distension of scenes of material life. He has also sculpted a large number of humans and animals together, revealing how the boundaries disappear between people and animals and between human behavior and animal behavior. In the psychological states expressed in the images, people's facial expressions assume animal-like simplicity and devotion, while his animals take on human moods and desires. Whether human or animal, all are similarly aberrant psychologically and hysterically overwrought. This approach entails the juxtaposition of "anthropomorphism" (personification) and "materialization" (hypostatization) and, in adopting these methods in his exploratory process, Chen Wenling also diversifies and augments the language he uses for these methods in his successive works, thereby delivering a self-contained internal force driving the trend of his artistic development.

Chen Wenling is, to a certain extent, an artist who is faithful to sculpture, unlike many artists of the same generation who are interested in constantly converting from one artistic medium to another, and he persists in sustained in-depth exploration of sculpture as an art form. The most distinctive feature of his work is his sculptural presentation of the sense of "distension." In shaping his images of people and animals, he generously uses tangible body mass and elastic curves, so that the abstract concept of "desire" saturates the body of the image, the sense of texture of the skin, and the lines throughout the body, and there is a sense that the sculpture flows from the inside outwards. With his works in recent years, he has been making use of much bulkier bodies or replicating single images to construct hallucinatory landscapes in which people and objects as well as plants and animals, are joined together wholly or in part to form a diffuse and continuous atmospheric environment that reflects the riotous colors of reality but is imbued with a strong illusory sense. In many cases, Chen Wenling is not producing sculpture embodying one specific image, but is using sculptural language to create scenes replete with life and the breath of life.

When an artist has a fresh and distinct formal language, the source of his or her art form is also susceptible to interrogation. This question is not only relevant to Chen Wenling, but is in fact applicable to Chinese contemporary art in its entirety, and to answer the questions raised or to find answers to them, it is necessary to proceed both from the sources of the ideas of the artist and from the sources of the language of the artist. From the perspective of Chen Wenling's life experience, both these sources are in the first instance identical. His works appear to embody the strong qualities of fable, while the people and objects in his works are the embodiment of proliferating "desire," but the soil in which the seeds of this desire were planted is not merely the urban soil of economic and social development, but also the soil of rural folkways and practices. The village of southern Fujian in which Chen Wenling spent his childhood is set in a countryside rich in folklore and imbued with the desires and ideals of wealth; as material life there continued to improve, people's material desires expanded and extended to become a social psychological trend, at the same time as they shaped a new view of life. These environmental elements have obviously and directly influenced Chen Wenling's consciousness, and even though he had no intention of documenting or producing an overall description of this lifestyle he did directly experience it. Yet he was able to express the "feel" of this sense of desire, and through the expression of this "sense" he created realistic scenarios that are specific and fresh. Thus, the language of his art is not simply an existing style drawn from the history of art, but one created from his own history and experience of real life; of course, in the process, the rich local cultural scenes and visual modeling inspired him. To a certain extent, the forms and language of Chen Wenling's works with their exaggerated shapes and voluptuous body forms have an unspoken affinity with southern Fujian's folk art traditions, and he sensitively captures the visual elements of his life experiences and subjects them to extreme reworking.

Chen Wenling has held many exhibitions, but this exhibition is different from past shows; in addition to his recent sculptures on display, he also documents a return visit to his hometown, to take part in the filming of a temple fair. In the riotous energy of these folk activities, we can clearly see the locale in which Chen Wenling's art originated. The teeming ritual site with the strength of its ostentatious material display forms an incredible visual spectacle. These two types of work (the video record and his sculpture) both in content and in form, are clearly related, and also reveal the root of the true mystery of Chen Wenling's creative work over recent years. In this sense, Chen Wenling's art can be said to be "a well grounded form." [2008]

陈文令：形有所据

范迪安

在中国当代艺术界，陈文令堪称一位迅速建立起自己艺术面貌的新锐人物。凭借着持续的努力和旺盛的创造力，他的作品一个系列接着一个系列面见艺坛，参加到多种展览活动之中，引人注目。更重要的是，他的作品因具有他自己艺术发展逻辑内在的牢靠性而获得鲜明的风格。在当代艺术创造中，观念的个性和风格的个性二者的统一至少是艺术成熟的基本标尺，在这个尺度上，陈文令构筑起了自己的世界。

已经有不少评论家指出陈文令的艺术源发于"消费社会"的现实土壤，事实上正是如此。对陈文令这一代艺术家来说，中国社会经济增长、物质富裕所带来的社会消费文化的发展，无论在视觉感性上还是在文化语境层面都给他们以深刻的影响，问题在于在传达自己对消费文化的感知上如何鞭辟入里，找到表达的方式，实现观念的陈述与形象的创造。从陈文令十多年来的作品中，可以看到他始终扣紧自己专注的感觉，也始终在艺术语言上探索与锤炼，力求用可视的形象表达精准的感知。在"消费社会"这个主题上，他的全部努力都落实在如何塑造"欲望的形象"这个具体的命题上，使一种社会现实的特征得到形象的表述。

可以说，陈文令的艺术透露出一种强烈的新现实主义的特征。他敏感于在一个极速膨胀的消费时代里社会滋生的享乐主义，一直在寻找表达、揭露并批判这种世俗现实的语言，其结果是在人与动物的"生物性"上找到了表达的契机。他的作品首先表现了人处于某种狂喜或者快乐的状态，在极度自我的状态中暴露出物欲的本性，这也可以视为是对物质生活场景的艺术放大。他也大量将人与动物塑造在一起，表达了人与动物、人的行为与动物的行为界限消失的情形。在形象的精神状态上，人的表情如动物般的简单和痴迷，而动物则有着拟人式的心境和欲望。而无论是人或者动物，都是那样精神异常，幸福亢奋。这是一种"拟人化"和"拟物化"并置的方法，陈文令在探索的过程中获得了这样一种方法，也按照这种方法在不断的作品系列中使语言获得增值与繁衍，由此形成一种自足的具有内在驱动力的发展态势。

在某种程度上，陈文令是一位信守雕塑力量的艺术家，他不像许多同代人对艺术的媒介有不断转换的兴趣，而是坚持在雕塑这种艺术形式上作深度的探寻。他的作品最鲜明的特征是对于"膨胀"这种感觉的造型。在人与动物的形象塑造上，他运用了宽厚浑实的体块和大量有弹性的曲线，使"欲望"这个抽象的概念透过形象的体积、肌肤的质感和通体的线条得以传达，并且有一种从内部涨溢出来的感性。在近年的作品中，他更多地使用庞大体量的作品或单个形象的重复构成一种种令人迷幻的景观，在那里，人与物、植物与动物、物的整体与细节粘连在一起，形成弥漫和延绵的氛境，折射出现实的斑斓光彩，又有强烈的虚幻性。在许多情况下，陈文令已经不是在雕塑一个具体的形象，而是运用雕塑的语言形成一种充满生活与生命气息的场景。

　　当一个艺术家拥有某种形式语言的鲜明特征时，对其艺术形式的来源也容易受到诘问。这个问题不仅对陈文令是可能发生的，其实对整个中国当代艺术都是通用的，回答这个问题或者找到这个问题的答案，需要既从艺术家的观念来源也要从艺术家的语言来源两个方面去做追寻。从陈文令的生活经历来看，这两个来源首先具有同一性。他的作品看上去有很强的寓言性，作品中的人和物都是被放大的"欲望"的体现，但是这种欲望所萌生的土壤不仅来自经济社会发展的都市土壤，也包括来自乡土的生活习俗。陈文令自幼生活在福建南部的乡村，在那里，浓郁的乡土习俗充满对于富裕的祈愿与理想，在物质生活得以不断提高的情形下，物质性欲望的膨胀与扩展成为一种社会心理趋势，也同时形成了新的生活景观。这些环境元素对陈文令的思想意识显然有着直接的感染，尽管他无意总体的描述这种活生生的情境，但是他却有着直接的感受。他所能做的也就是表达欲望感的"感"字，并且通过对"感"的表达使现实的情境变得具体而又鲜活。在这个意义上，他的艺术语言不是简单地来自艺术史中已有的风格，而是来自他自己经历和体验过的生活气息，当然在这个过程中，乡土文化浓郁的场景和视觉的造型也给予他以启发。在某种程度上，陈文令作品中夸张的造型和浑圆的体块等形式语言与闽南民间艺术中的传统有着暗合的关系，他敏感地捕捉到了生活经验中的视觉元素，并且将这些元素予以推向极端的处理。

　　陈文令已经举办过多次展览，但是这次展览与以往不同的是除了展出他新近的雕塑作品，同时还展现他重返故里、参加家乡庙会所拍摄的场景。在极为热烈的民俗活动中，我们可以清楚地看到陈文令艺术的本土来源。在那里铺天盖地的祭祀场面所展现出物质的力量，已匪夷所思地形成一种视觉奇观。这两类作品——影像的纪录与他的雕塑，无论在内容上还是在形式上都具有清晰的关联，也揭示出陈文令这些年艺术创作的真正谜底。在这个意义上，陈文令的艺术可以说是"形有所据"。

[2008]

Page 6
The Illusor Part / 幻界局部, 2012

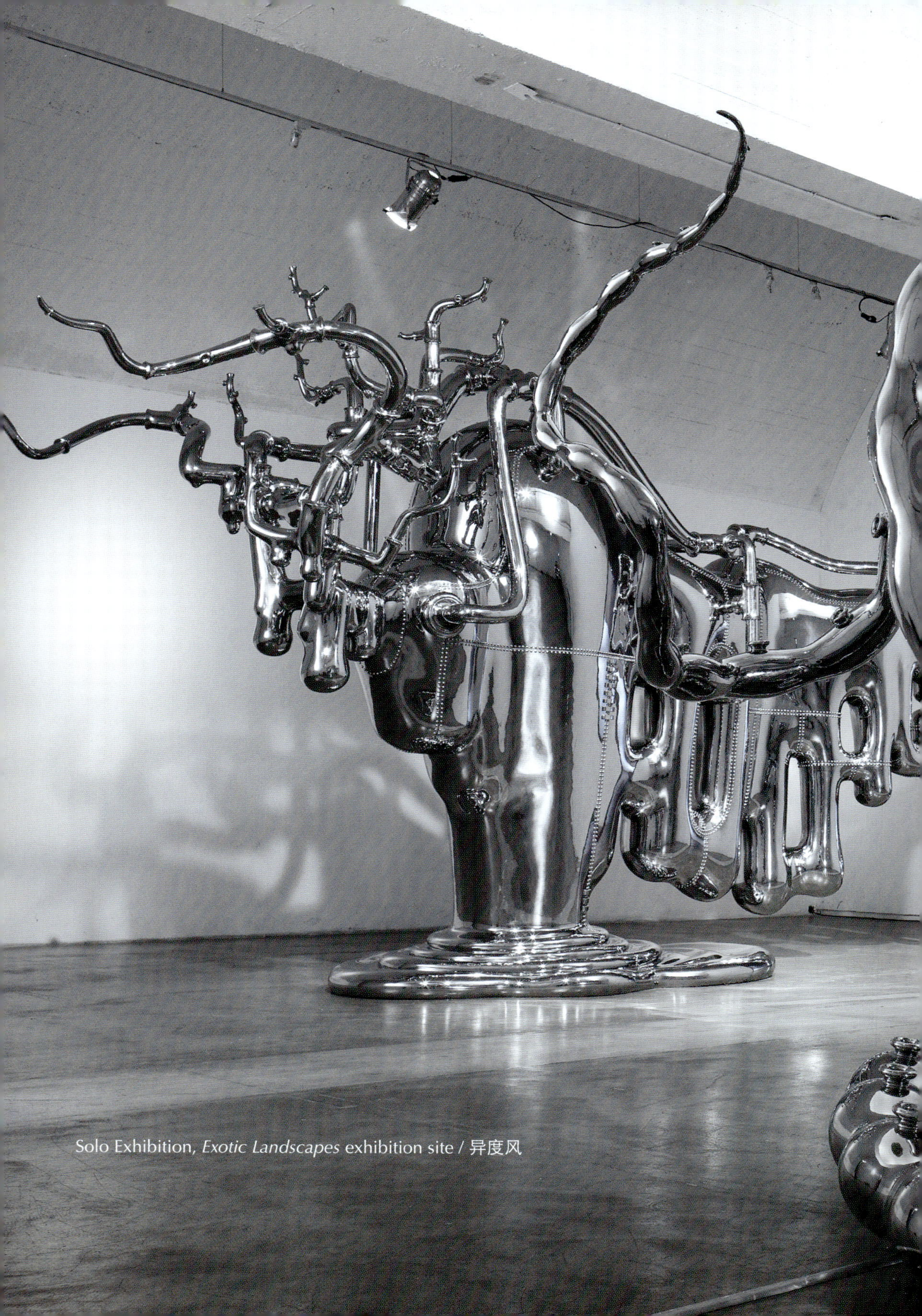

Solo Exhibition, *Exotic Landscapes* exhibition site / 异度风

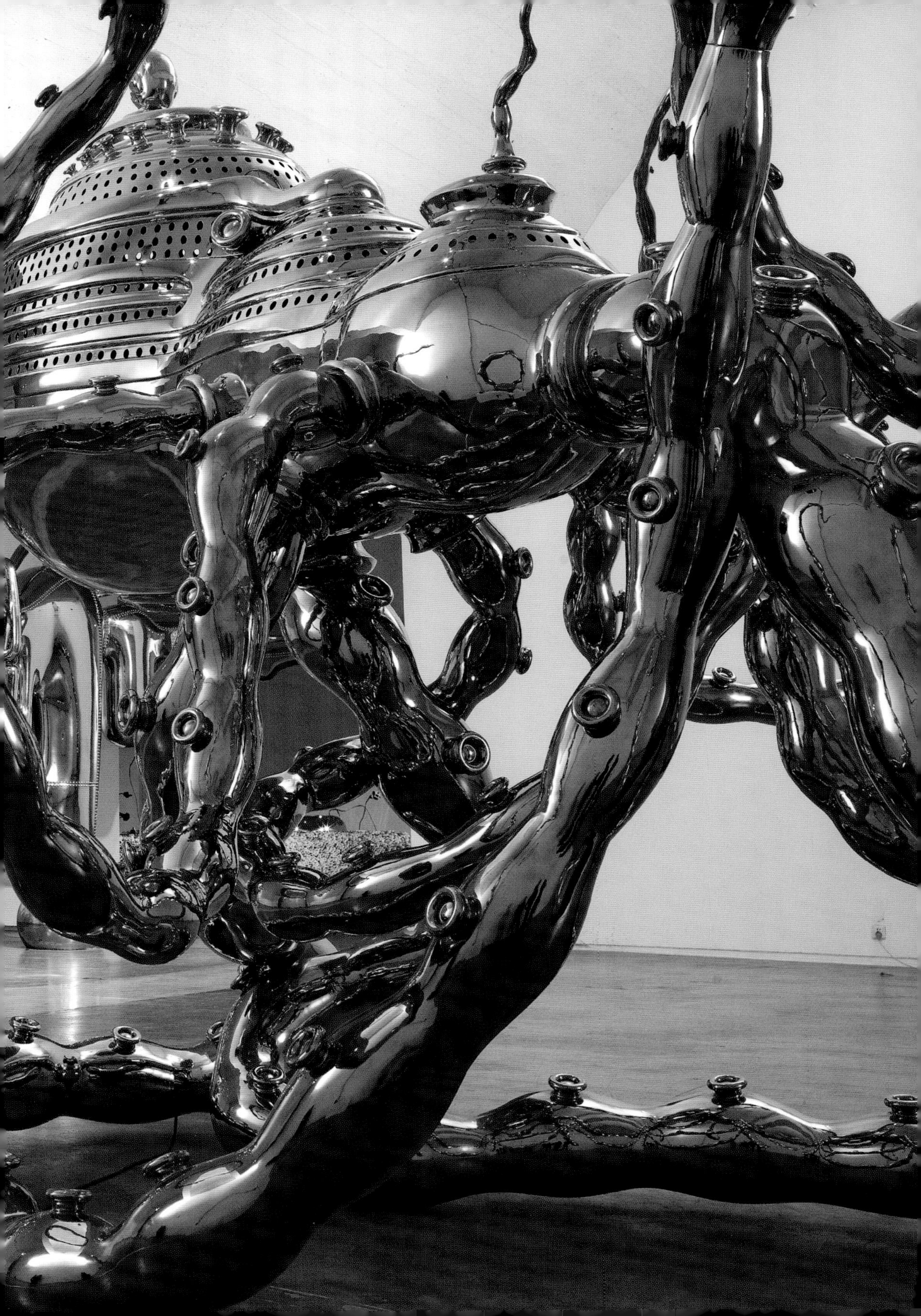

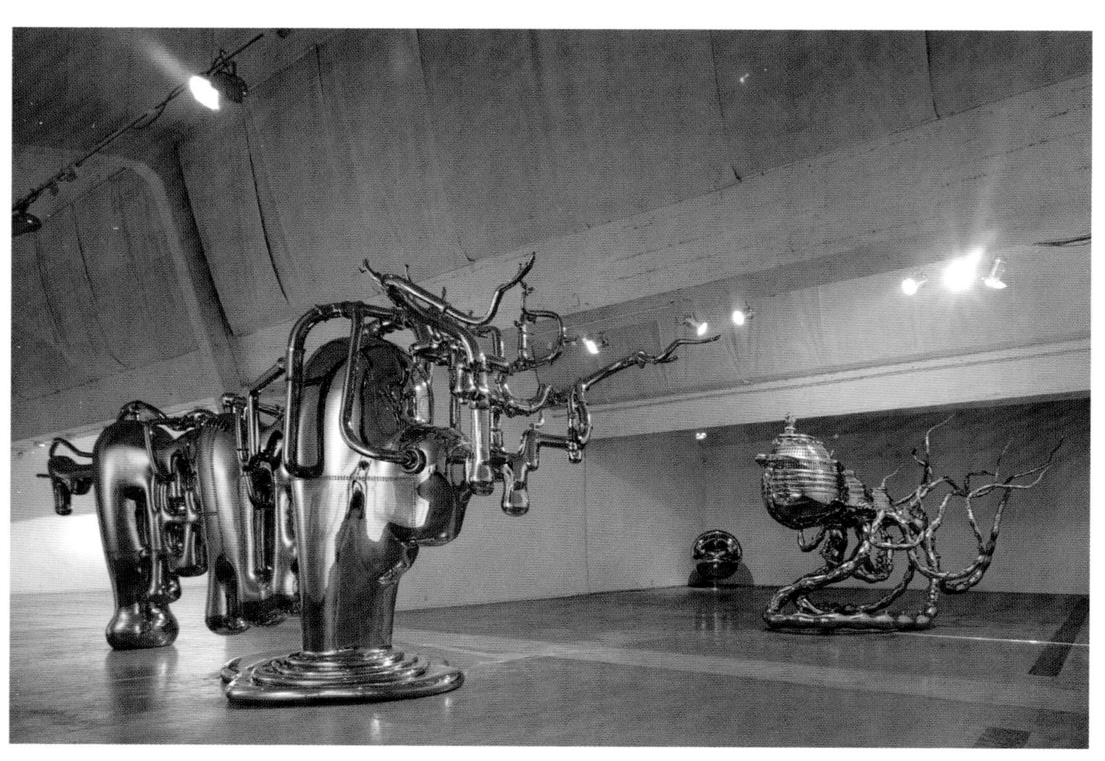

Solo Exhibition, *Exotic Landscapes* exhibition site / 异度风景个展现场

pp. 15, 16
Ark of Transcendence / 超验的方舟, 2012

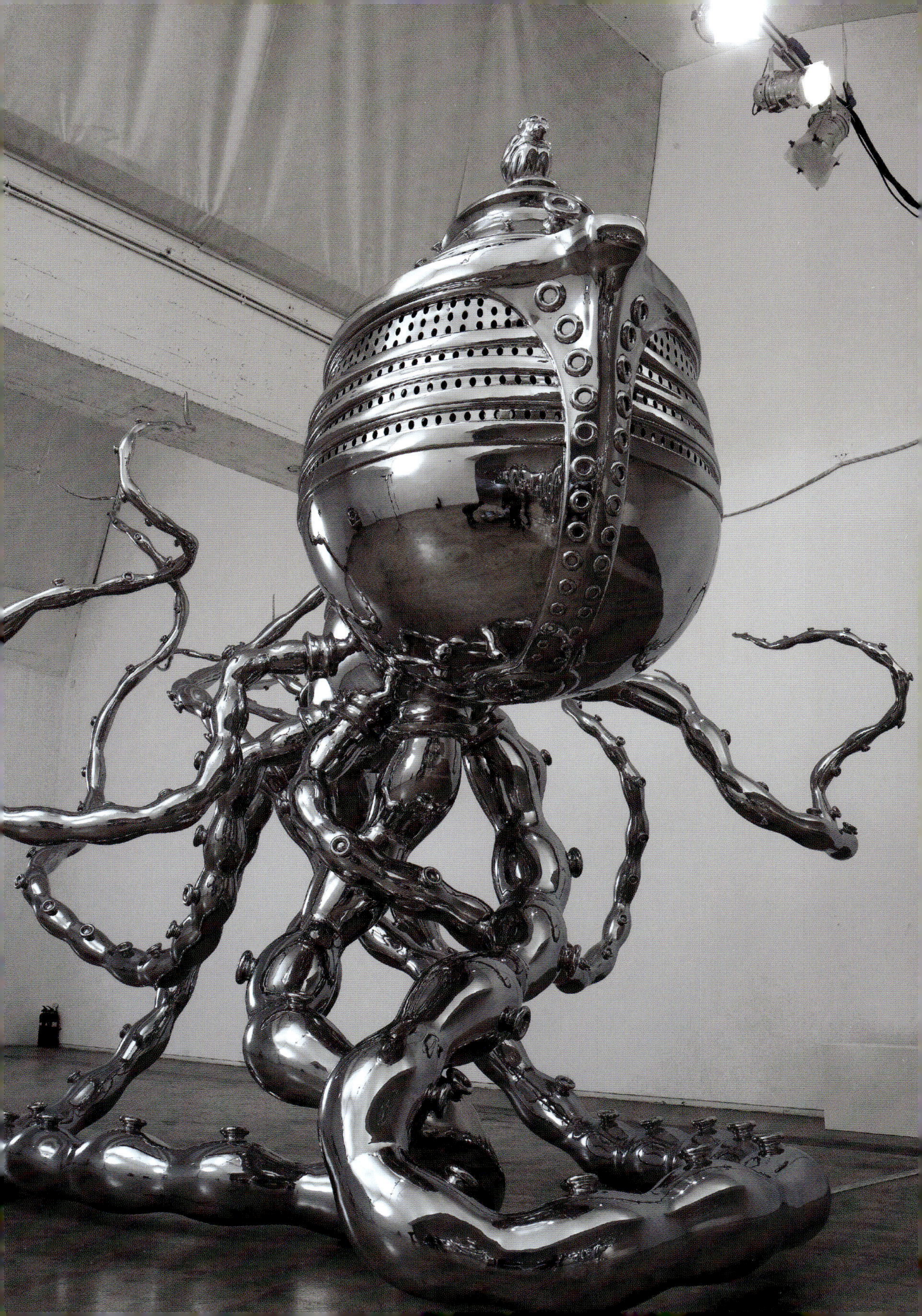

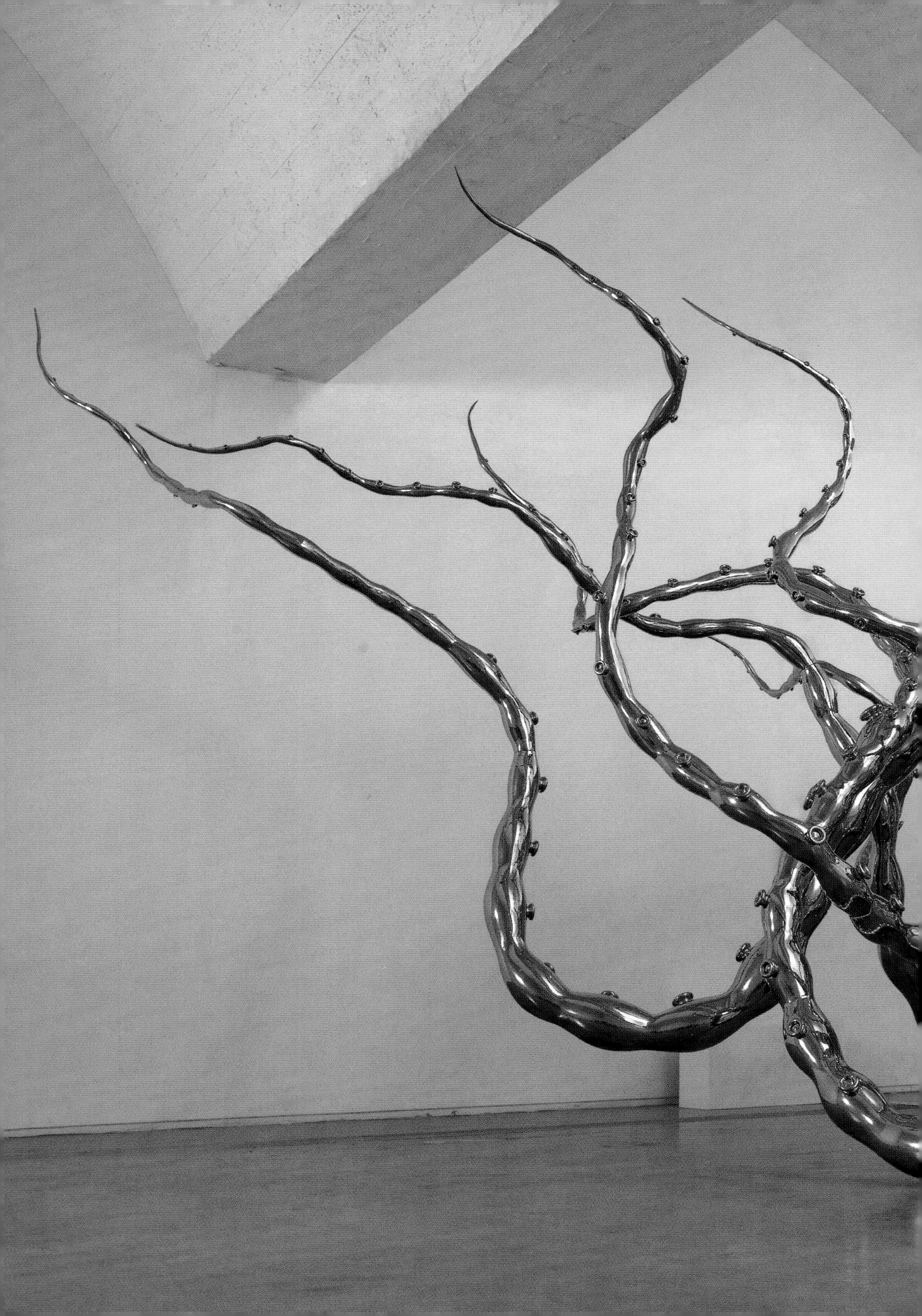

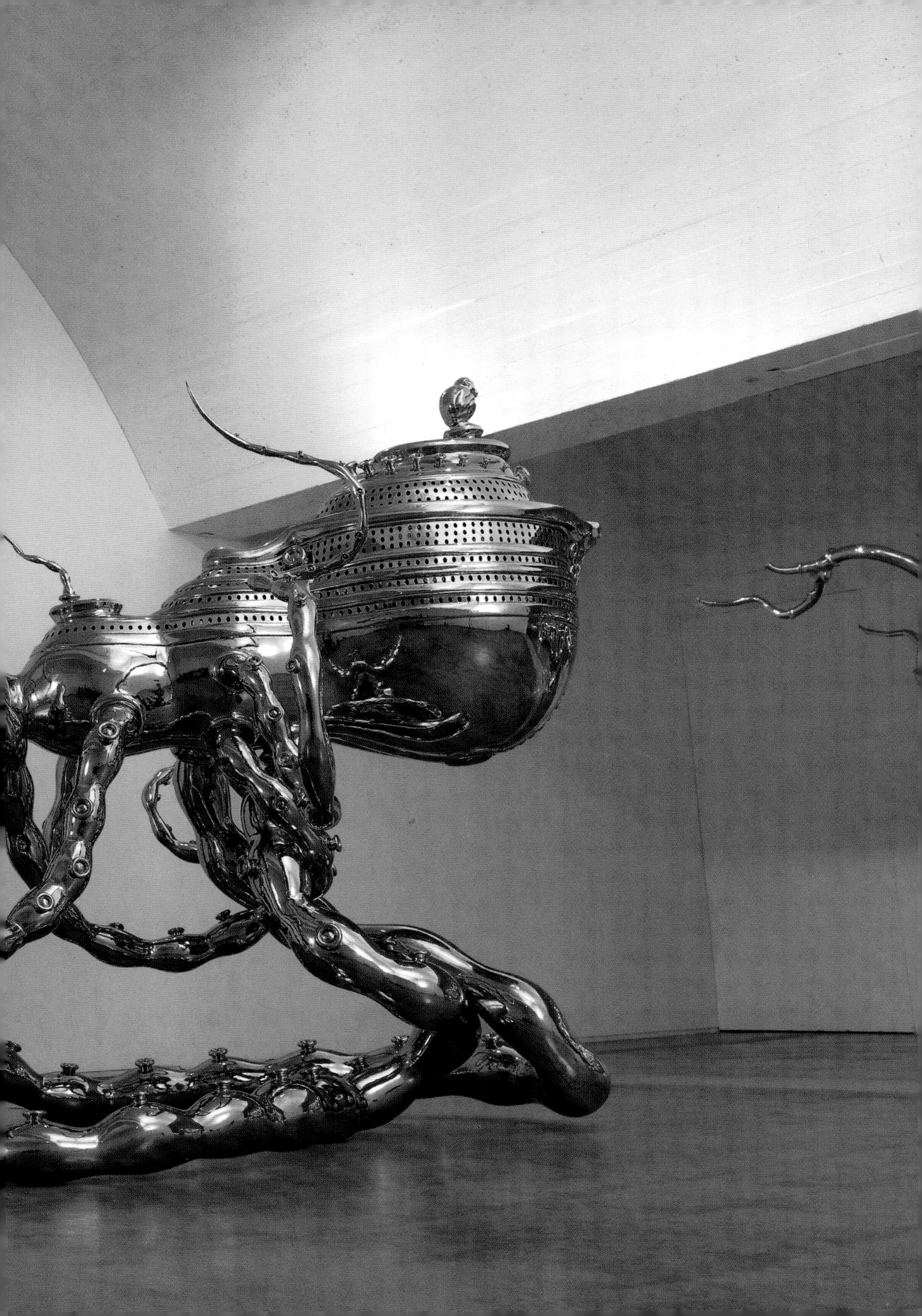

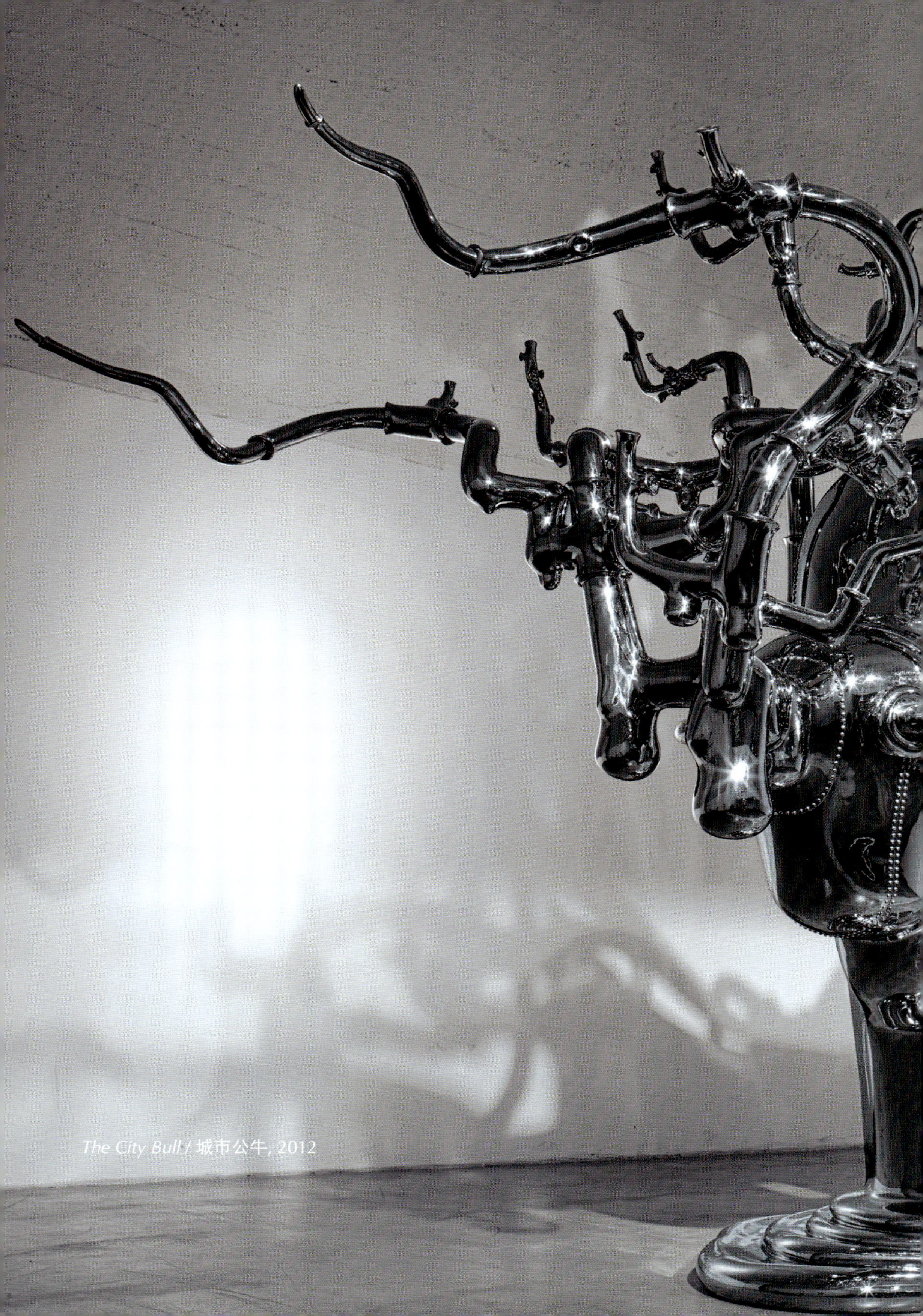

The City Bull / 城市公牛, 2012

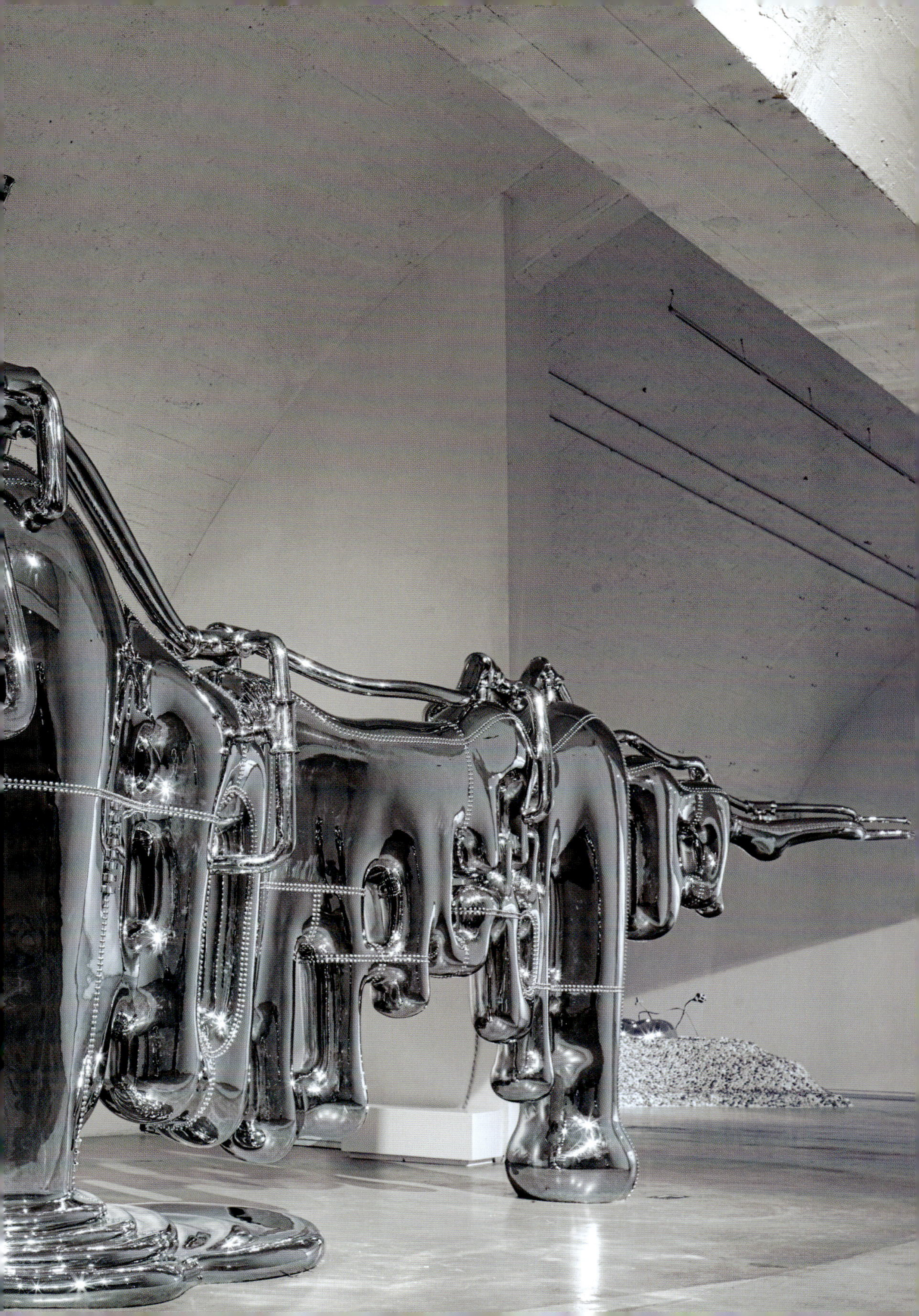

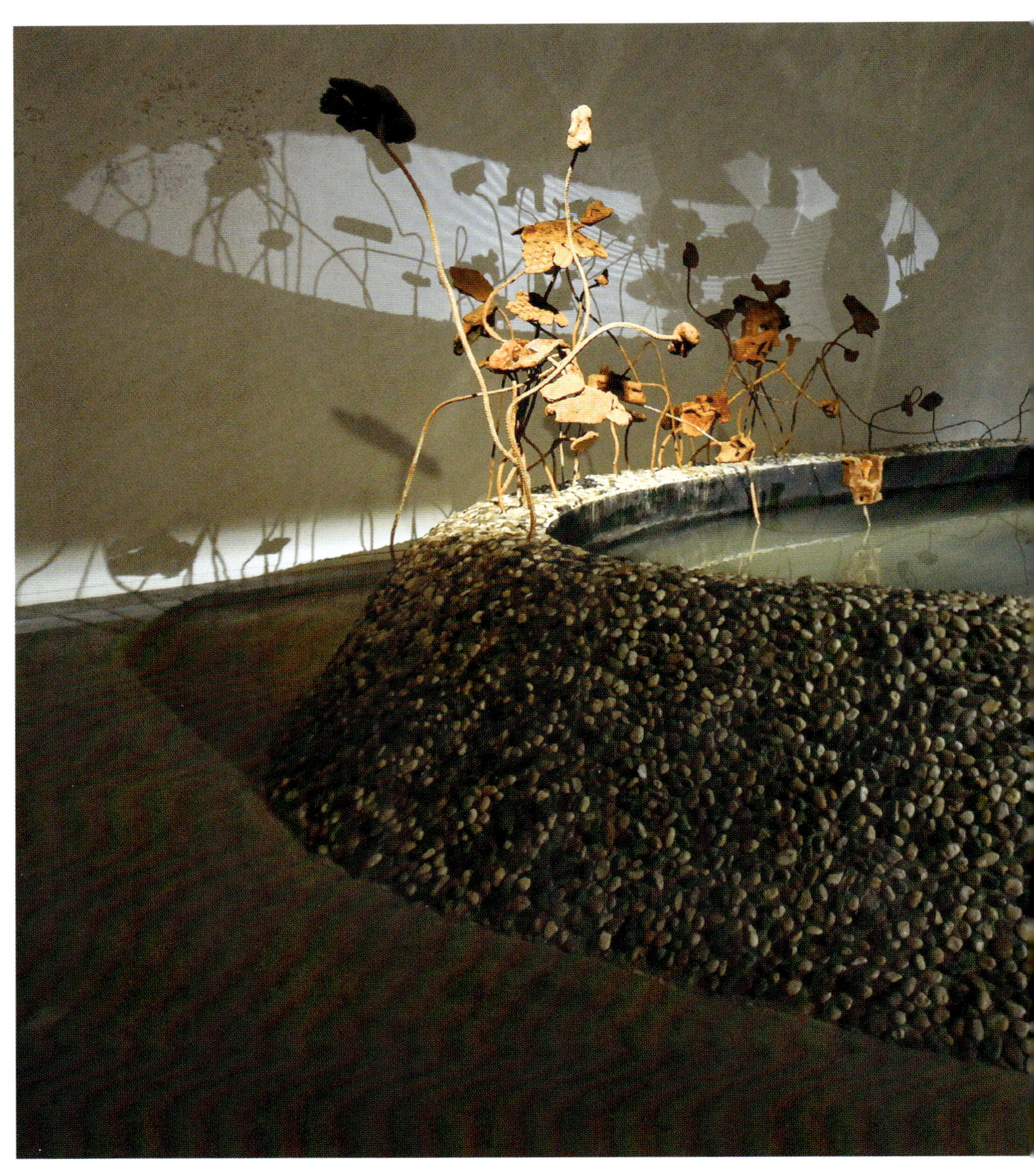

Building the Garden / 造园, 2012

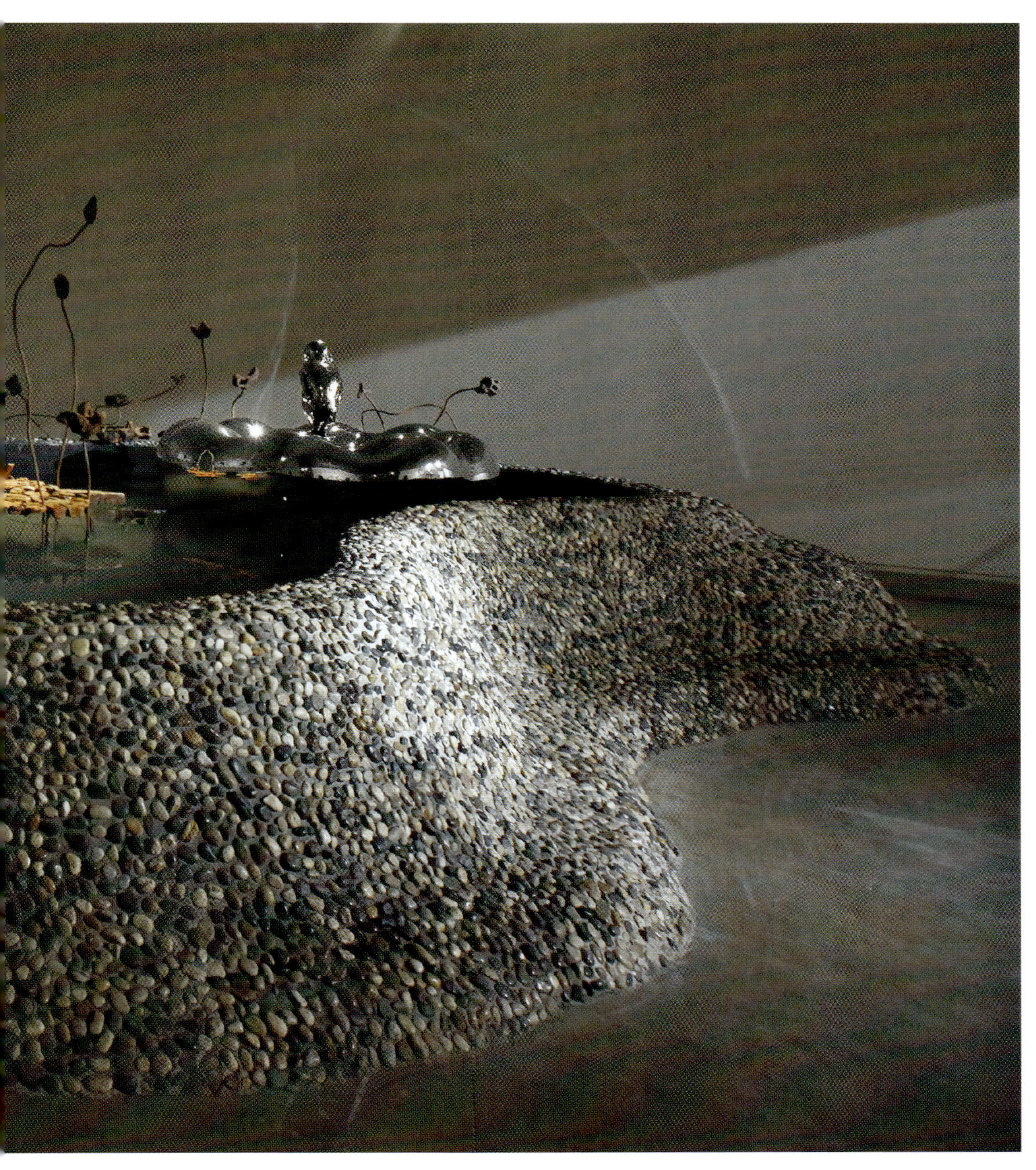

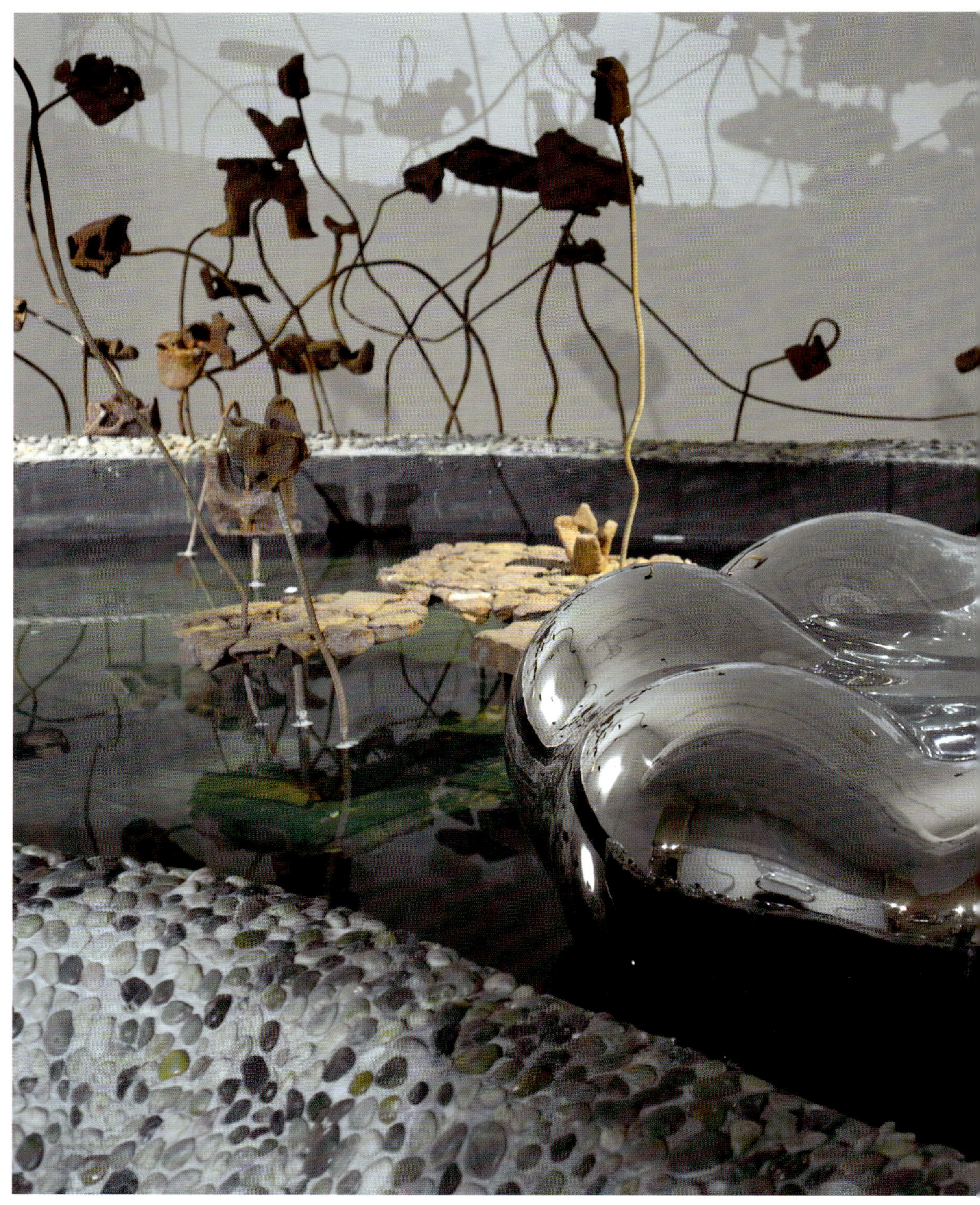

Building the Garden Part / 造园局部, 2012

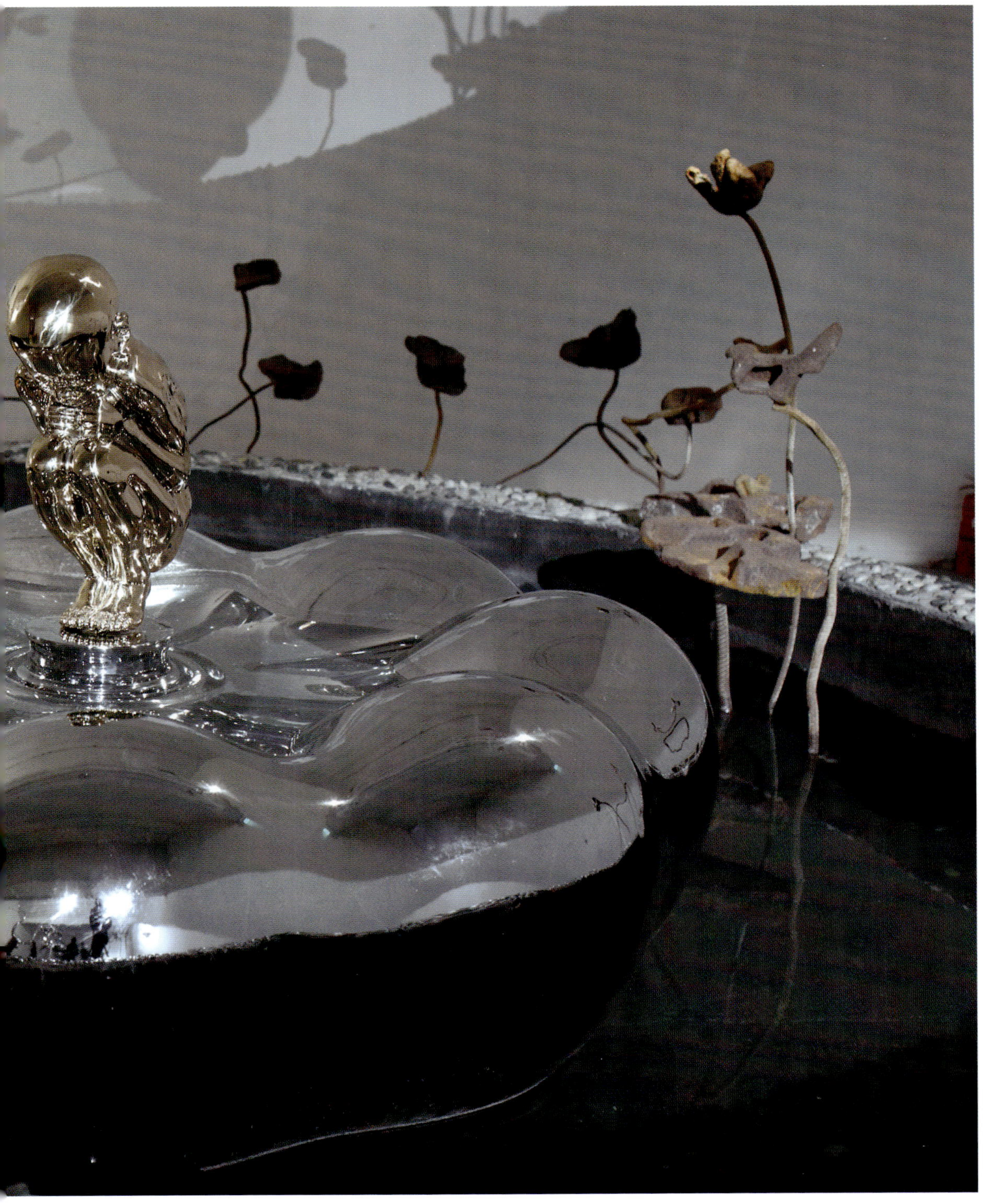

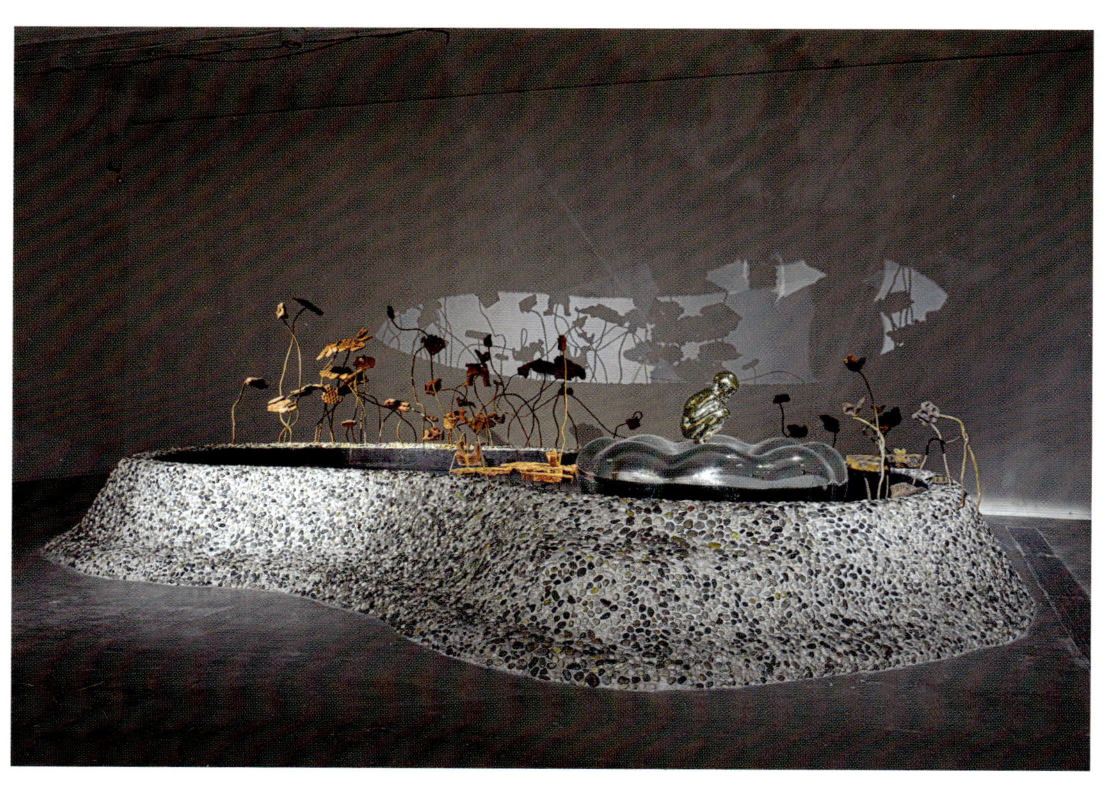

Building the Garden / 造园, 2012

pp. 25, 26
Building the Garden Part / 造园局部, 2012

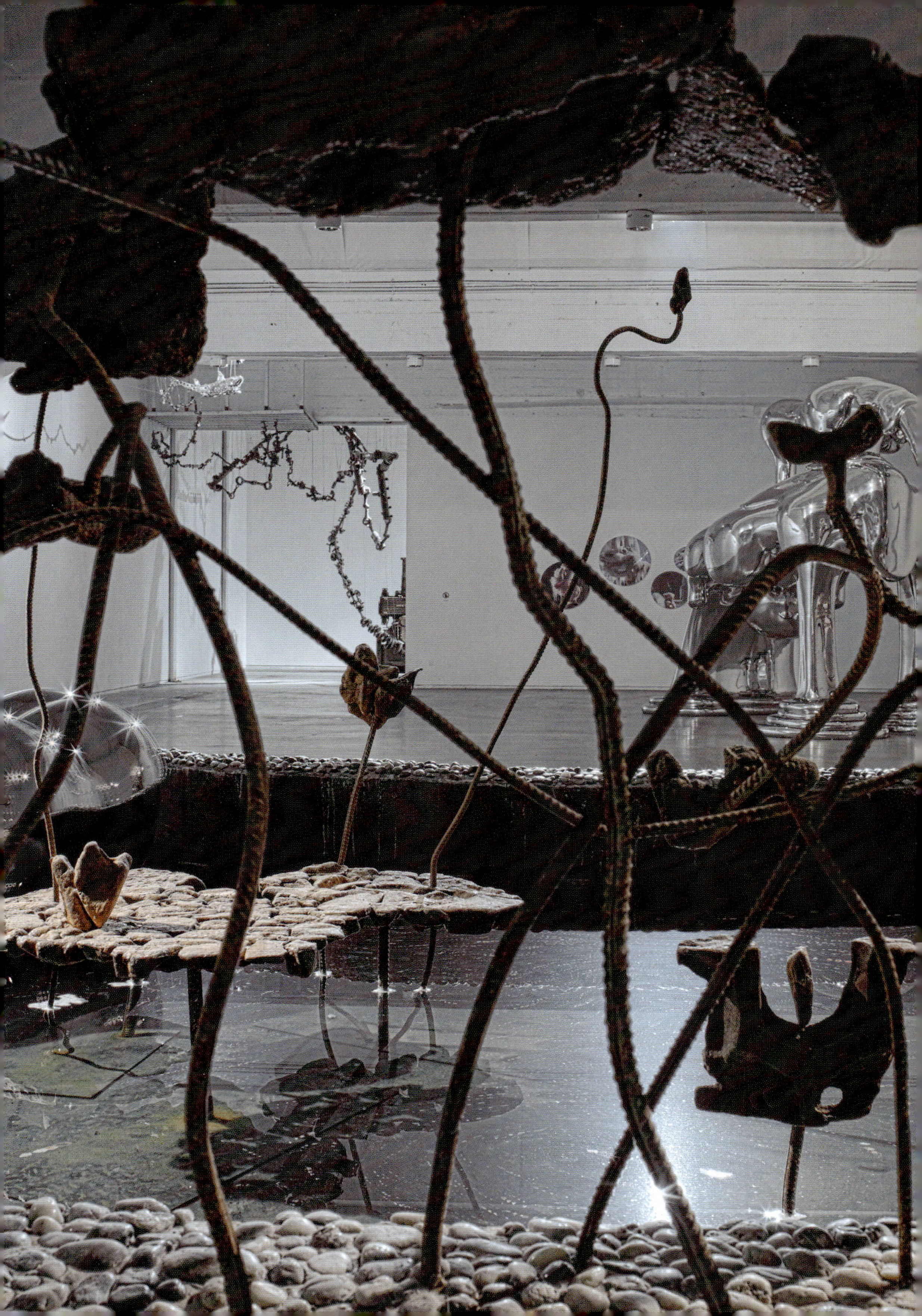

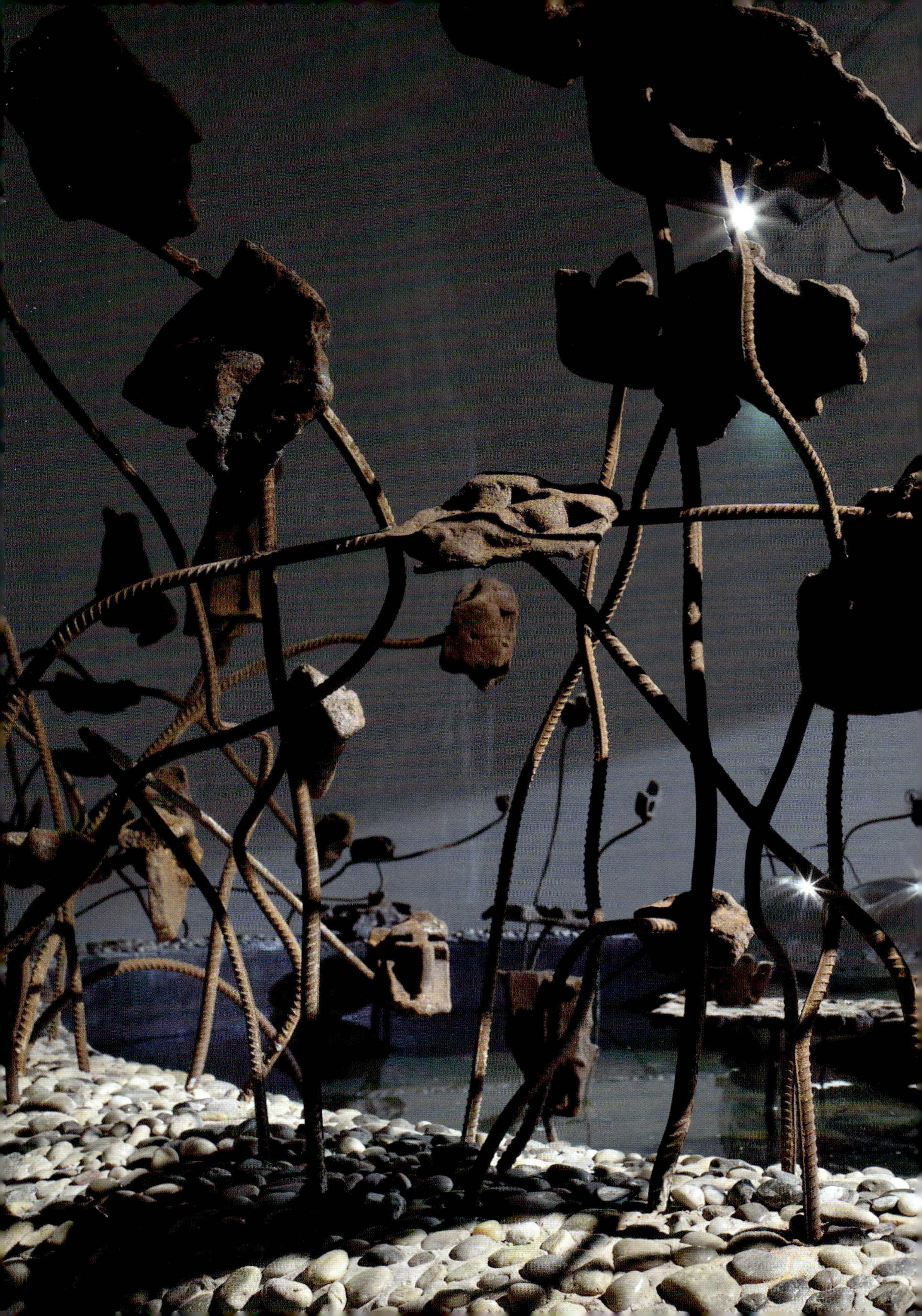

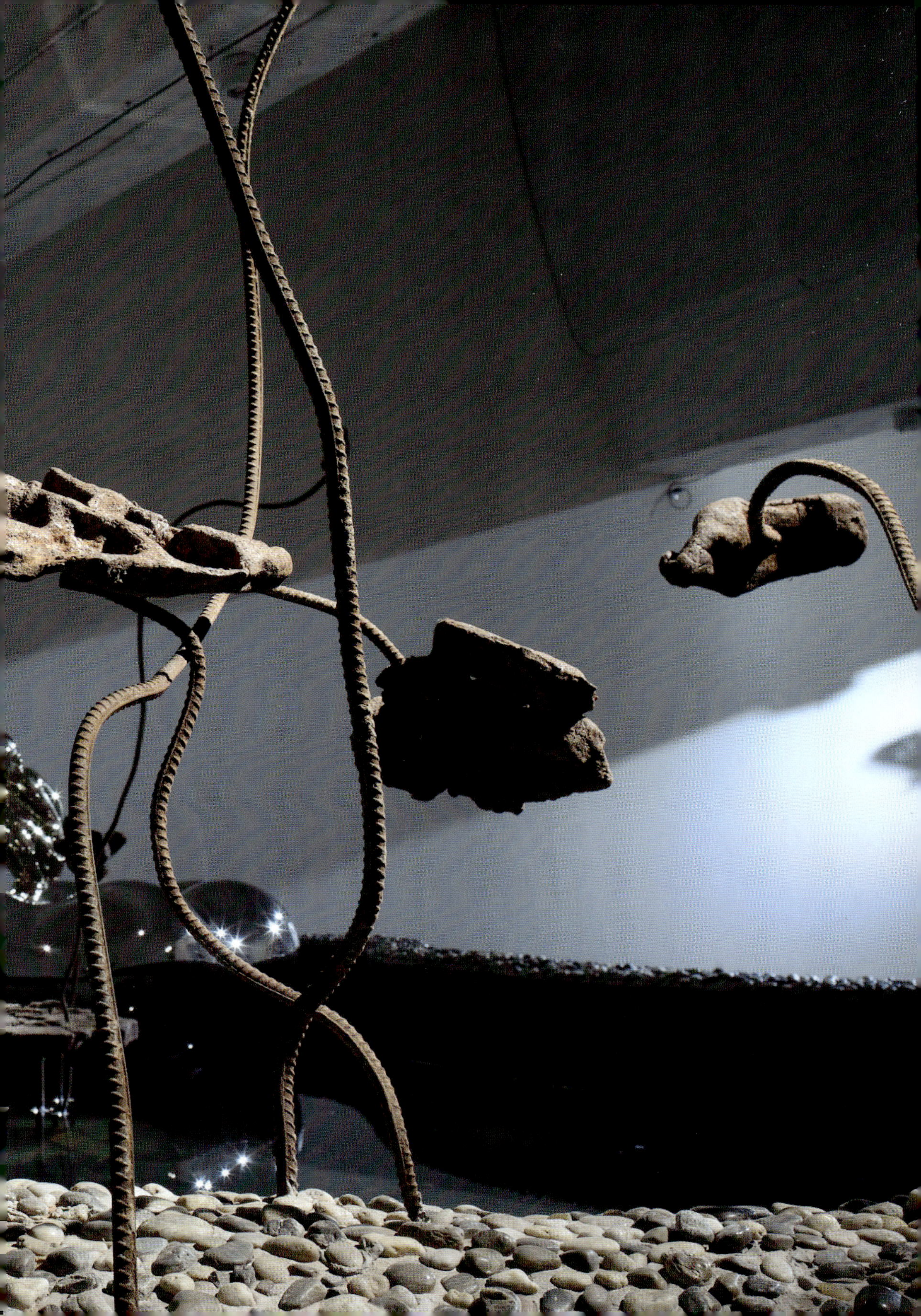

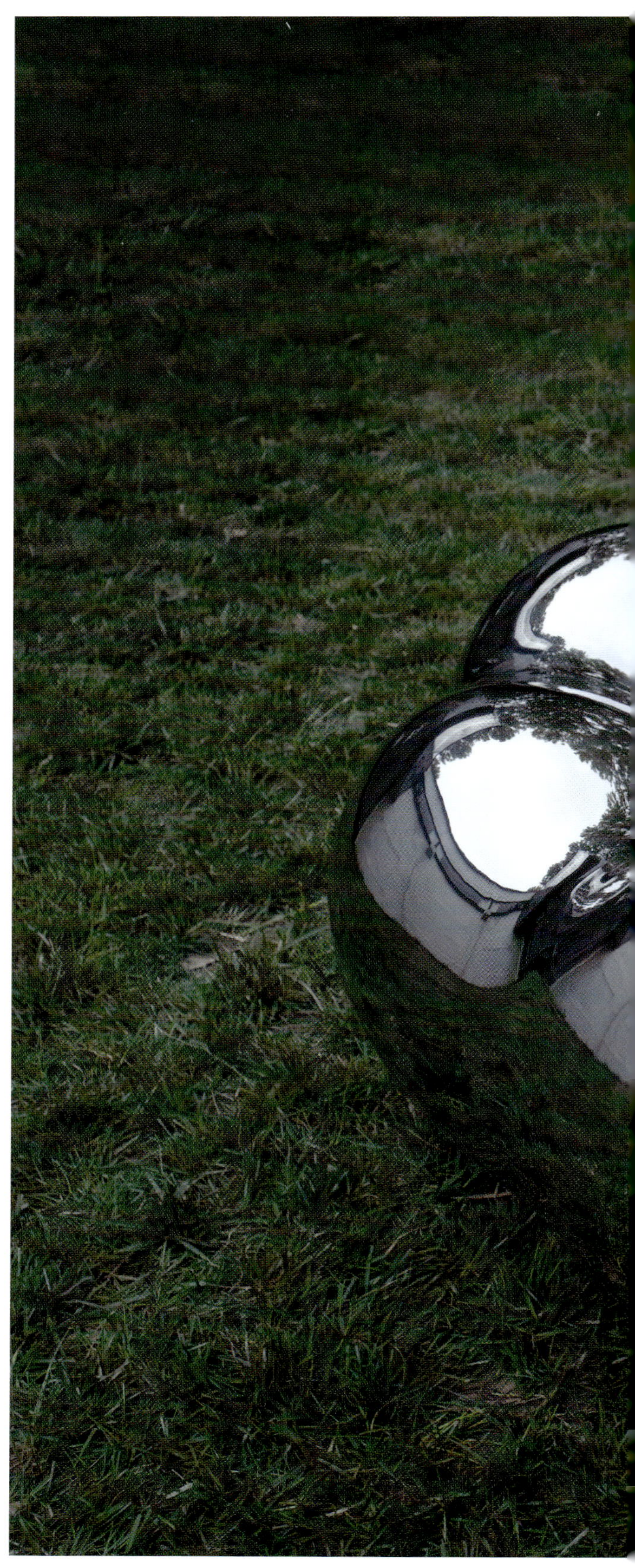

The Floating Room of Desire /
漂流欲室, 2012

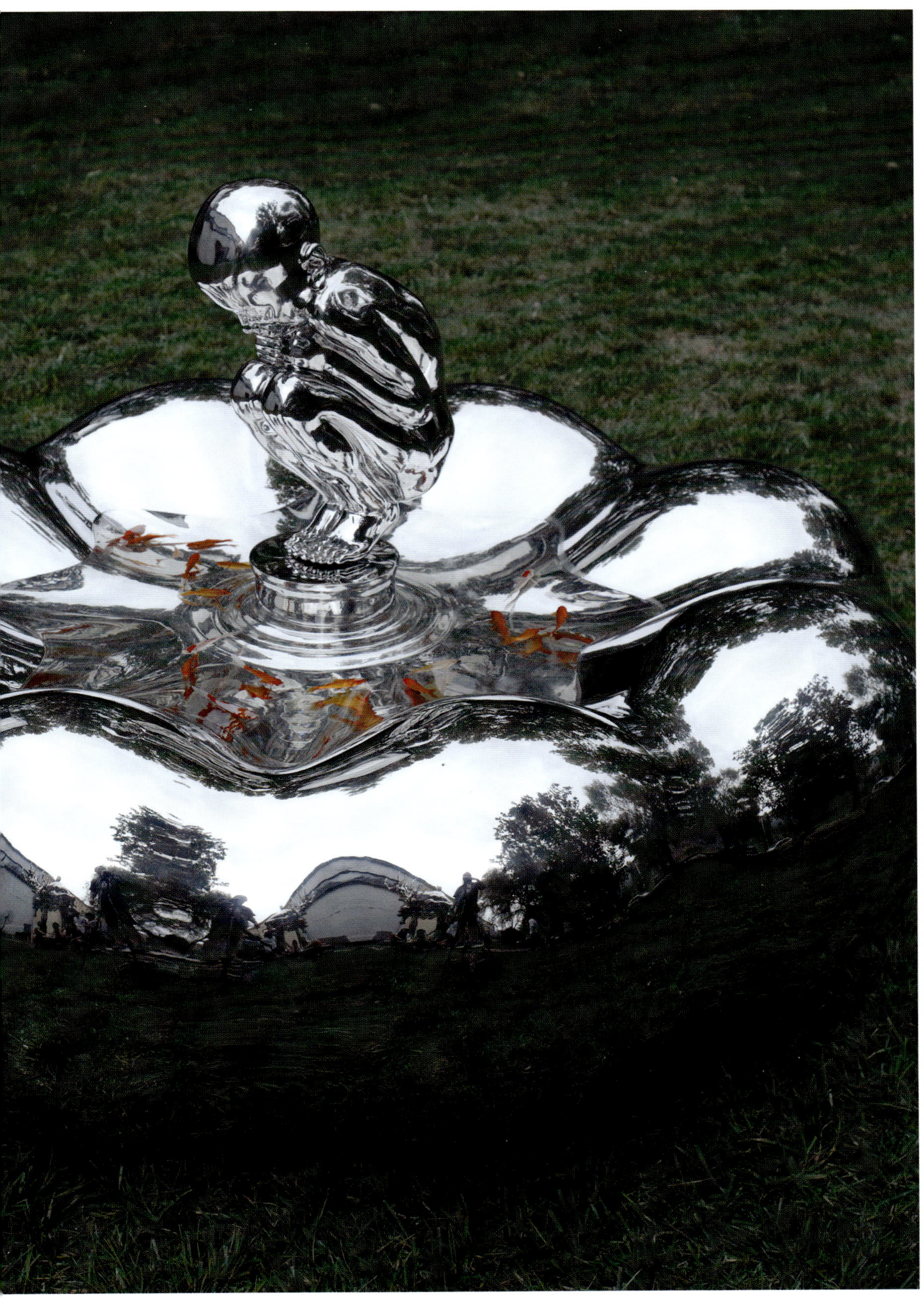

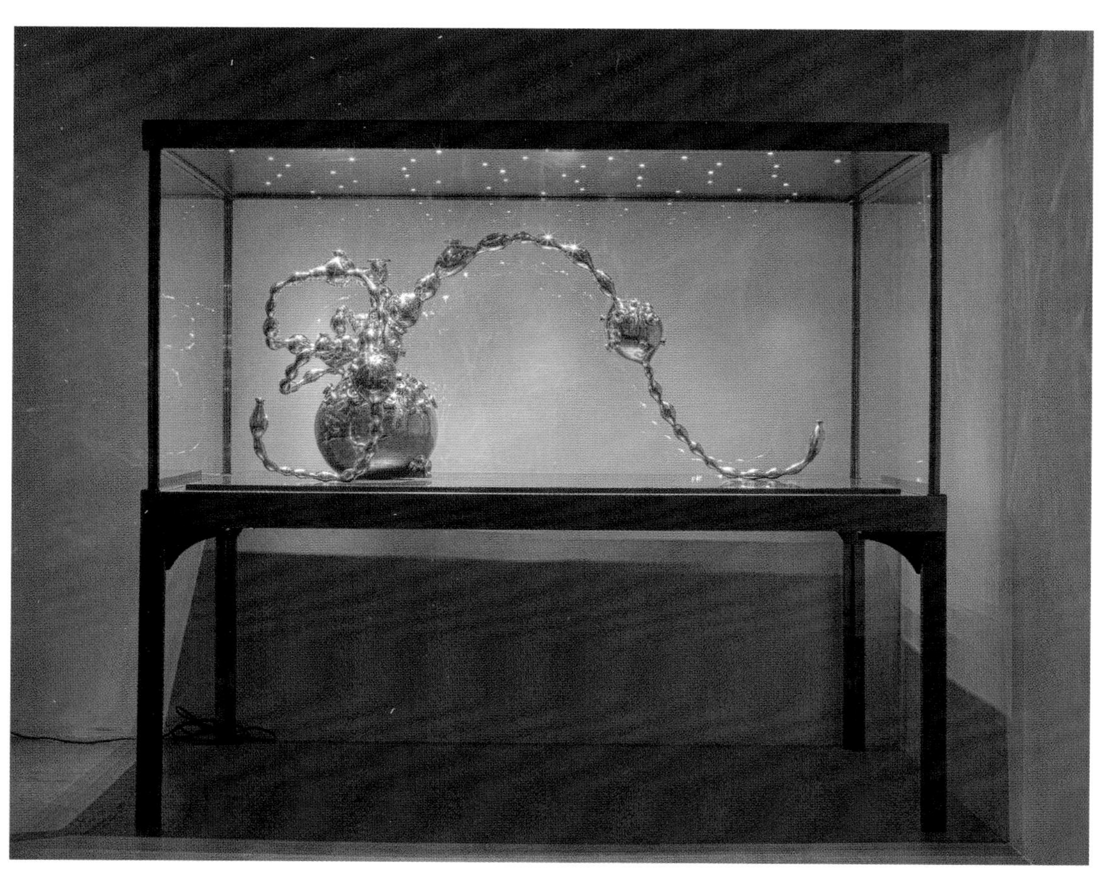

Heterogeneous Space / 异度空间, 2012

pp. 31, 32
Heterogeneous Space Part / 异度空间局部, 2012

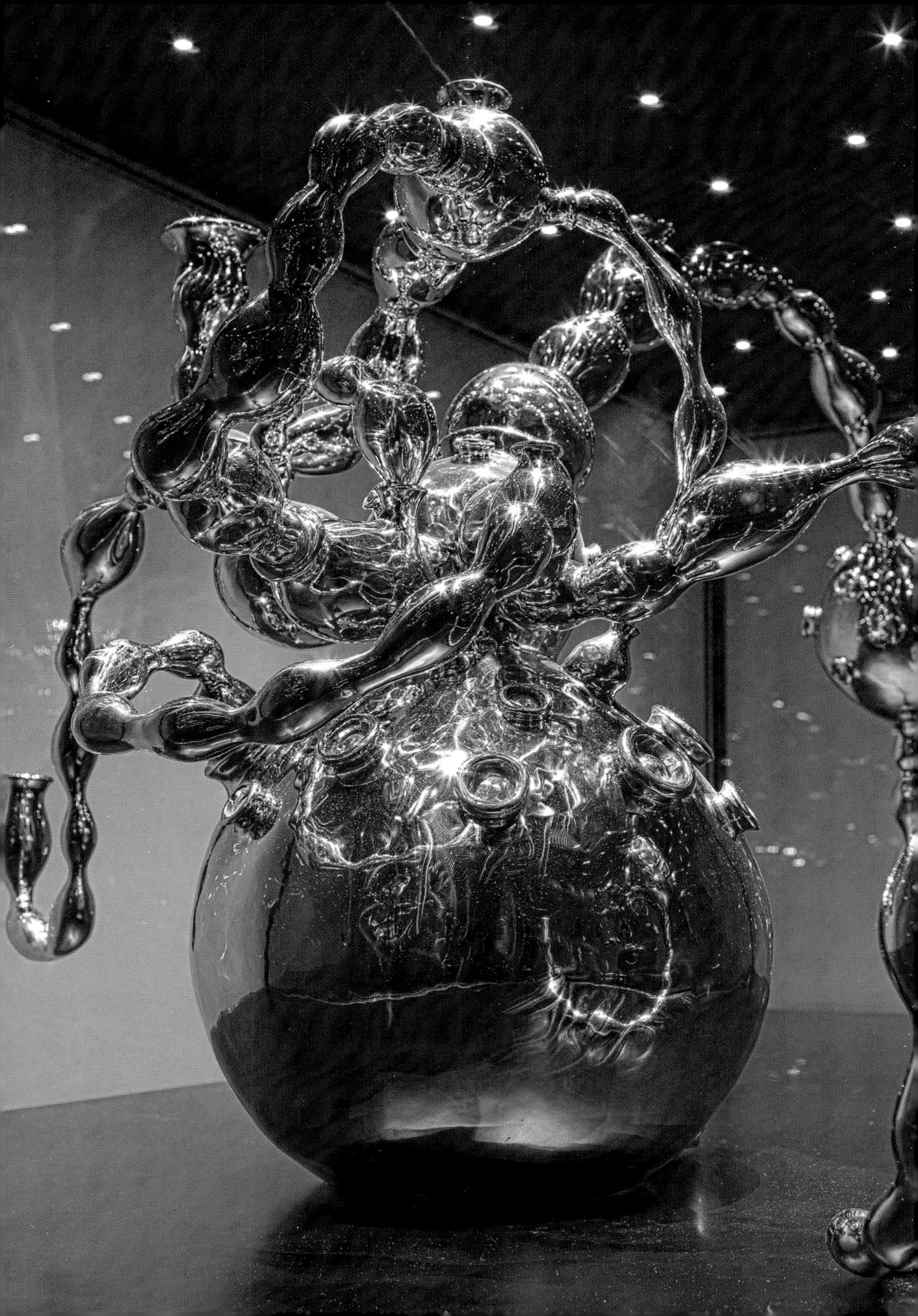

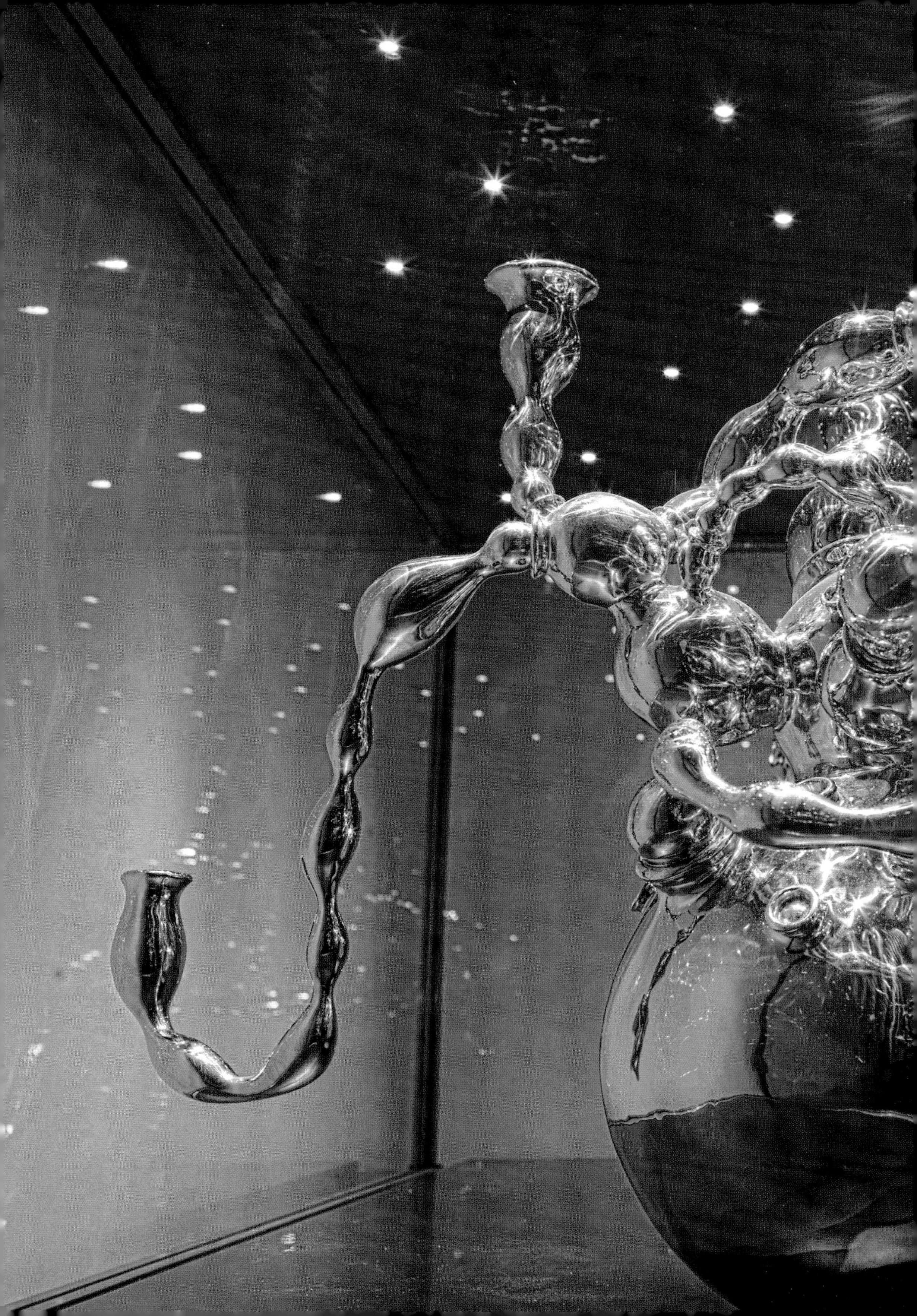

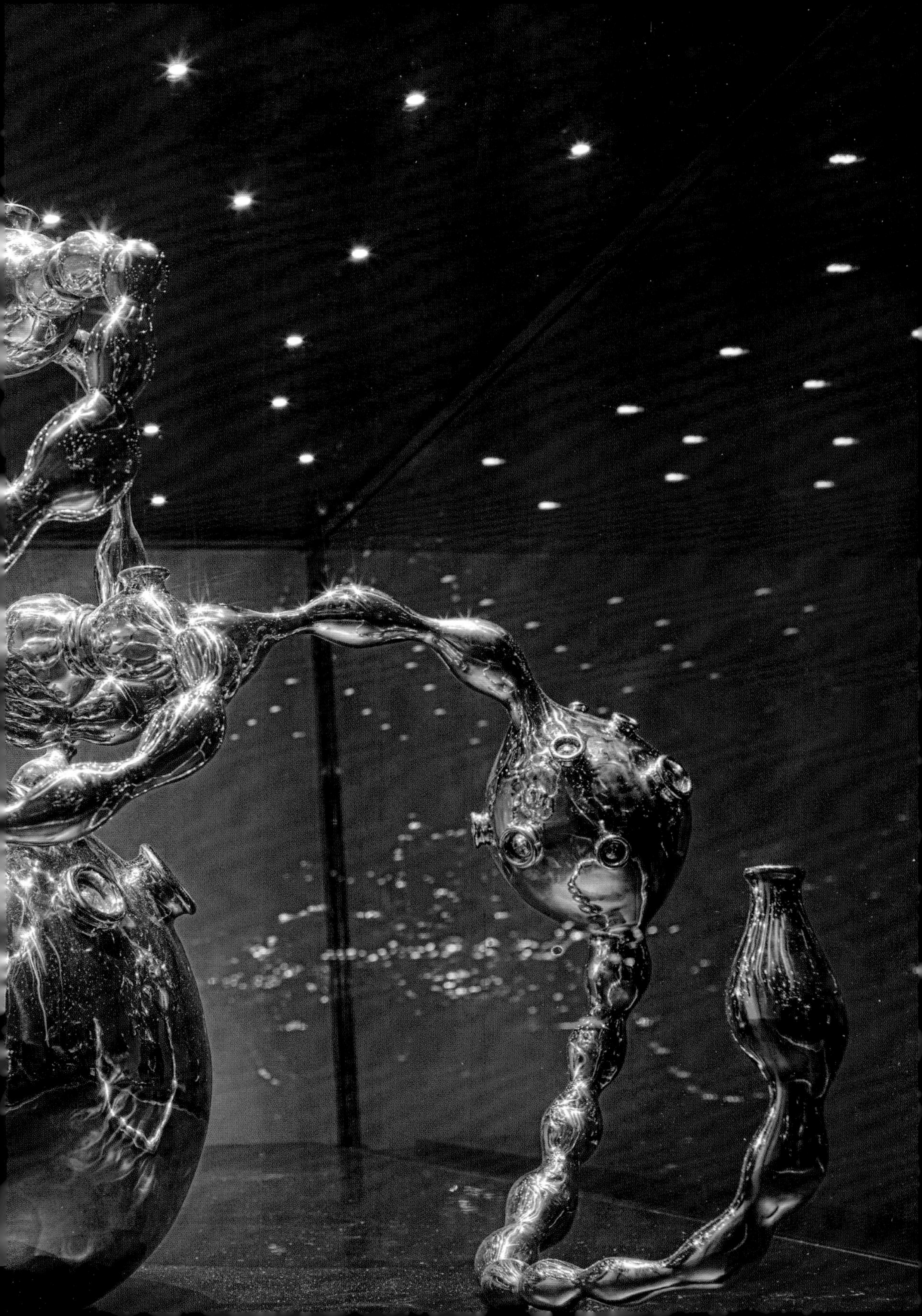

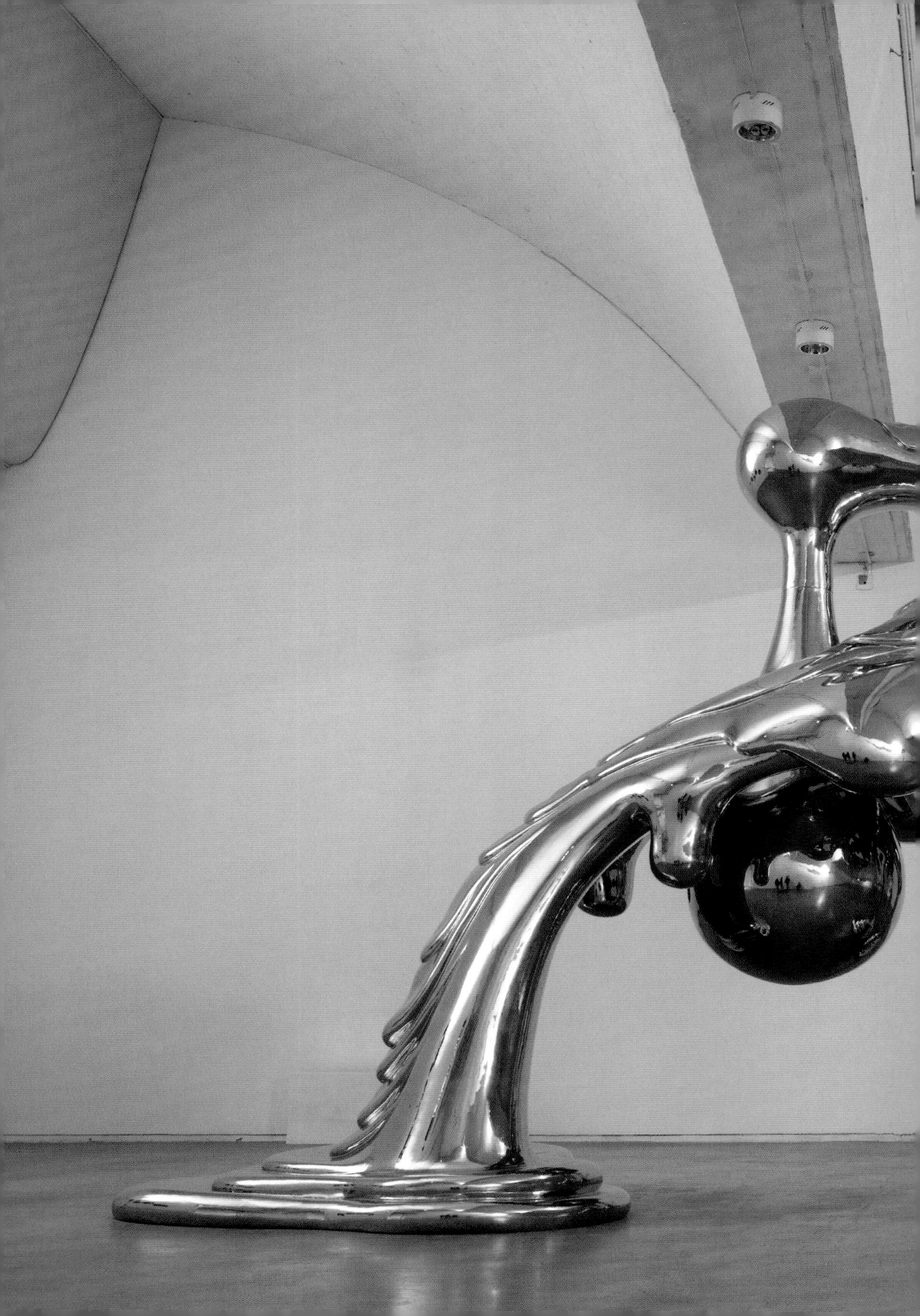

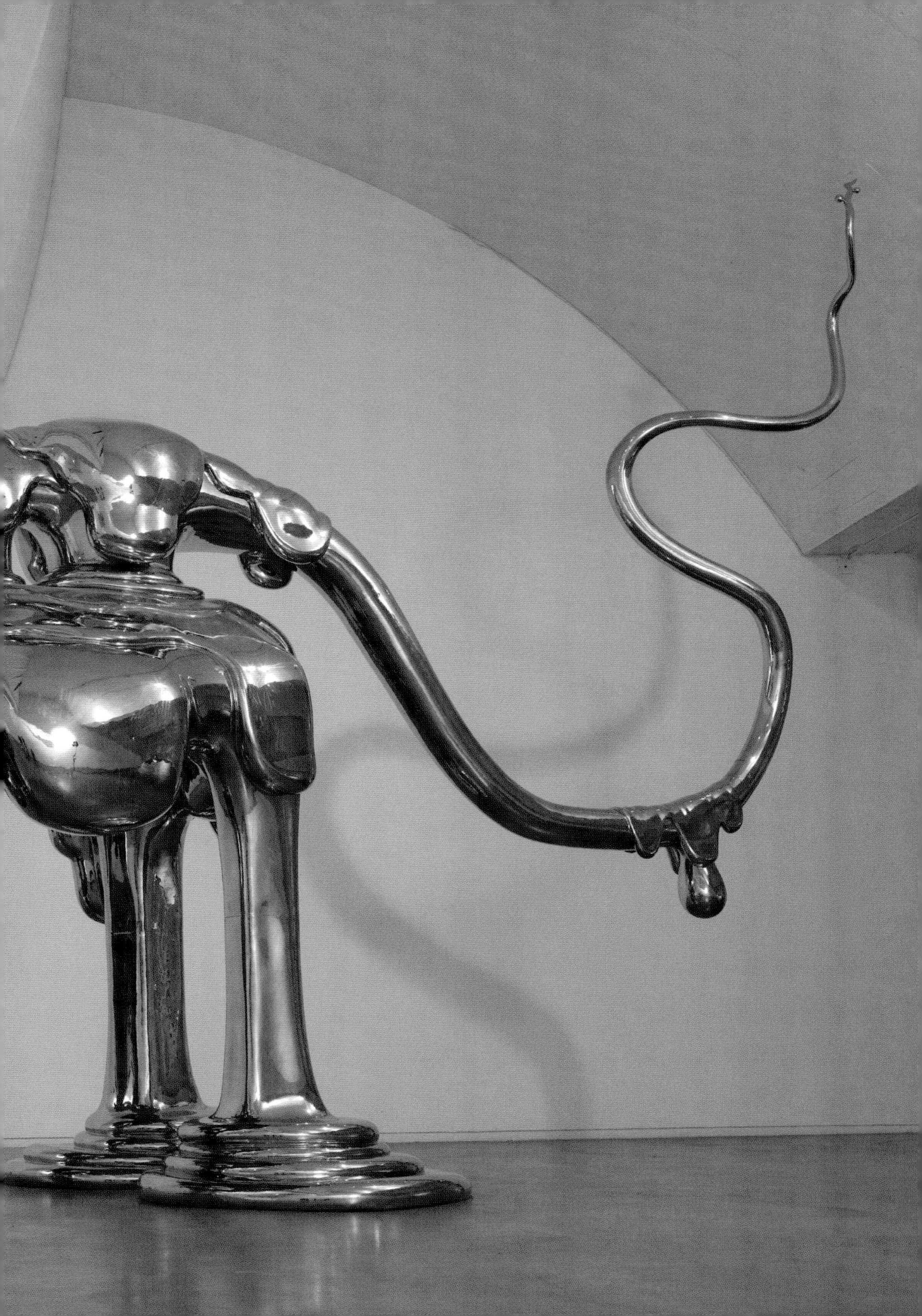

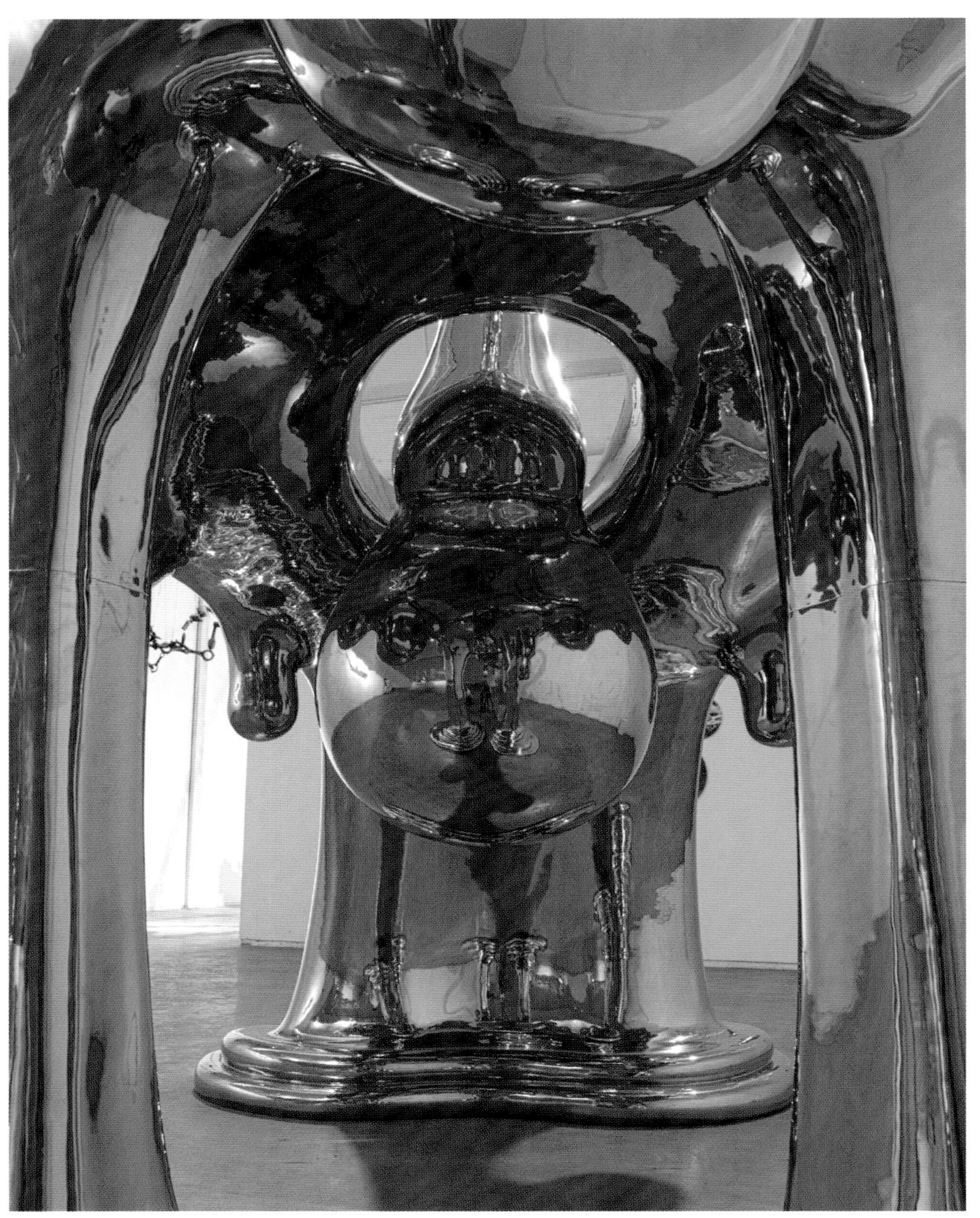

pp. 34, 37
Reincarnation of Mammoth / 猛犸复活, 2012

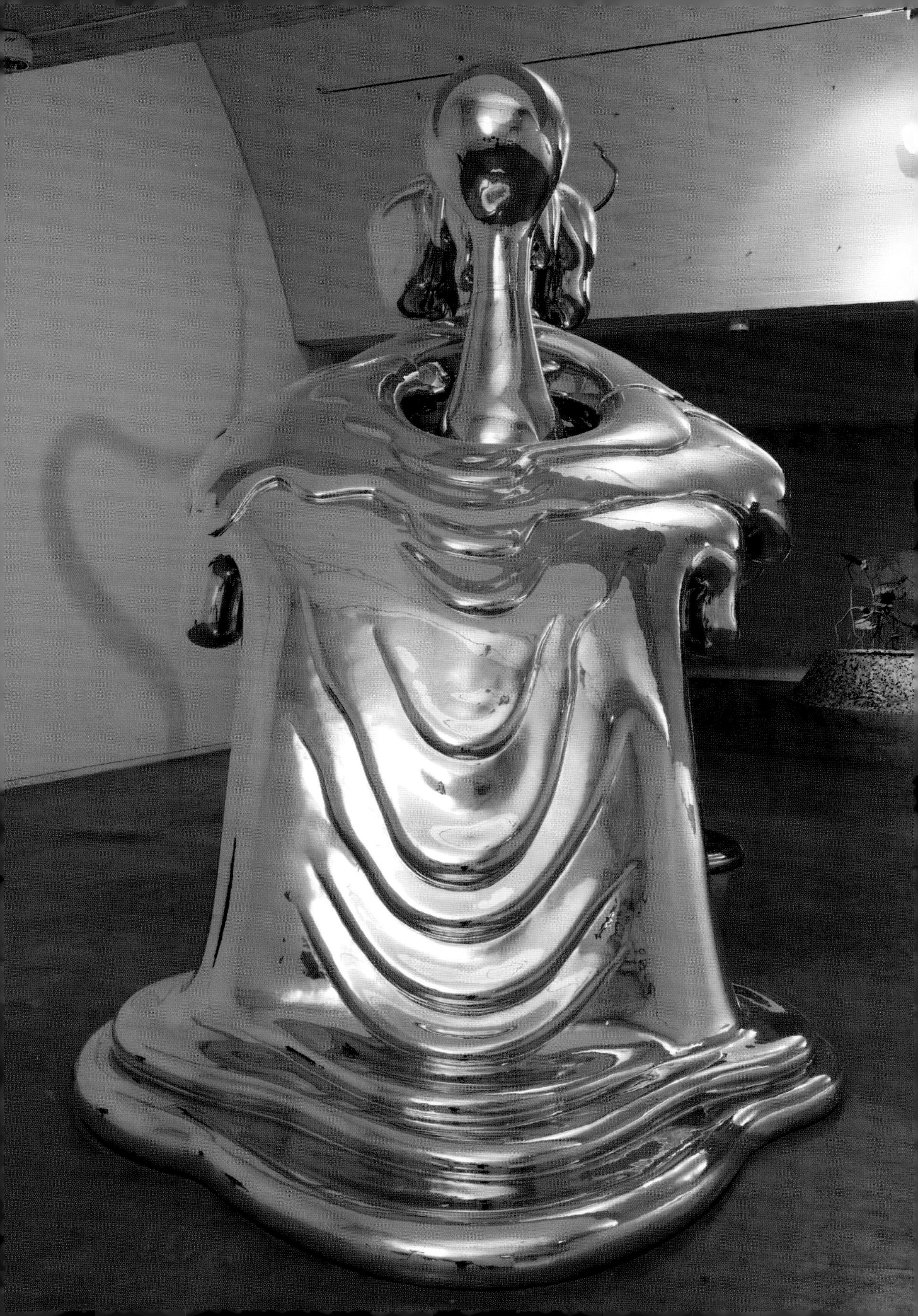

Shark of the Ocean Mixed / 海洋之鲨, 2012

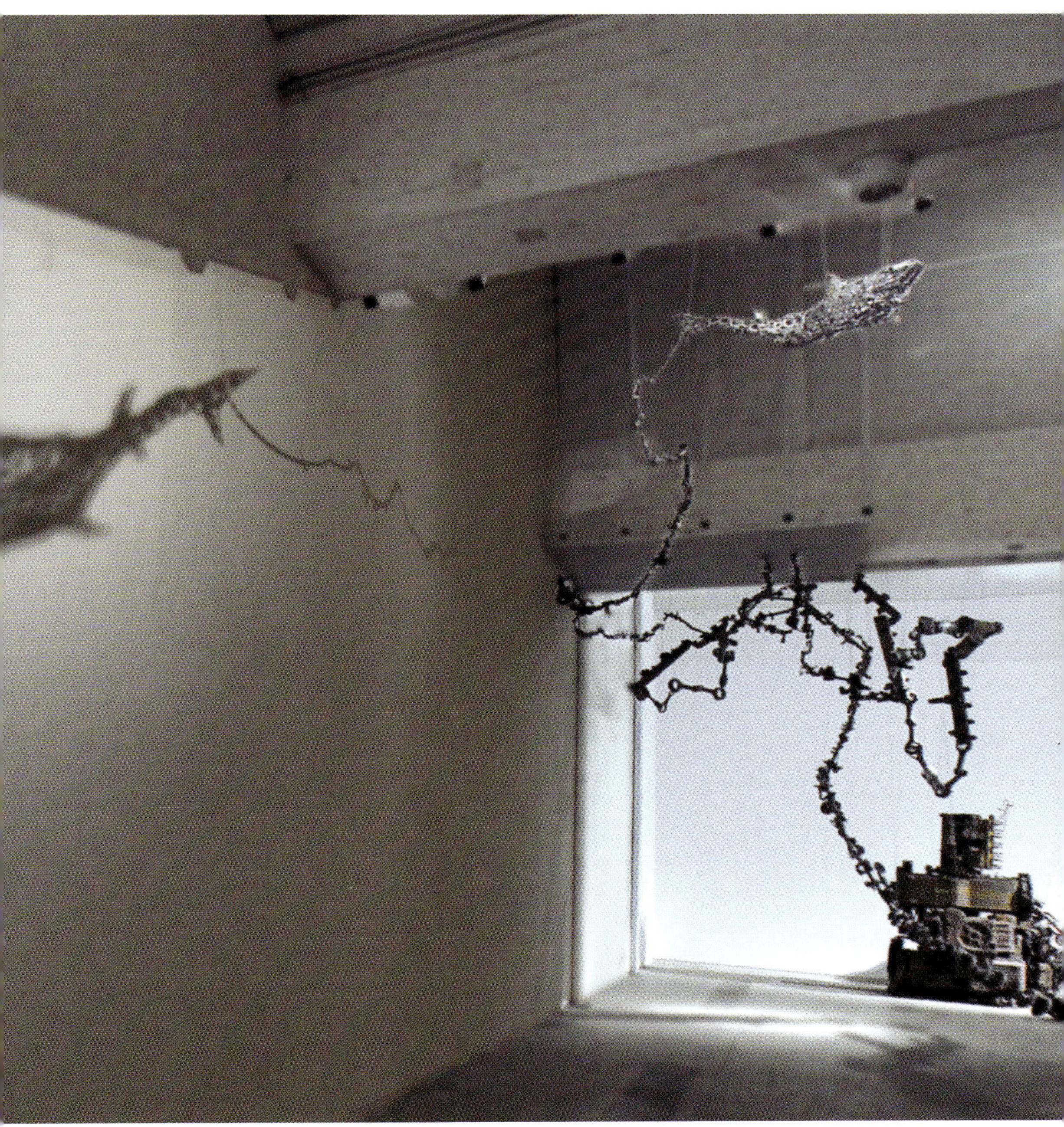

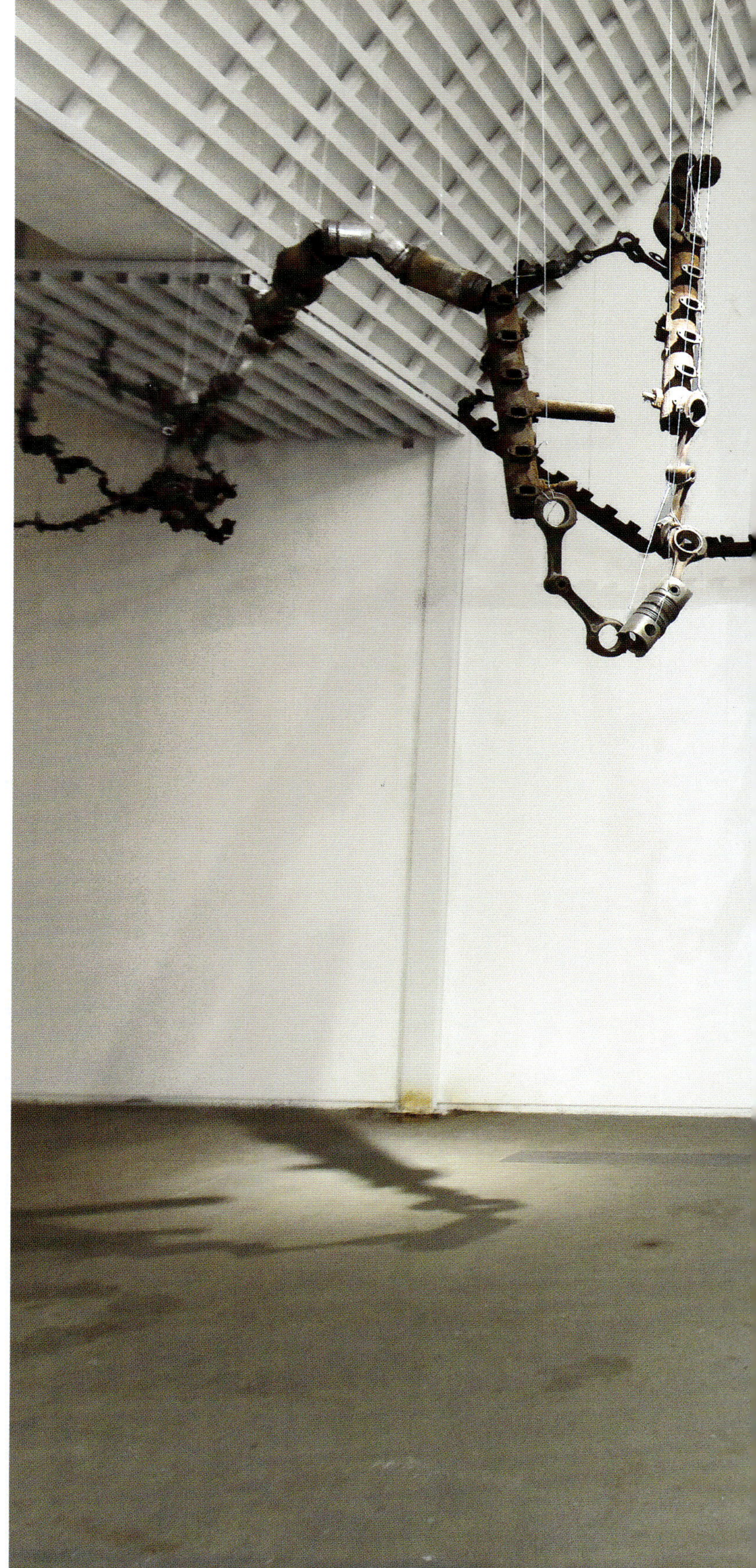

Shark of the Ocean Mixed /
海洋之鲨, 2012

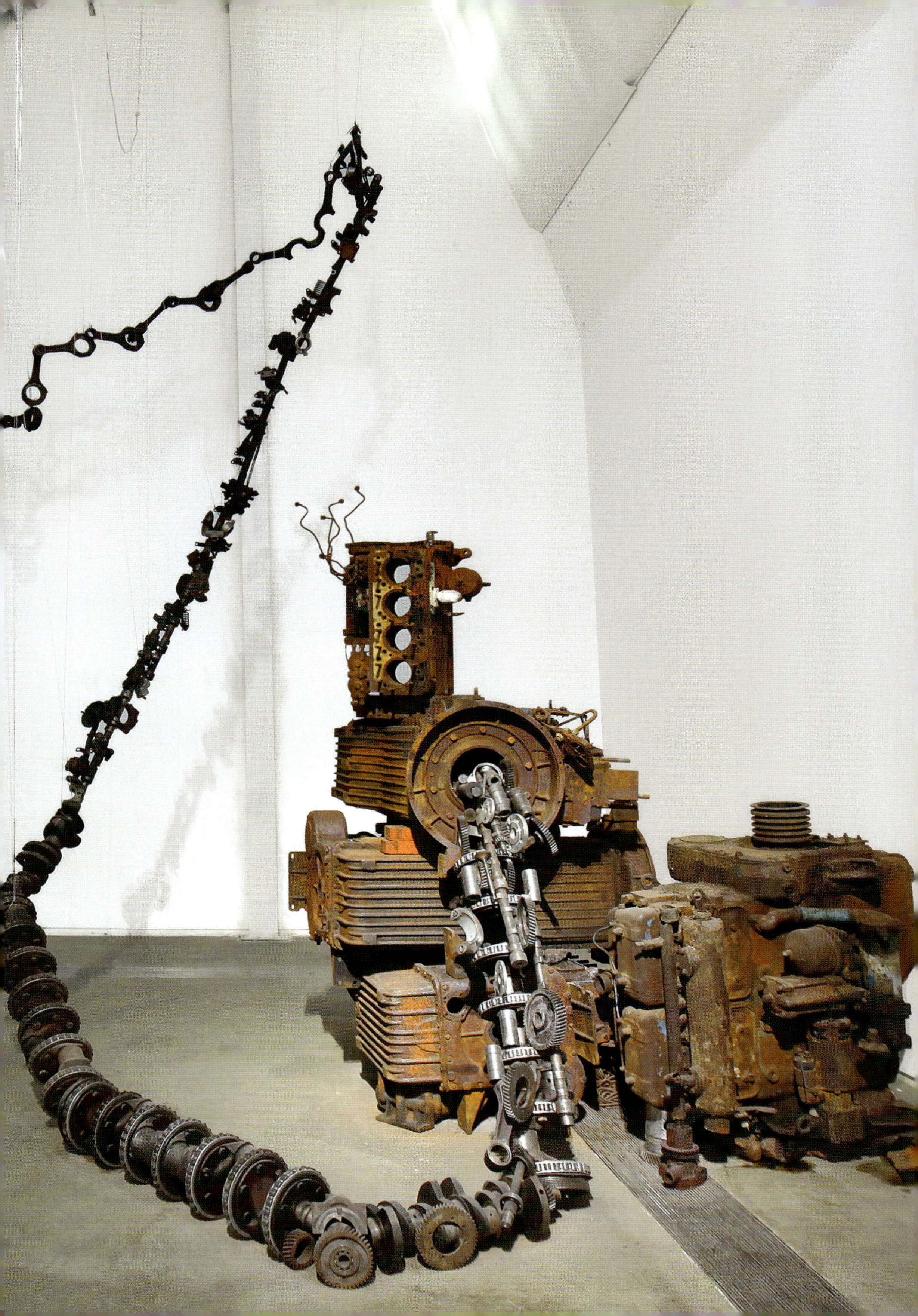

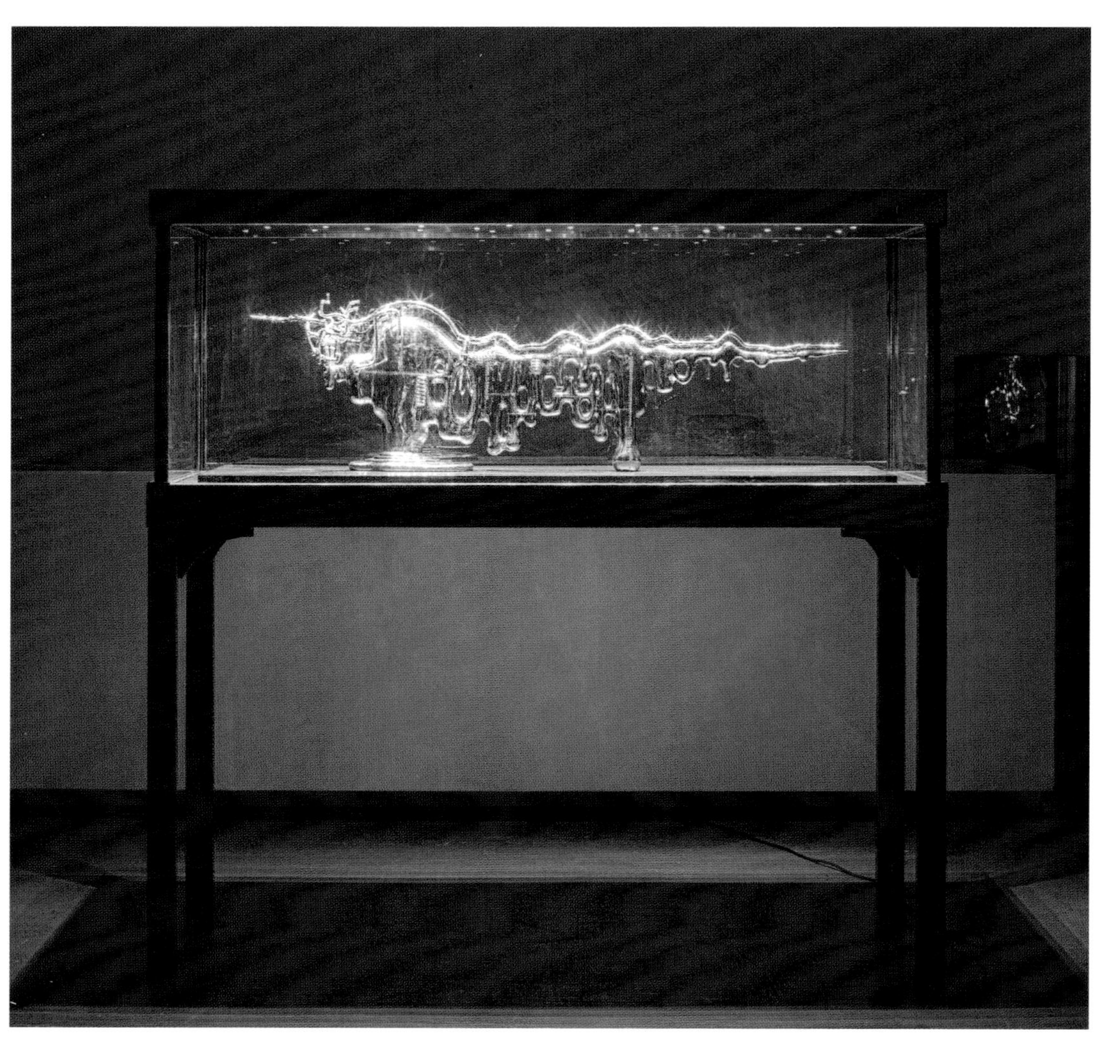

The City Bull / 城市公牛, 2012

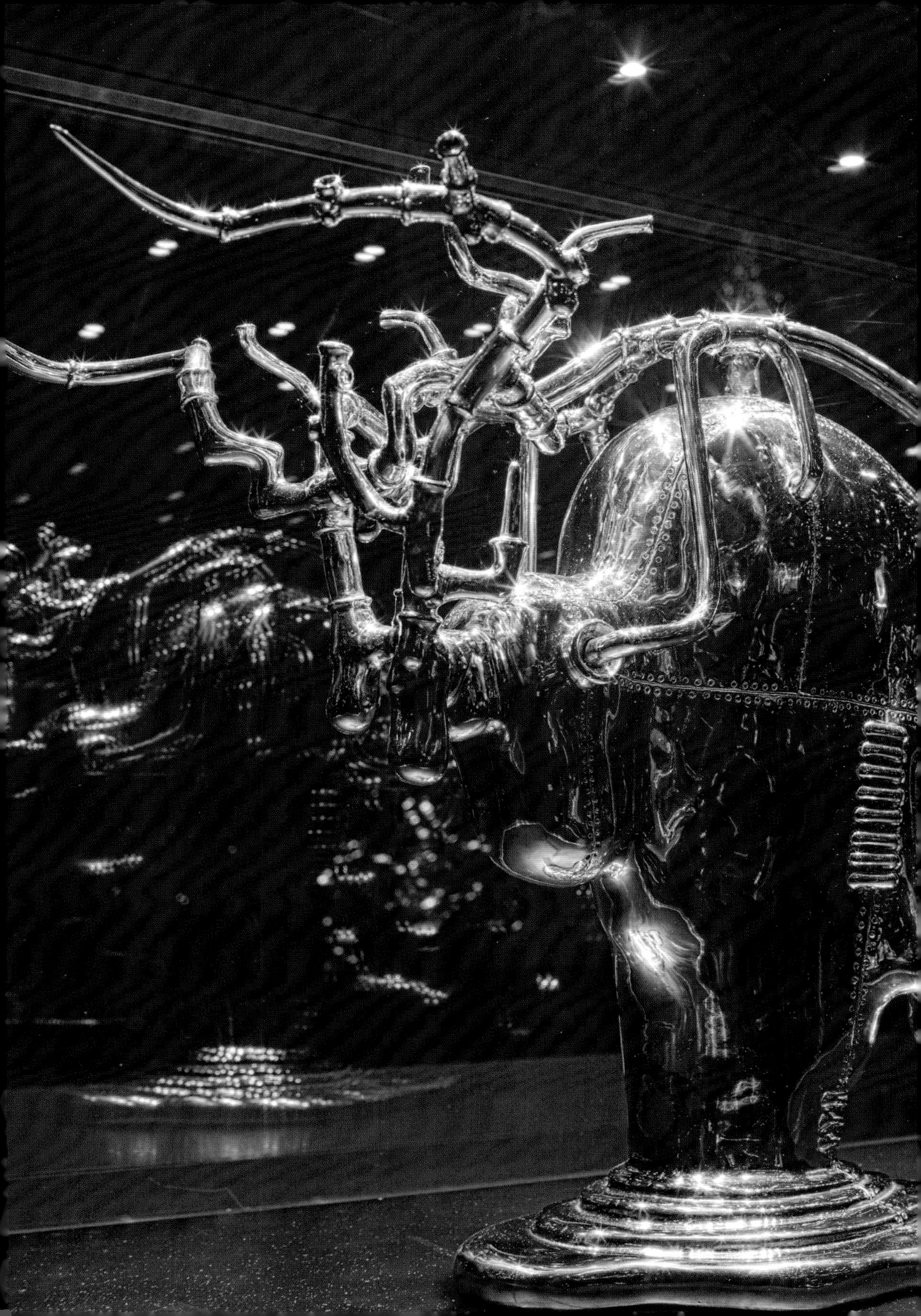

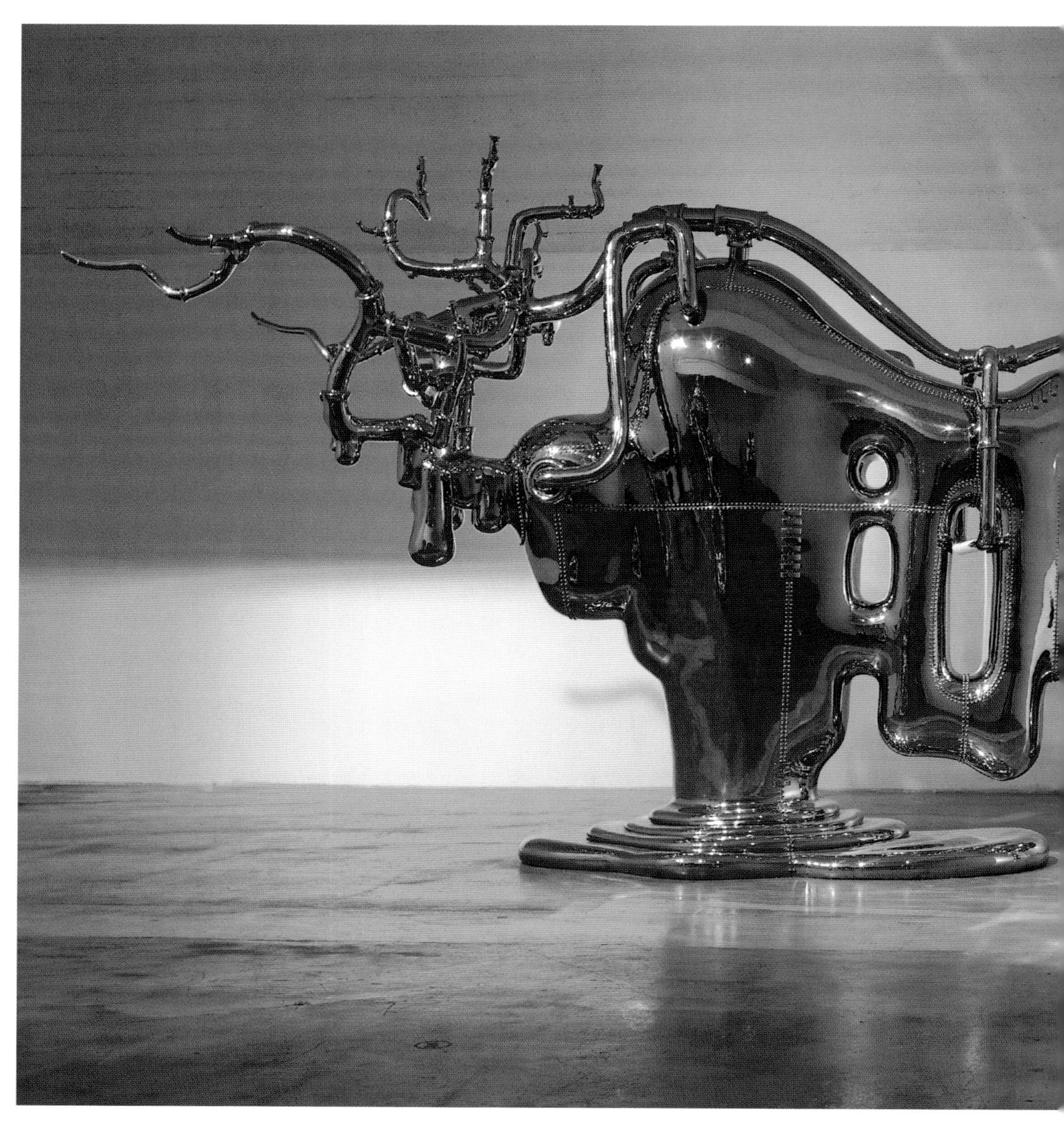

The City Bull / 城市公牛, 2012

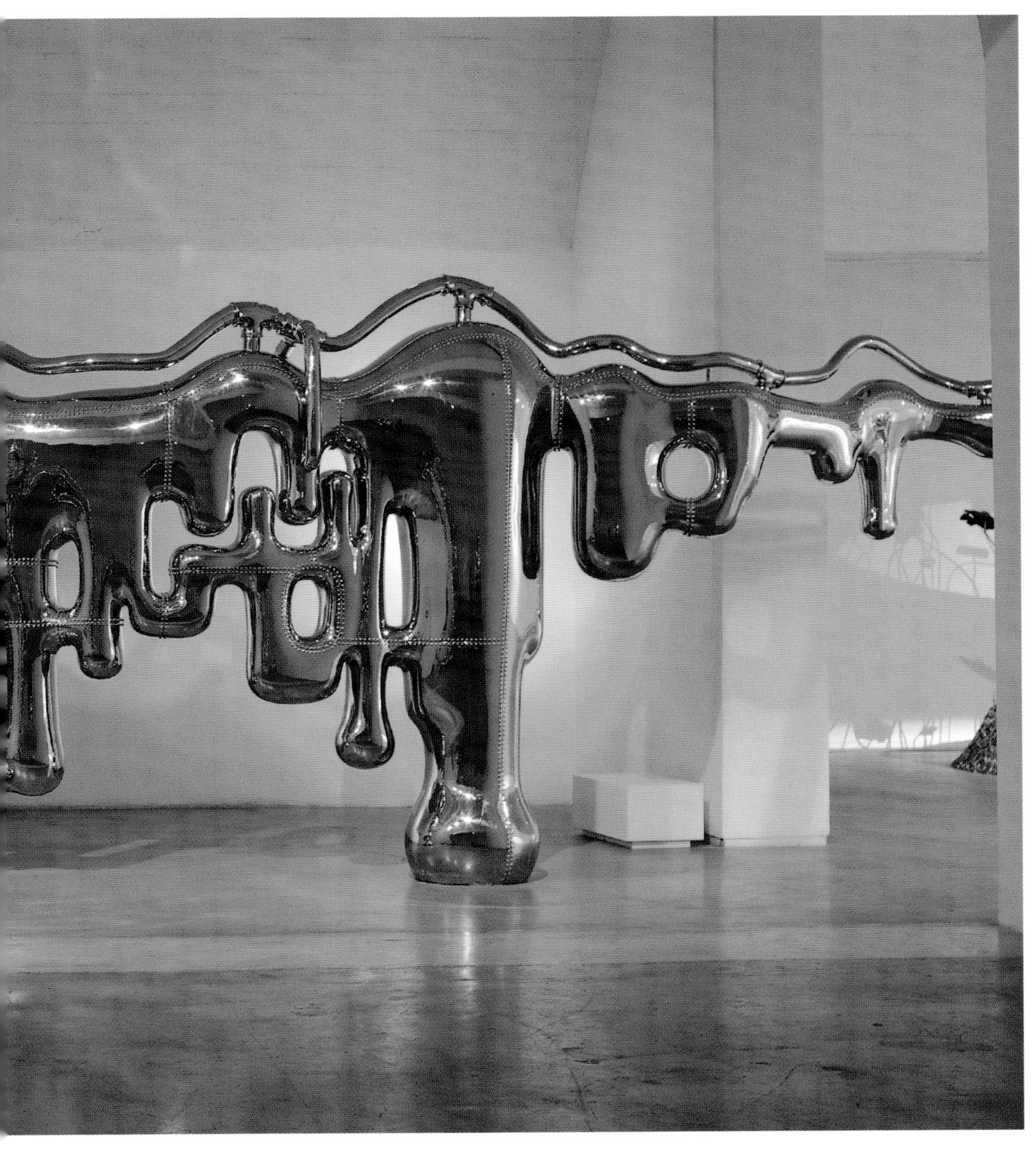

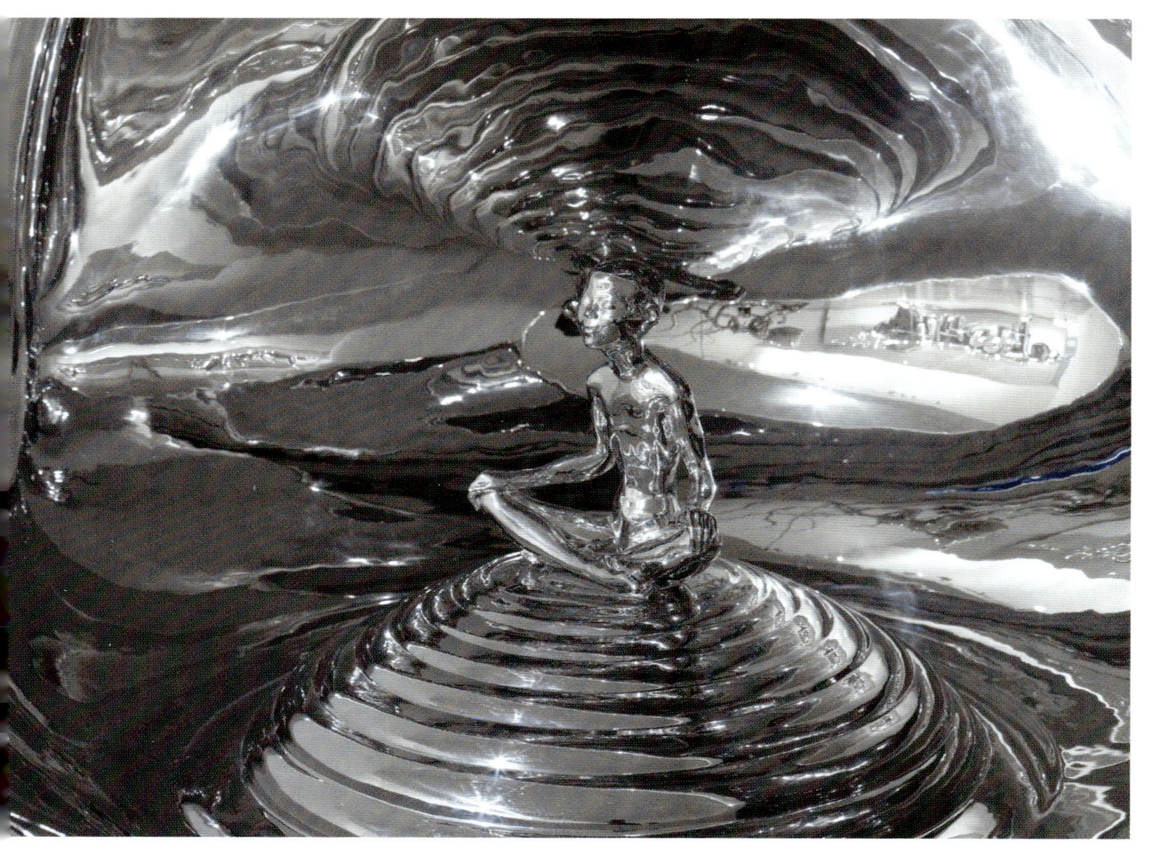

The Illusor / 幻界, 2012

pp. 48, 49
Reincarnation of Mammoth in Kassel / 猛犸复活在卡塞尔展

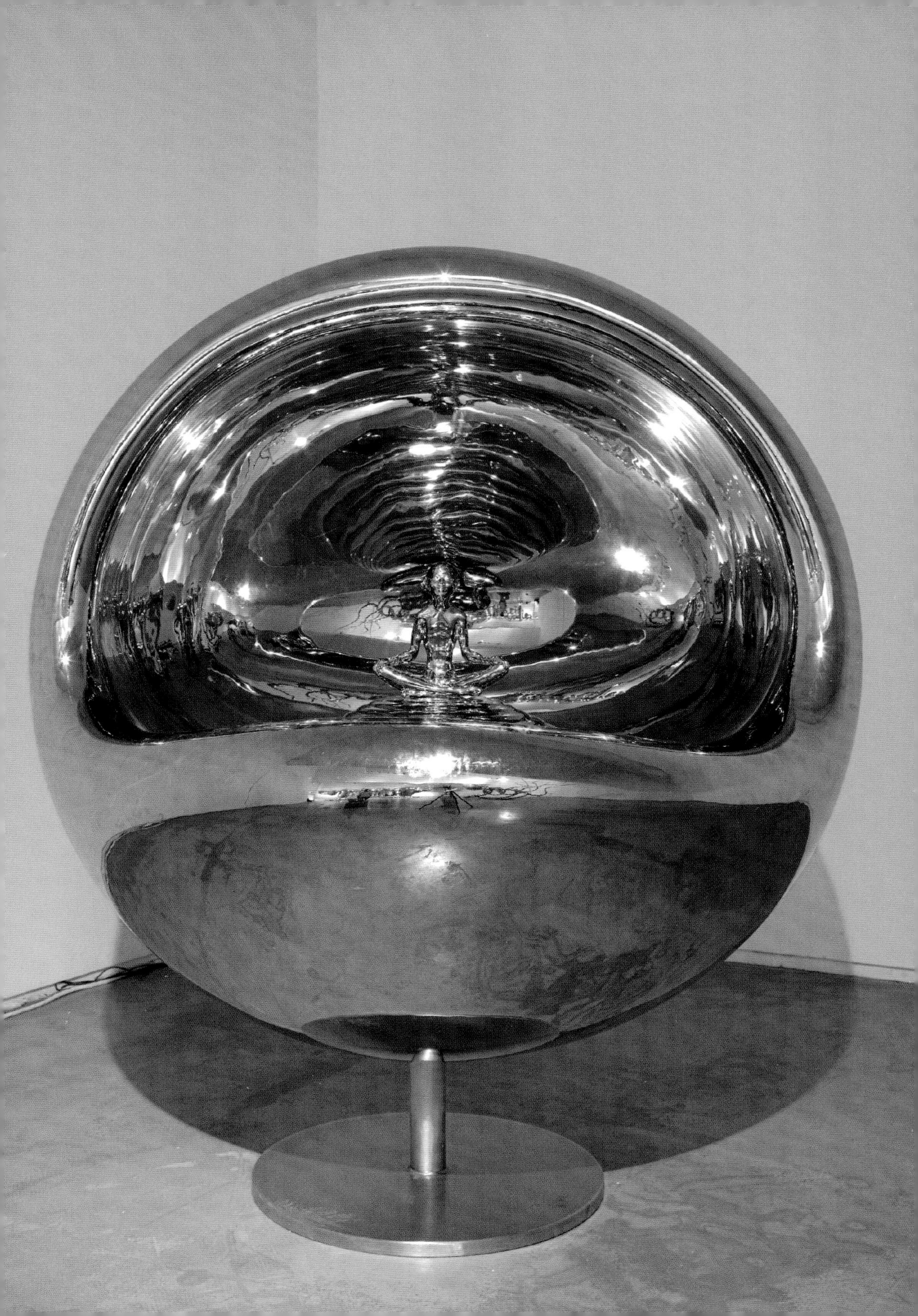

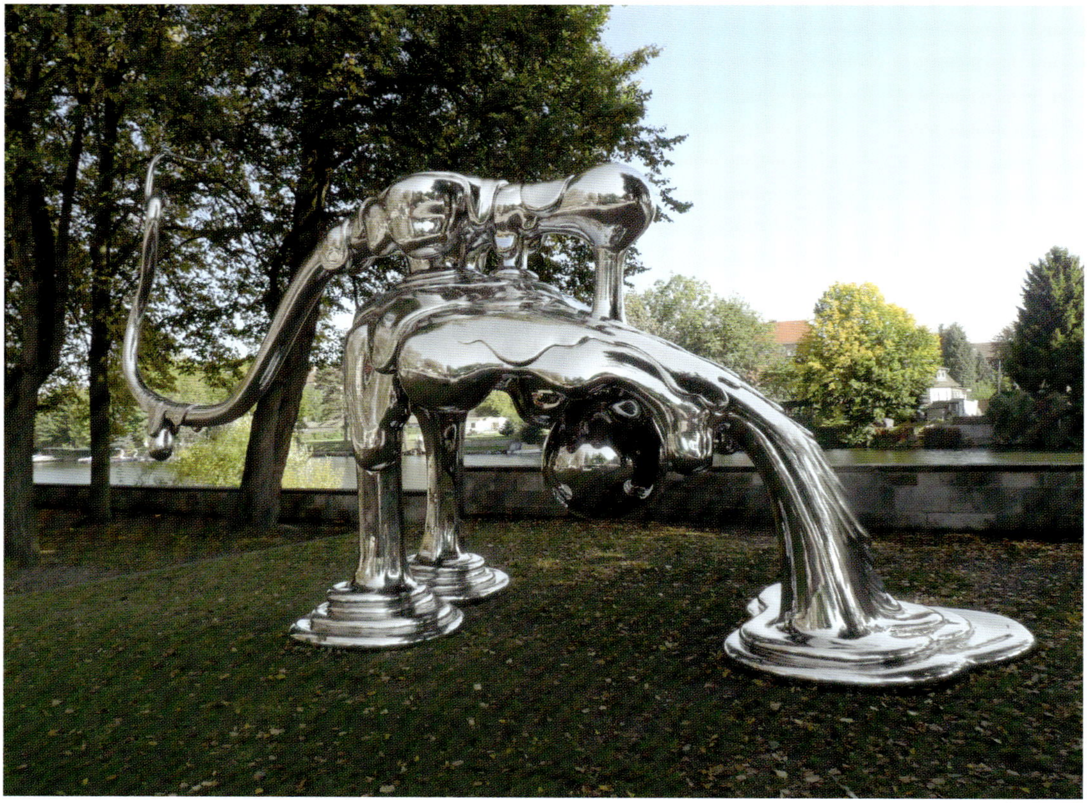

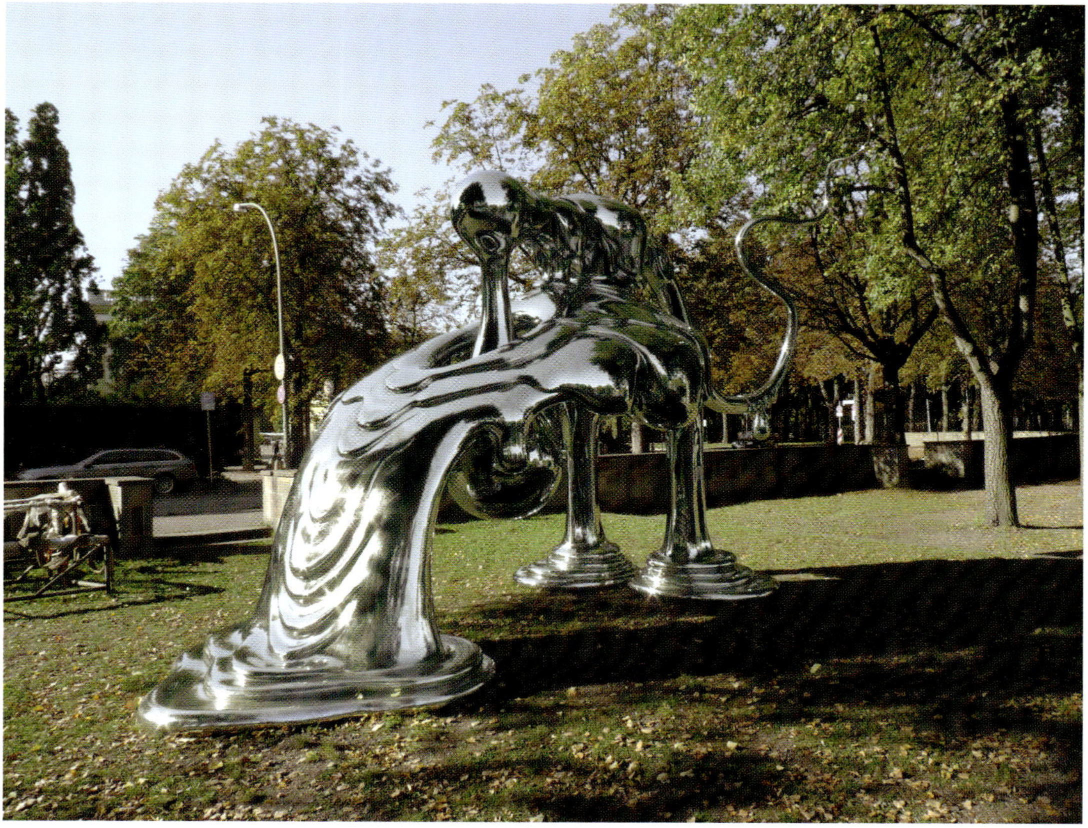

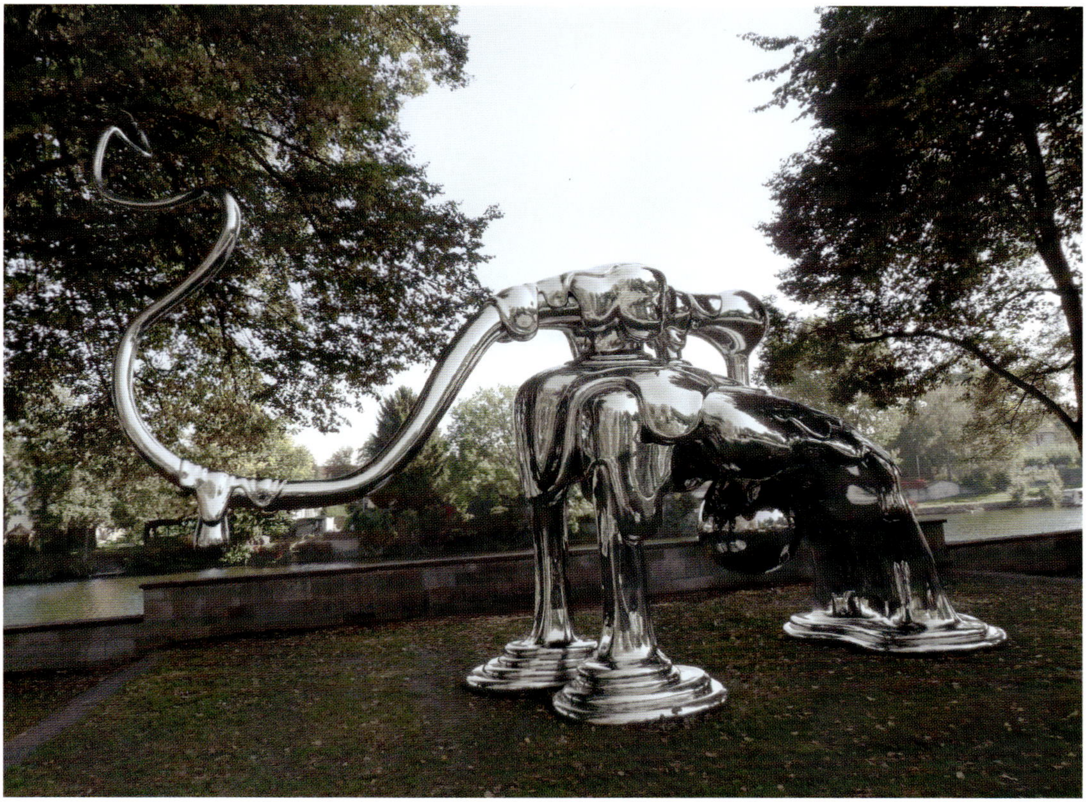

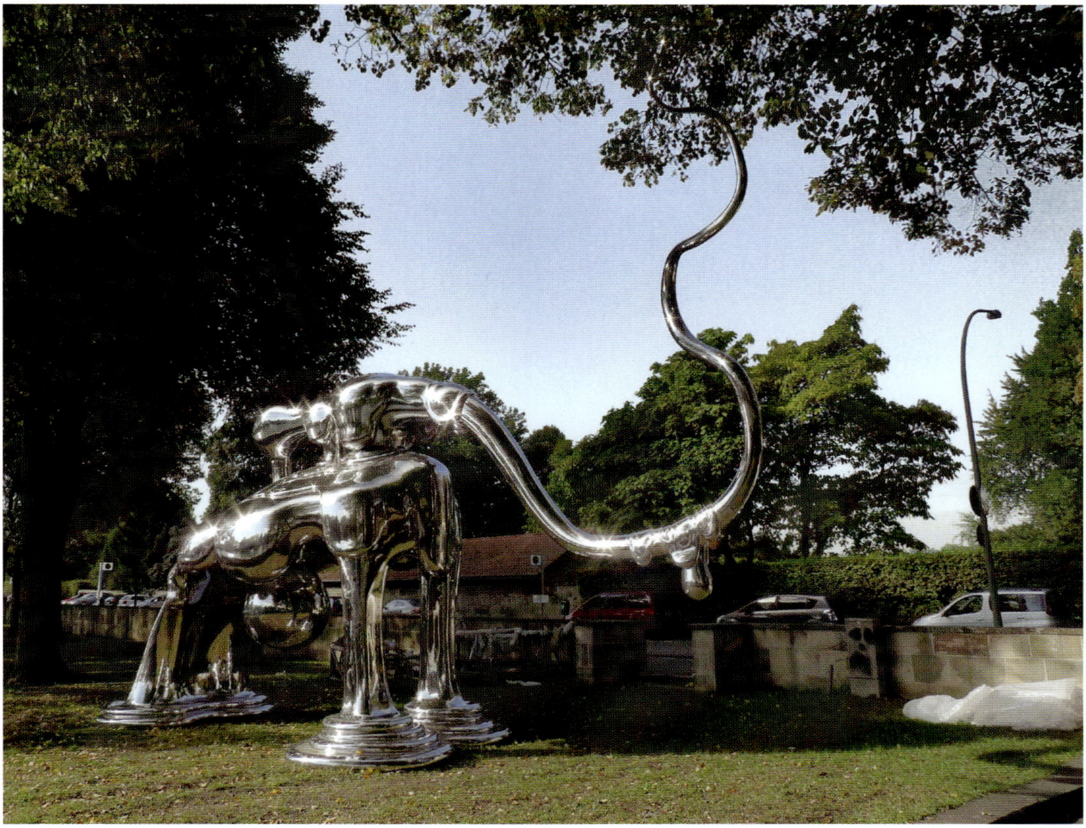

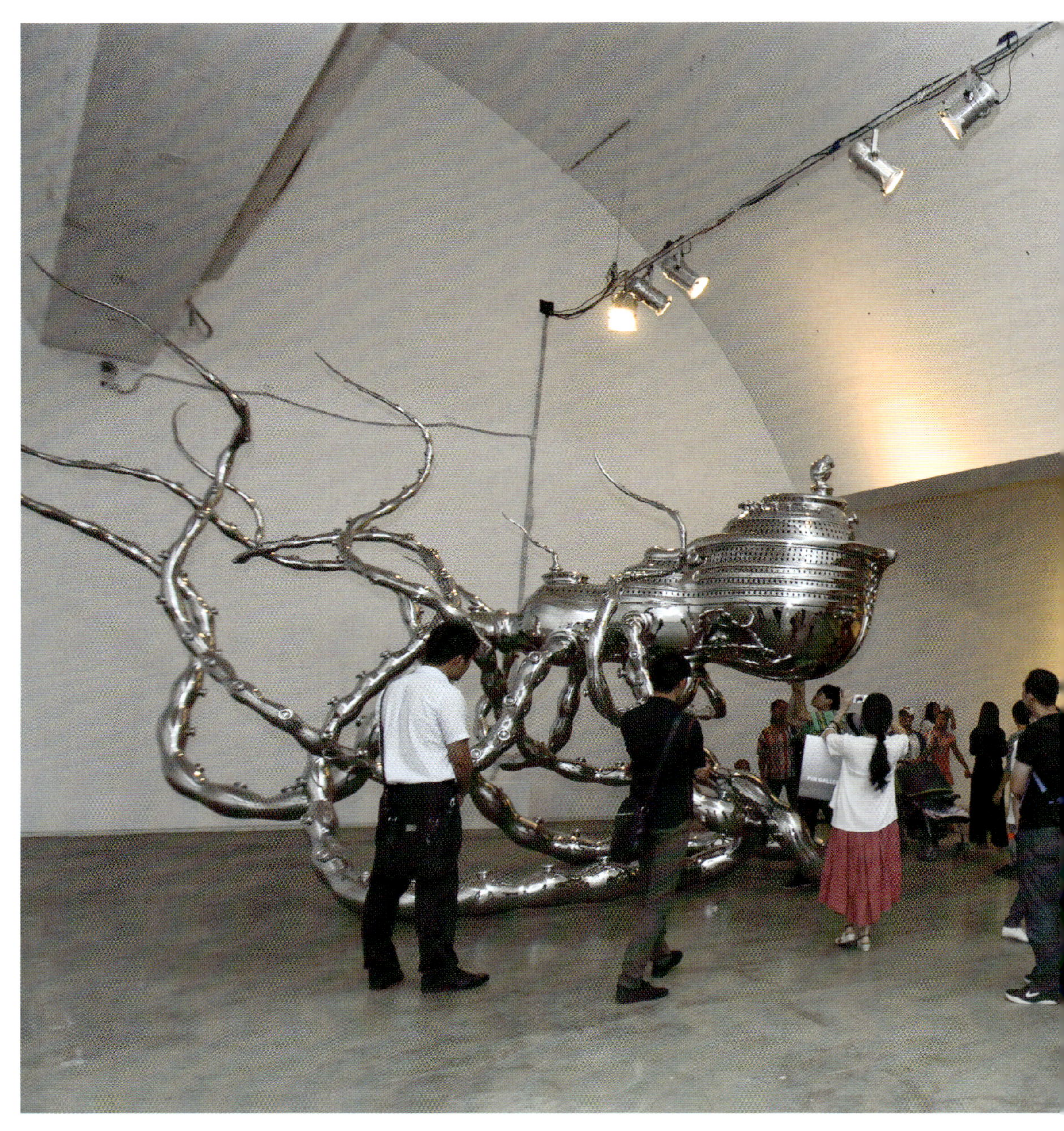

Solo Exhibition, *Exotic Landscapes* exhibition site / 异度风景个展现场, 2012

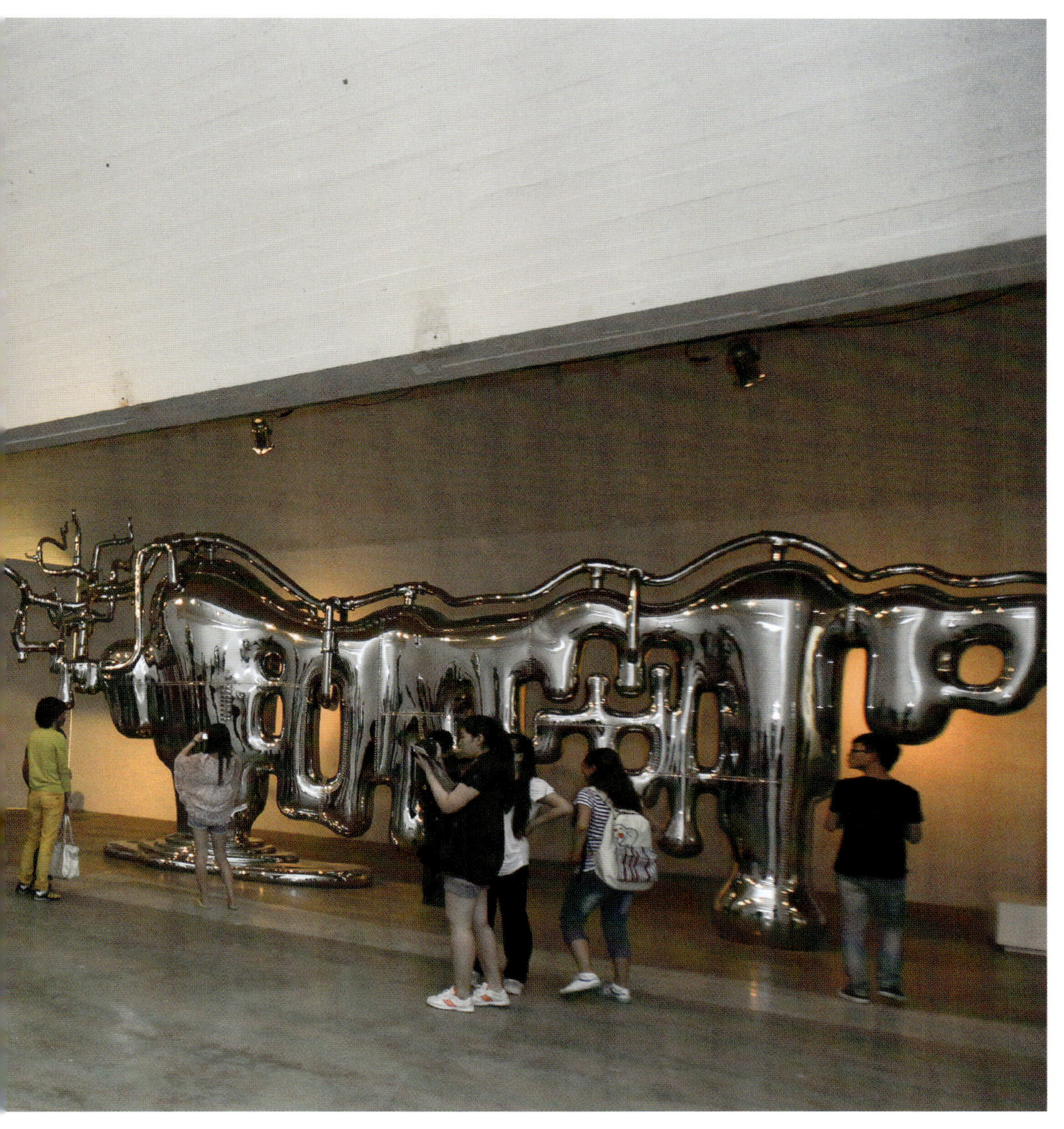

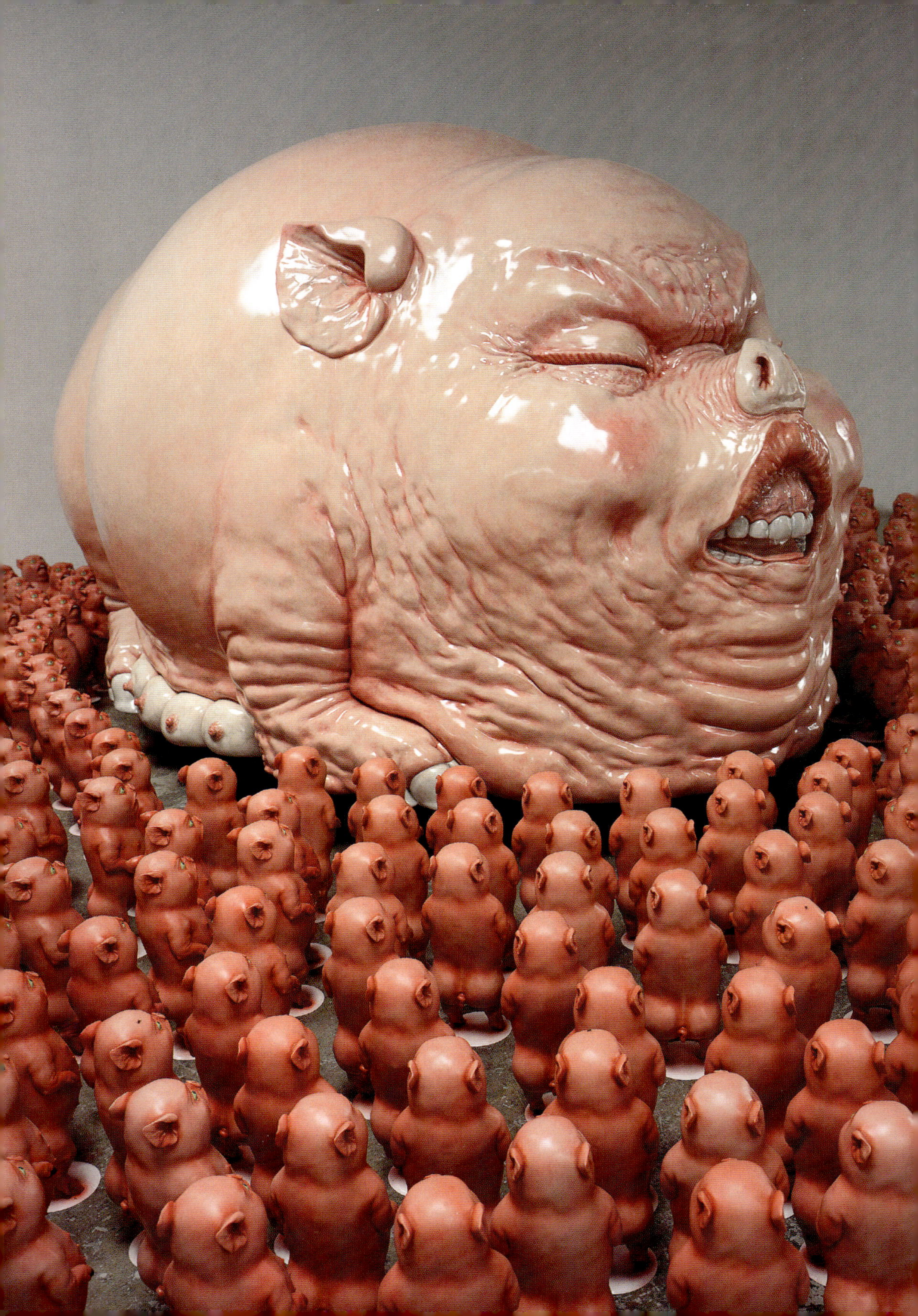

What Is Made-in-China Fantasy?

Huang Du

Chen Wenling is an extremely imaginative and creative artist. His sculptures invariably place animals and people in a relationship, achieved through the noncommittal or tense connections between hysterical people and stout animals. He pushes these images of ecstasy, movement, strength, and desire to the extreme, to give expression to worldly pleasures, humor, and fun, and he reproduces the expansion of human material desires and the state of endlessly proliferating desire in consumer society, thereby satirizing the game system that links desire and money, flesh and power. In *Happy Life, Heroic Struggle*, and other works, he firmly grasps spontaneous vignettes of the dynamic engagement of obese people with wild rampant animals, and exerts control over their dynamic tension to form groupings with plump and unnamed pigs, ferocious dogs, and sexy beautiful mermaids. However, the key issue is not simply these relationships, but more importantly how these animals are fetishized as objects of human desire to directly ask the rhetorical questions: What is desire? Where does desire come from? Obviously, the artist hints at the answer to this question through the exaggeration and deformation of his sculptural language, and human desire is nothing more than the attempt to gain hedonistic benefits through possession and exchange. From a grassroots position, he upholds an awareness of social justice and uses cynicism and black humor to express his contempt and criticism of irrational desire, vanity, power, and violence. Chen Wenling's sculpture does not simply use realism as its only creative method, and to the base of realism he blends folk images, pop culture images, and historical images, and using simple, pure, straightforward, and exaggerated techniques handles sculptural language as black comedy that is absurd, satirical, and humorous.

In *Chinese Landscape*, Chen Wenling's artistic concepts have undergone a shift, enhancing the experimental and public aspects of his sculpture, giving full play to personal imagination, and making use of such modes of expression as appropriation, bricolage, and retranslation. Mixing and converting images of nature, tradition, and the modern age, he has succeeded in creating a surreal landscape of bizarre rocks, subjectively processed to form ambiguous images. They resemble ice and snow that has melted to form icebergs; some resemble large deer and others a traditional garden pavilion from the base of which melting ice is flowing and on the eaves of which crystal-clear water droplets form. This is a distorted and broken illusory image with no sense of realism, and it vividly reproduces a quiet and ethereal pure world and a sense of distance from reality. At the same time, the sculpture *Chinese Landscape* makes full use of the rounded and smooth surfaces and flowing lines of stainless steel produced by industrial civilization to create the sense of apathy and order of modern society through melting, flowing, and solidified forms that cause people to all experience the variability of time and the disorder of space. In fact, the artist's sculpture concept stresses the harmony of nature, and the cold feeling and sense of power of the modern age (stainless steel), while traditional poetic beauty advances the deconstruction and integration. This is the visual metaphor of the transitional period in which Chinese society finds itself in which agricultural society, industrial society, and post-industrial society conflict, overlap, and blend. The artist accurately grasps the organic relationships between cultural concepts, historical consciousness, and the real world. This is a body of surreal sculpture that blends nature, tradition, and industry, and is both interactive and public. When the audience is in the work, the light reflects the audience on the surface of stainless steel sculpture and enables them to feel the singular fantasy world structured by light and shadow. In this sense, it tries to prompt people to re-examine the frame of reference of their everyday experience and the entirety of changes in the external environment, and to continually reflect on subjective consciousness and observe changes in the objective world. Therefore, through Chen Wenling's open sculptural language we can better recognize and understand the value and significance of Chinese contemporary art in the conversion of traditional aesthetics and modern aesthetics.

In 2008, a recent work by Chen Wenling attained a new height, when he boldly and adventurously challenged his easily immobilized personal artistic style by further deepening and extending his art's connotations and implications, and was able to analyze human relations with society from a microscopic point of departure and to directly borrow or absorb technology, ready-mades, material objects, and elements of installation to form a new artistic language. At the same time, Chen Wenling challenged himself but also reflected criticism of the fashion for the repetition and replication of works in Chinese contemporary art. So, how does Chen Wenling's new work embody his new intentions? We can feel the shift in attitudes from the imagery of his work; he has returned to secular reality from a poeticized world. Because he has realized the strength and depth of the language of art from the complexity and dynamism of reality, his art reflects not only the artist's self-creation, self-expression, and self-realization, but art's aesthetic activities have also played a "healing" role. In other words, art not only embodies the expressive tension of the artist's form and language, but also reflects art's significance as social intervention, and its analysis and critique of social reality.

His work *Fetish,* in which Chen Wenling mixes humans and pigs, creates ambiguous visages that are neither porcine nor human, and this language should be regarded as "post-pop" in Chinese contemporary art. On the surface of his art, his works appear to be part of popular culture, but in fact his key ideas stress that "the most important objects of worship are not spiritual but material." This materiality borrows the image of the pig which in Chinese society is seen as a symbol of wealth and desires, and his stance of social criticism presents a heightened sense of China's social problems in daily life, an ironic take on the characteristics of China's entry into the madness of material consumption. For humans, pigs have no brains and are animals to be eaten, so this animal has become an object of human consumption. In this sense, in his "post-pop" language he attempts to draw on folk language as an alternative to capitalistic pop culture. As a consequence, Chen Wenling's *Fetish* is a scientific genetic fable, as well as an allegory and critique of a society with untrammeled material desires.

In another piece, *Weightless*, Chen Wenling treats the body as an immensity that finds it difficult to stand tall like a mountain as it is wrapped in unlimited desires and the unsteady collapse of the body presages the unlimited expansion of the material that will result in imbalance of the spirit and the flesh, and loss of control over the spiritual and material. It is a questioning of the inherent nature of the body: What led to the desires of the body? What is causing the imbalance in the body? What dominates or controls the body?

Chen Wenling's work, *The Breast-feeding Pig*, is a departure from the realistic context, creating a weird object that expresses the sense of beauty that scientific and technological progress bring to the body, at the same time as it is a metaphor for the damage it inflicts on the body, and then extends and links this phenomenon to Chinese reality - society as a whole is in a process of material transformation, suggesting that the development of China's modernization is one of deficit and pain.

In *China Fantasy*, Chen Wenling blends southern Fujian's *feng-shui* balls, tea art, folk culture, and new media into an artistic integration, thereby creating an entertaining and ironic work that links installation, sculpture, new media, and performance in a work of interdisciplinary significance. The new contemporary art language constructed from folk and the folkloric as the driving force is replete with inspirational significance, raising the question: Can folk customs and folk art be translated into contemporary art? In fact, Chen Wenling, through his continuous artistic experiments, fully demonstrates the possibility of creating a new art.

[2009]

什么是中国式幻想？

黄 笃

陈文令是一位非常有想象力和创造力的艺术家。他的雕塑作品总是把动物和人置于一种关系之中，这种关系通过狂乱的人和肥硕的动物之间的暧昧或紧张关系得以实现，他借此把这种狂欢、运动、力量和欲望的表象推向了极致，既表达了一种世俗的快乐，一种世俗的幽默，一种世俗的好玩，又再现了消费社会中人的物欲膨胀和人的欲望的无止境状态，进而讽刺了欲望与金钱、肉体和权力相关的游戏系统。在《幸福生活》和《英勇奋斗》等作品中，他紧紧抓住肥硕丰满的人和狂野、运动的动物的瞬间，肥硕狂野的猪、凶猛的狗和性感漂亮的美人鱼与控制它们的人组成了作品的张力。然而，问题的关键点并不只在于这种关系，而更重要的在于他把这些动物处理成人的欲望的恋物对象，并向我们直接发出了这样的反问，什么是欲望？欲望从何而来？显然，艺术家通过雕塑语言夸张和变形提示性地回答了这一问题，人的欲望无非是在占有与交换中试图获得享乐性的利益。他从草根立场出发，秉持社会公正意识，以愤世嫉俗和黑色幽默的态度表达了对非理性的欲望、虚荣、权力和暴力的蔑视和批判。陈文令的雕塑不只是把现实主义作为唯一的创作方法，而是在现实主义的基础上将民间图像、流行文化图像和历史图像加以糅合，以简洁、朴实、率真、夸张的手法将雕塑语言处理成具有荒诞、讽刺、幽默的黑色喜剧。

在《中国风景》中，陈文令的艺术观念有了一个转变，更让自己的雕塑具有实验性和公共性的特征，他充分发挥了个人的想象力，借用挪用、拼贴和转译的表现方法，即对自然、传统和现代的图像进行混合和转换，从而创造了一种超现实的奇异的山石之景，怪异山石被主观处理成了模棱两可的物象，类似于冰雪消融流淌所形成的冰山，又类似于一头硕大的鹿，也类似于传统园林中的亭子，而底部则像融化的冰，亭子上有正在流淌的晶莹剔透的水滴，这是一种扭曲和破碎的毫无真实感的幻象，生动再现了一个寂静空灵的洁净世界及与现实的疏离感。同时，雕塑《中国风景》充分利用了工业文明的不锈钢材质圆润光滑的曲面和流畅的线条，营造出的是一种现代社会的冷漠感和秩序感，表现出的融化、流淌、凝固的形式让人无不体验到时间的可变性和空间的无序性。事实上，艺术家的雕塑观念就在于他把自然的和谐性，现代（不锈钢材料）的冰冷感和力量感，传统的诗意美感进行了解构和整合。这也正是对中国社会处于农业社会、工业社会和后工业社会间相互冲突、重叠、混合的过渡时期的视觉化隐喻。艺术家准确地把握住了文化观念、历史意识和现实世界的有机联系。这是一件集自然、传统、工业于一体的超现实雕塑作品，具有互动性和公共性。当观众置身于作品中的时候，不锈钢的雕塑表面会对观众产生光的反射，使其感受到由光和影构成的奇异梦幻世界。在这个意义上，它试图提示人重新审视日常经验的参照系和整个外部环境的变化，并不断反视主体意识和洞察客观世界的变化。因此，我们通过陈文令的开放雕塑语言案例可以进一步认识和理解中国当代艺术在传统美学与现代美学的转换过程中的价值和意义。

2008年，陈文令的新作品再次迈向一个高度，他大胆而冒险地向那种易于固定化的个人艺术风格发起挑战，将艺术的内涵和外延进一步深化和延伸，既能从微观角度出发剖析人与社会的关系，又能直接借用或融入了技术、现成品、物体、装置的要素，从而形成了新的艺术语言。与此同时，陈文令的自我挑战也折射出对中国当代艺术中

盛行的作品重复和复制的批评。那么，陈文令在新作中又如何体现出新的意图呢？我们可以从他作品图像中感受到观念的转变——他从那种诗化世界中又重返世俗现实，因为他能从复杂而动感的现实中领悟到艺术语言的力度和深度，艺术不仅反映出艺术家的自我创造、自我展现和自我实现的过程，而且艺术的审美活动起到对人的"疗伤"作用。也就是说，艺术不仅要体现艺术家形式语言的表现张力，而且还要反映出艺术的社会干预意义，即对社会现实的解析与批判性。

在作品《物神》中，陈文令把人与猪混而为一，营造出一种非猪非人的模糊面孔，这种语言应被看作是中国当代艺术的"后波普"个案，他的作品在艺术表面上看起来是一种流行文化，实际上其的理念关键强调的是"最重要的崇拜对象不是精神而是物质"。这种物质性则借用了猪的形象，猪在中国社会中被看作是财富和欲望的象征物，并以社会批判的姿态强化了日常生活中的中国社会问题——反讽了中国进入疯狂的物质消费时代的特征。对人类来说，猪是一种没有脑子的只是吃的动物，而这个动物又成为被人类吃的对象。在这样的意义上，他的这种"后波普"语言，试图借用一种民俗性的语言替代资本主义式的流行文化。因此，陈文令的《物神》既是对科学基因的寓言，也是对无度的物欲社会的讽喻和批判。

在另一件作品《失重》中，陈文令把身体看作是像山一般的难以屹立的巨大躯体中包裹着无限的欲望，不稳重的下滑的身体预示了物的无限扩张，并导致了灵与肉的失衡以及精神与物质的失控。它是对身体内在本质的质疑，是什么导致身体的欲望？是什么造成身体失衡？又是什么支配或控制着身体？

陈文令的作品《丰胸猪》则是从现实语境出发，创造出了一个怪异的艺术表征，既表现了科技进步对身体带来的美感，同时也隐喻了它对人的身体造成的一定伤害，进而把这种现象延伸和联系到中国现实——整个社会到处充满着物化的过程，并暗示了中国现代化发展中的透支和隐痛。

　　在《中国幻想》中，陈文令将闽南风水球、茶艺、民俗文化和新媒体艺术融为一体，创造出了一个集装置、雕塑、新媒体、行为等组成的跨学科意义的娱乐性和反讽性的作品，这种源自民间和民俗的艺术原动力建构起了一种新的当代艺术语言，具有很多启发意义，民俗或民间艺术在当代艺术中能否有被转译的作用？事实上，陈文令通过不断的艺术实验充分证明了开创一个新的艺术的可能性。

[2009]

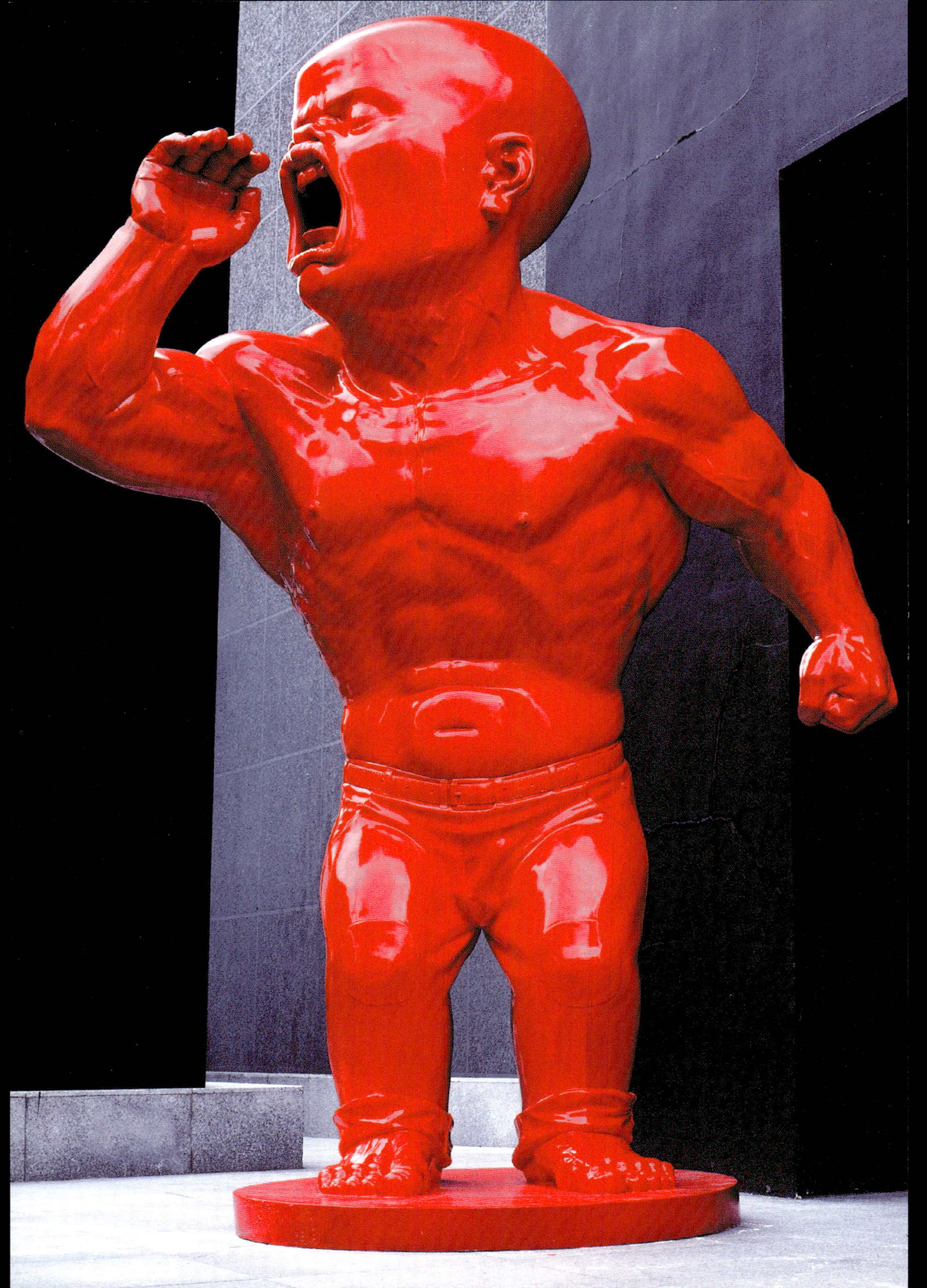

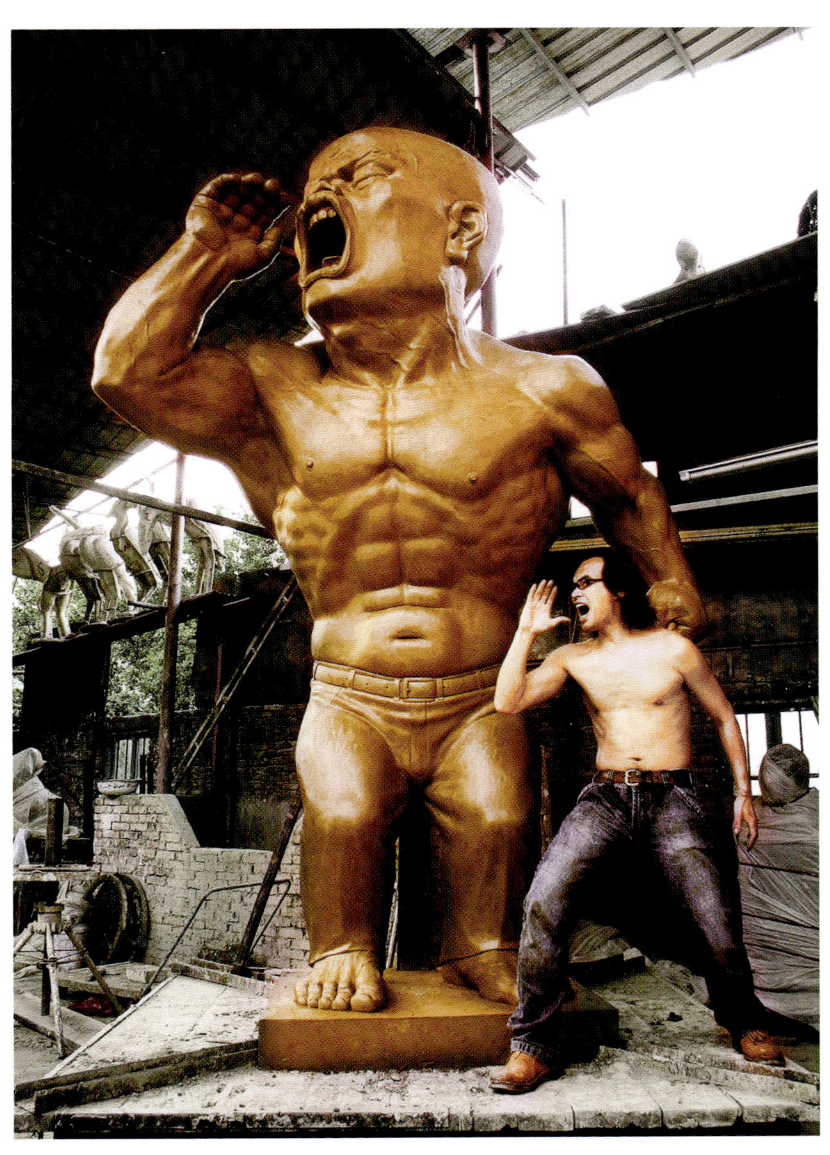

Homunculus / 侏儒, 2005   *Homunculus Draft* / 侏儒, 2005

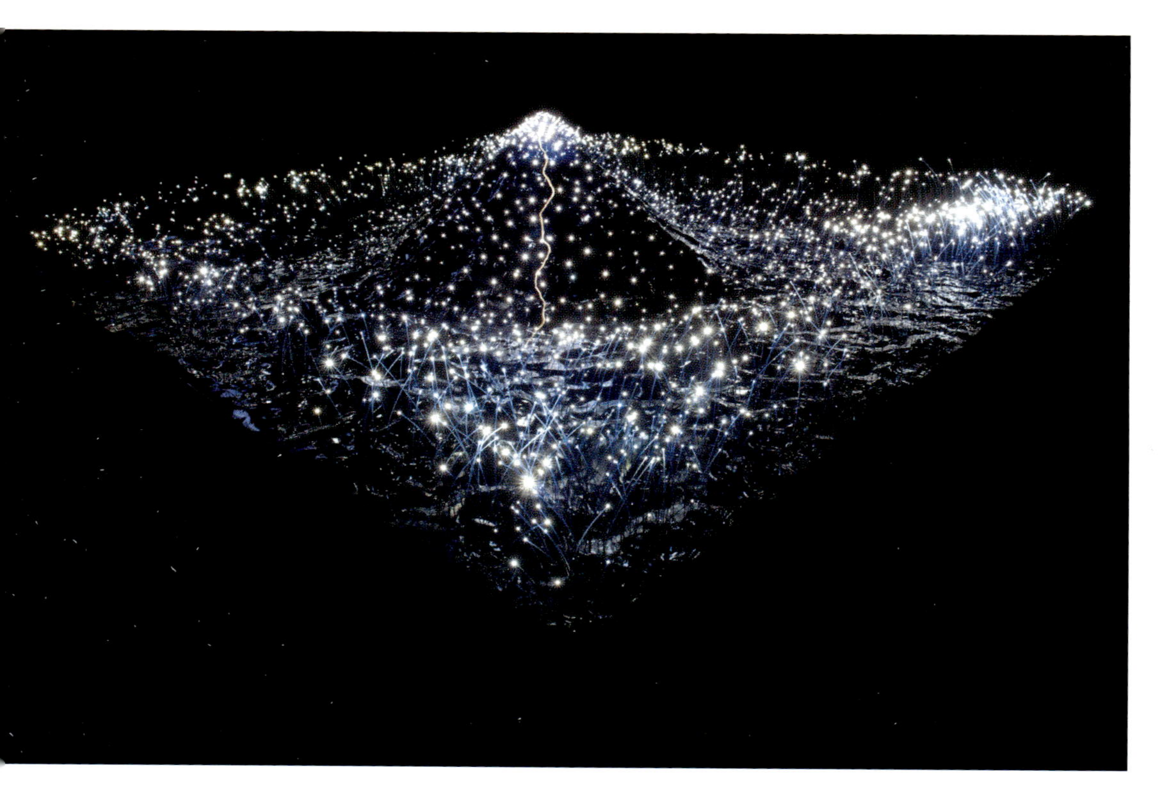

5.12 NO. 1 12th May No. 1, 2008

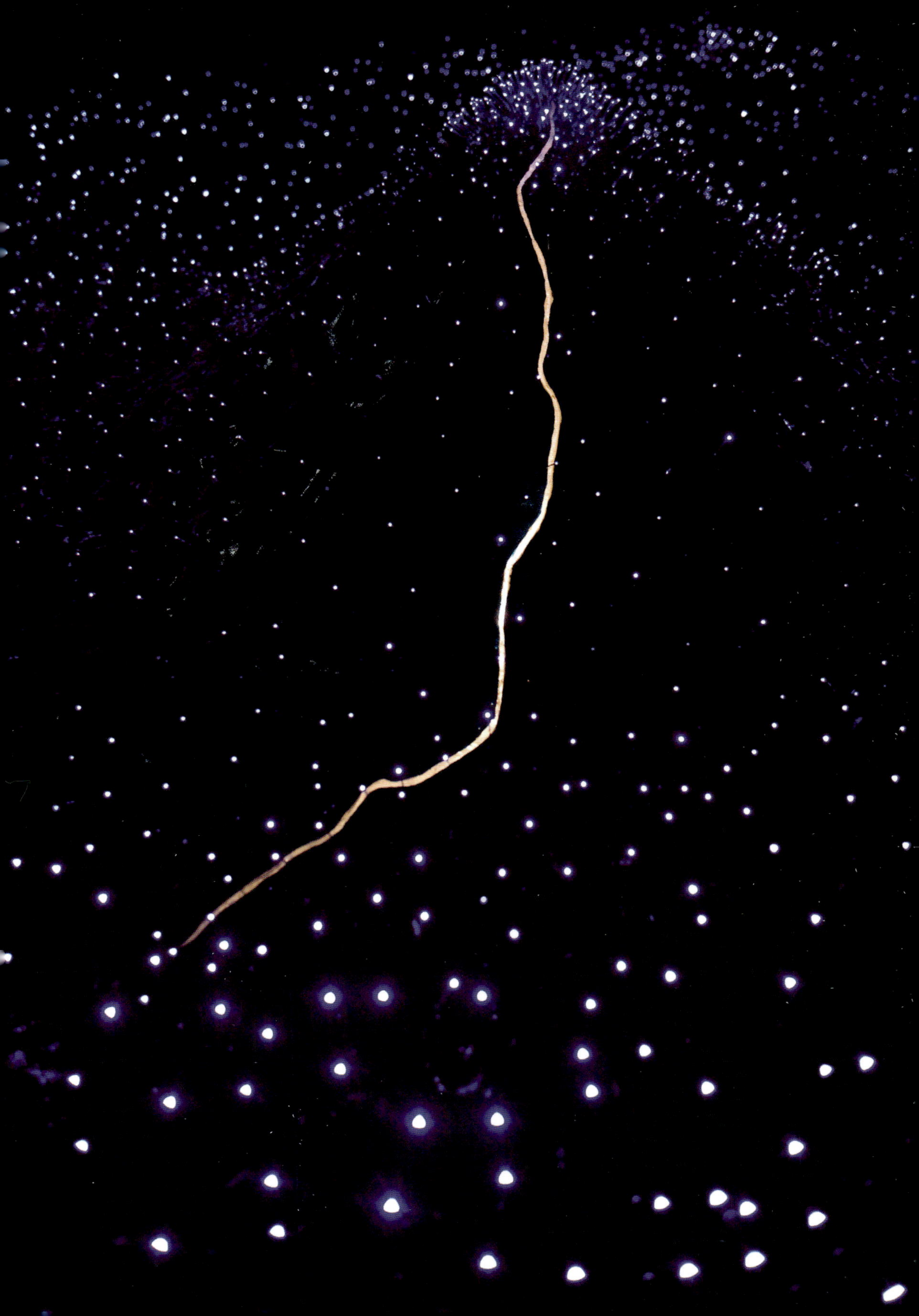

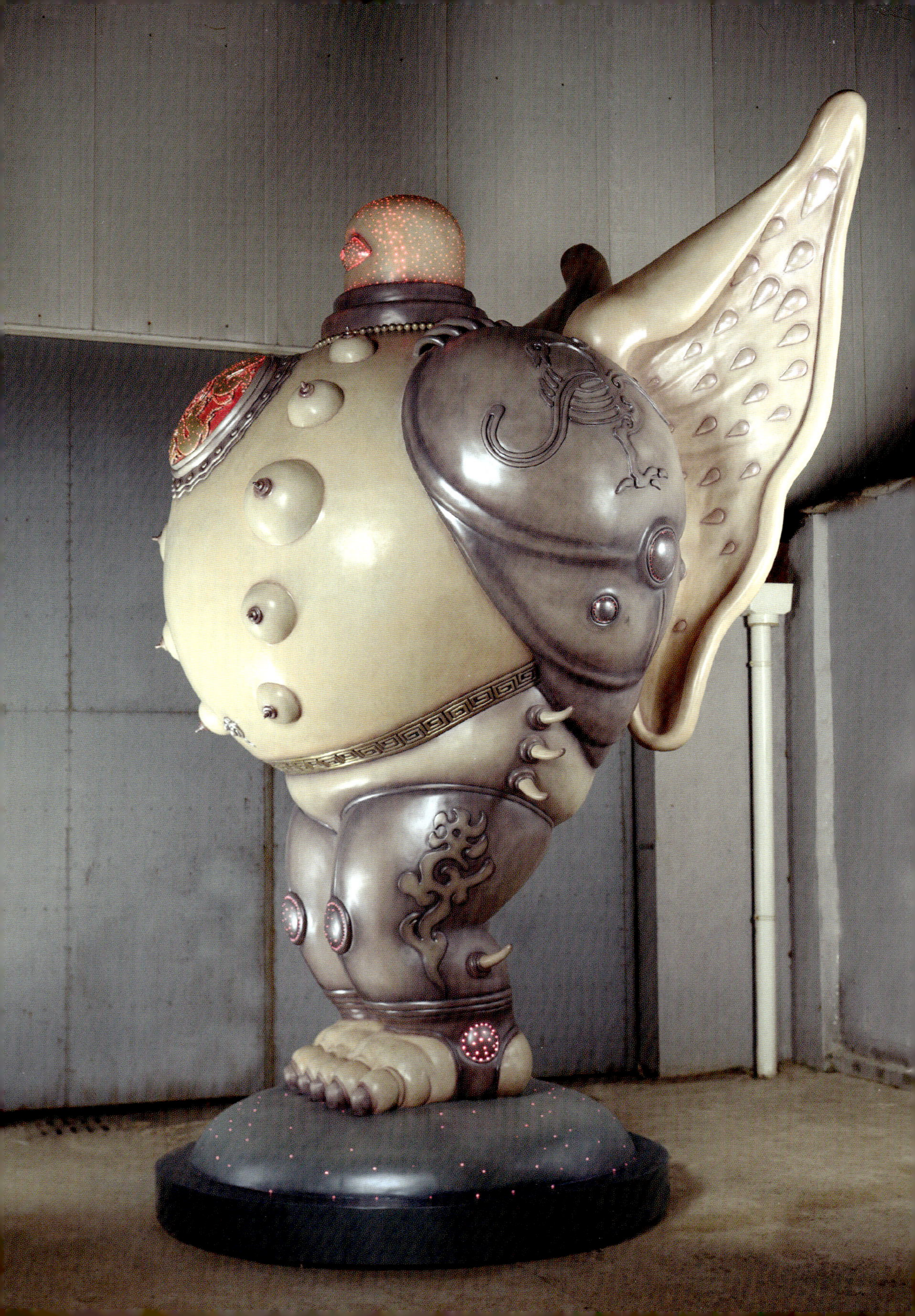

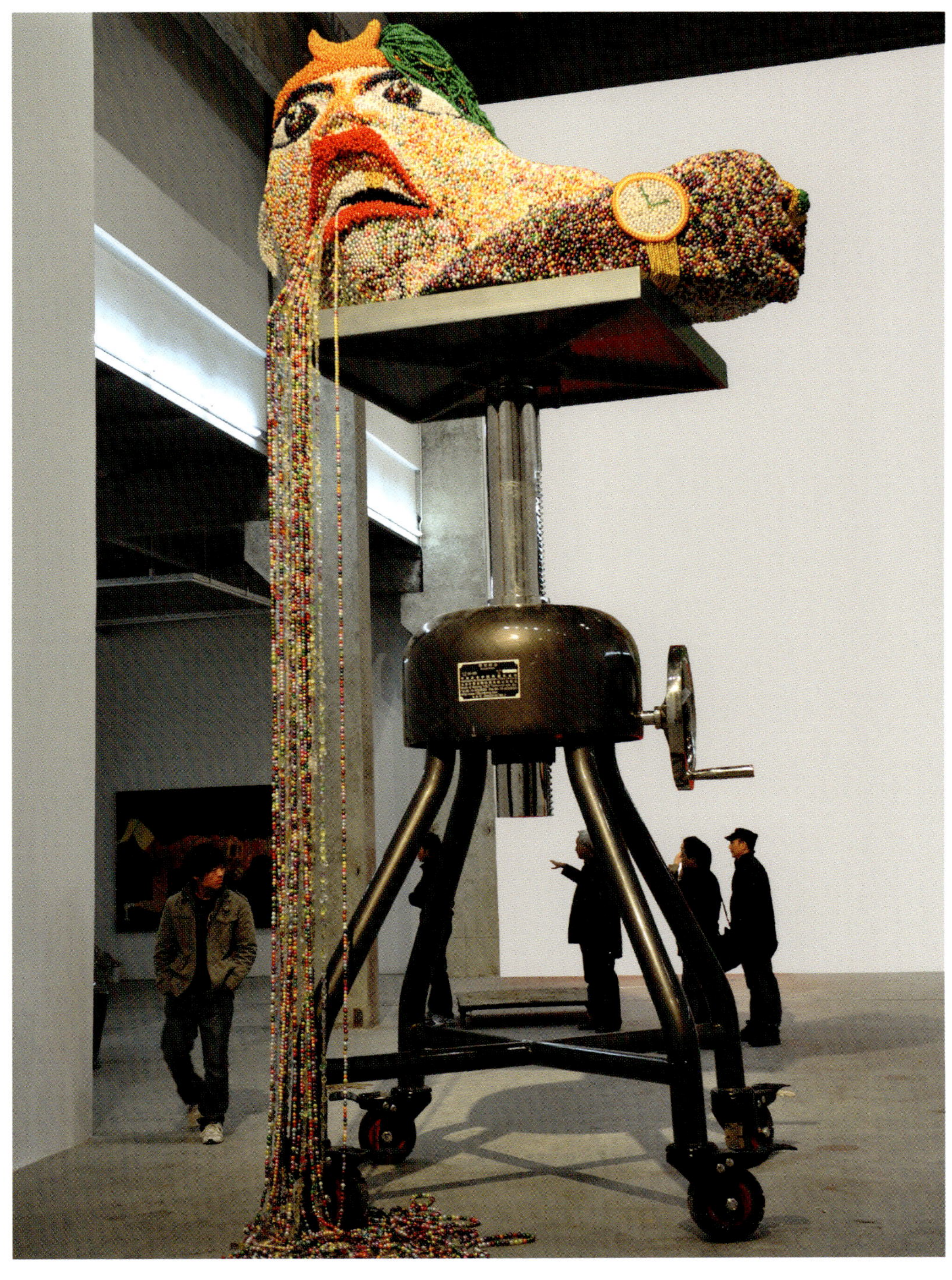

Uninvited Guest / 不速之客, 2008   *Altar* / 祭坛, 2008

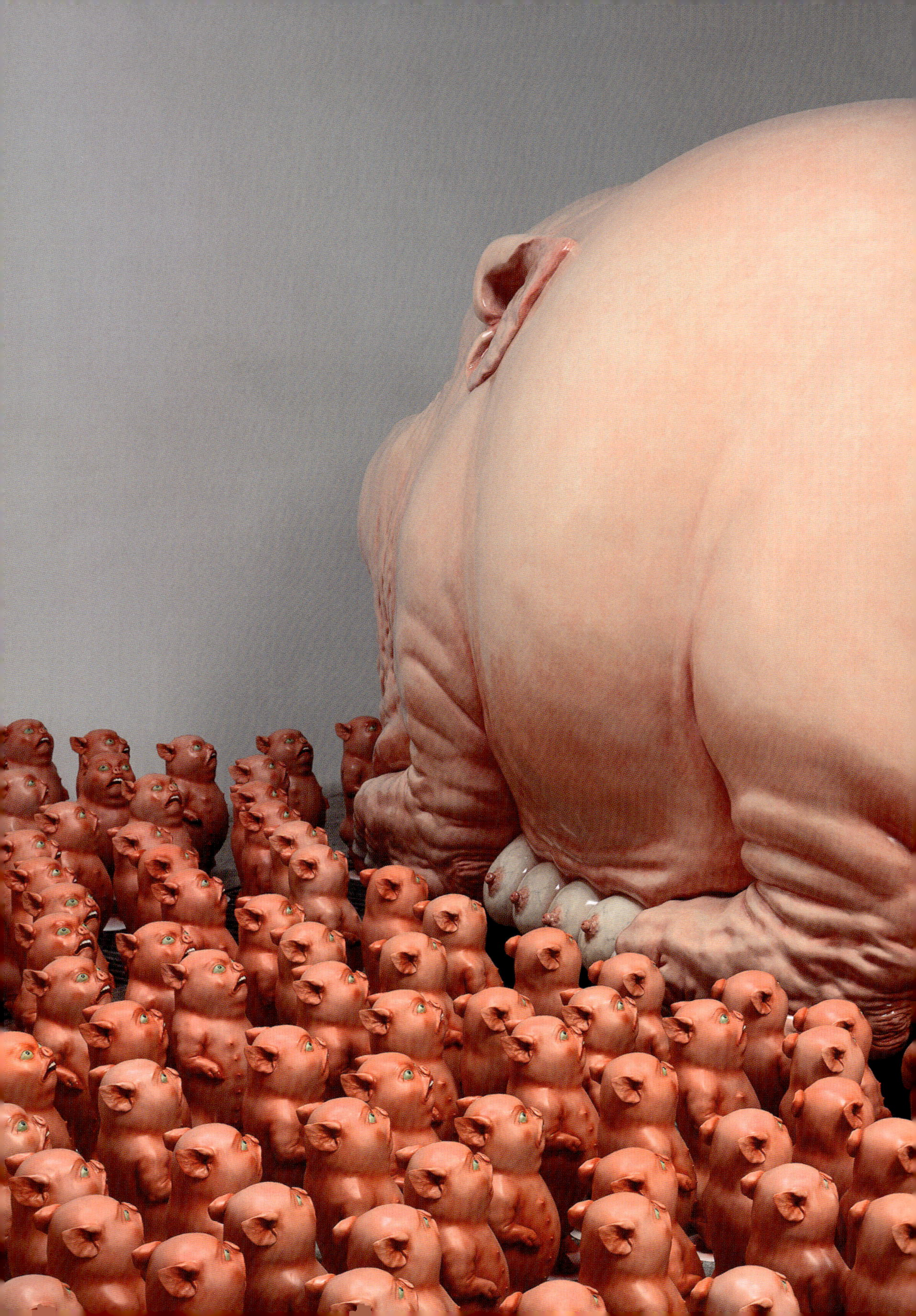

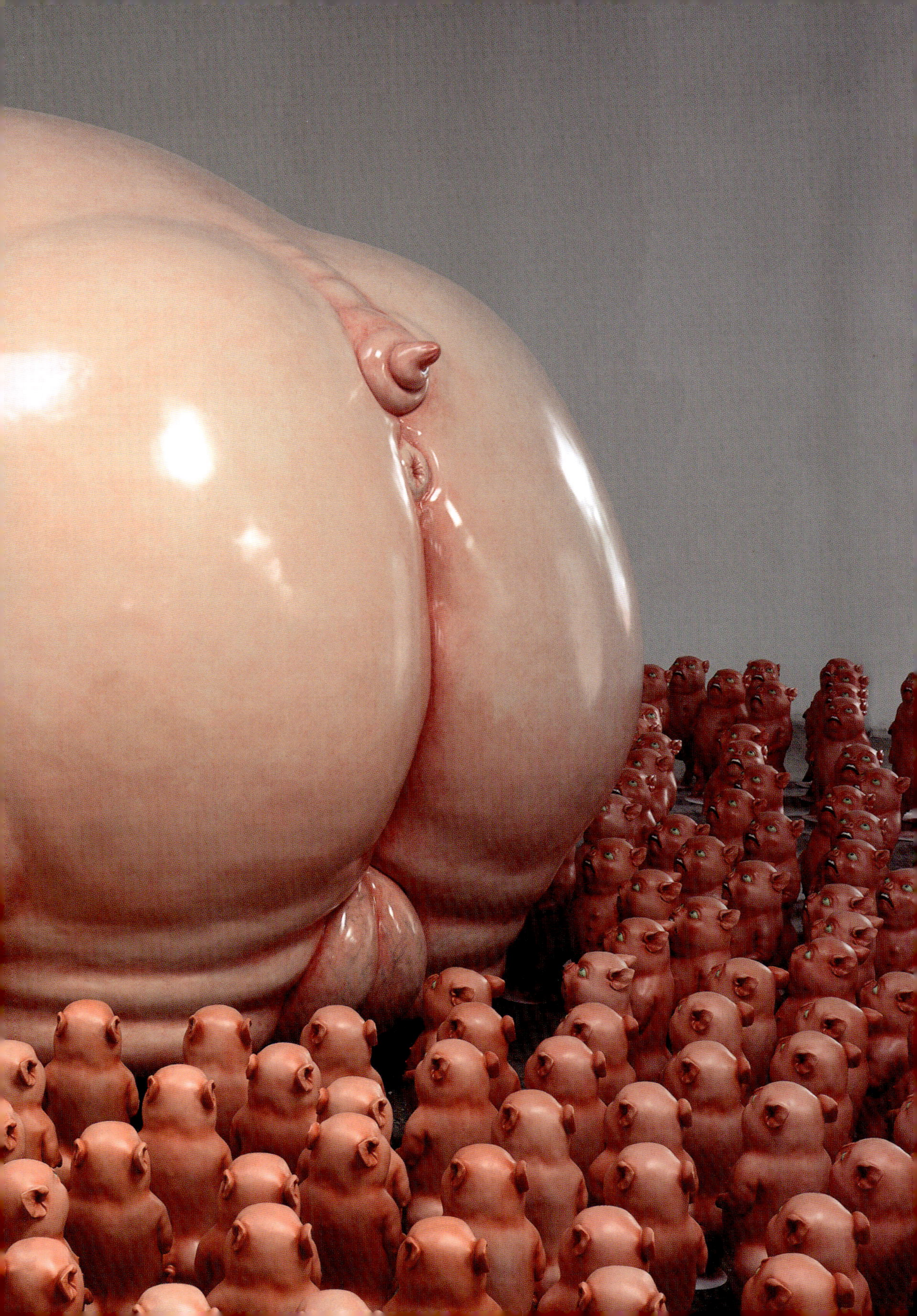

pp. 66-67
God of Materialism / 物神, 2008

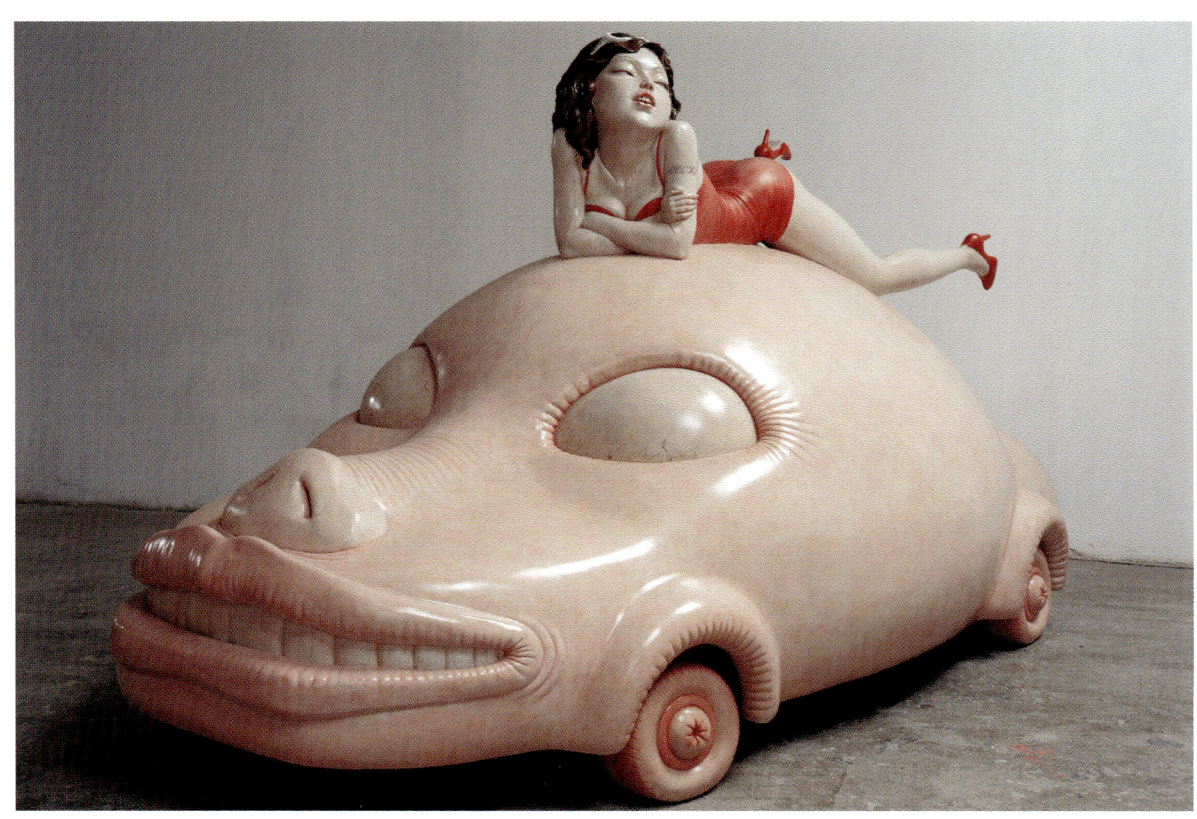

Handsome Car and Pretty Girl / 香车美女, 2008

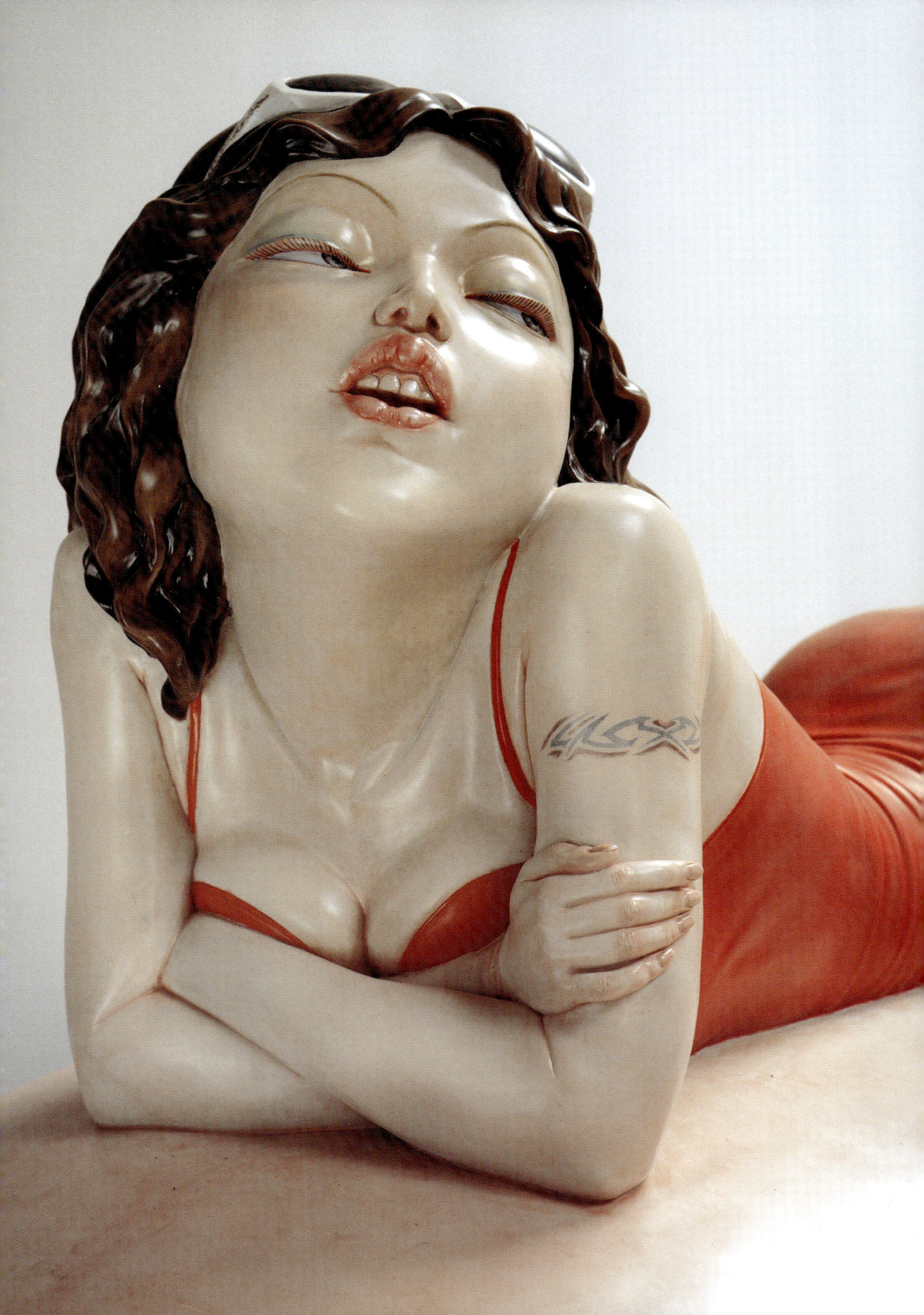

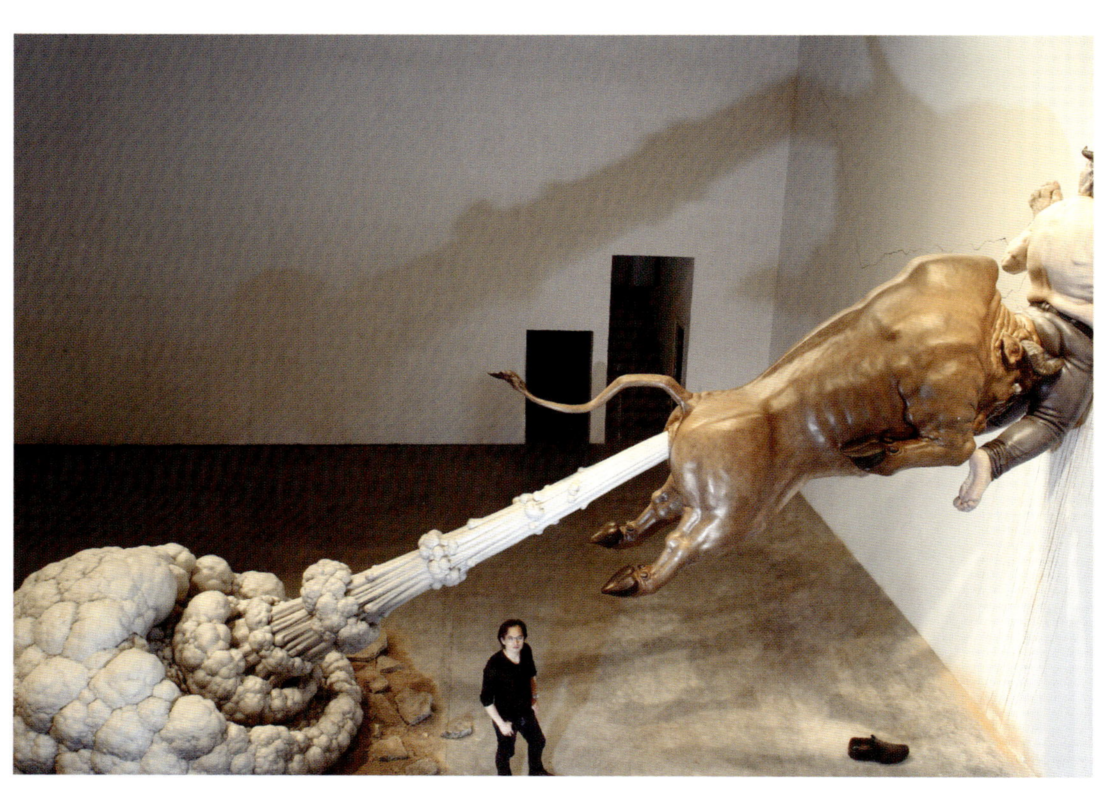

What You See is not Necessarily True / 你看到未必是真实的, 2009

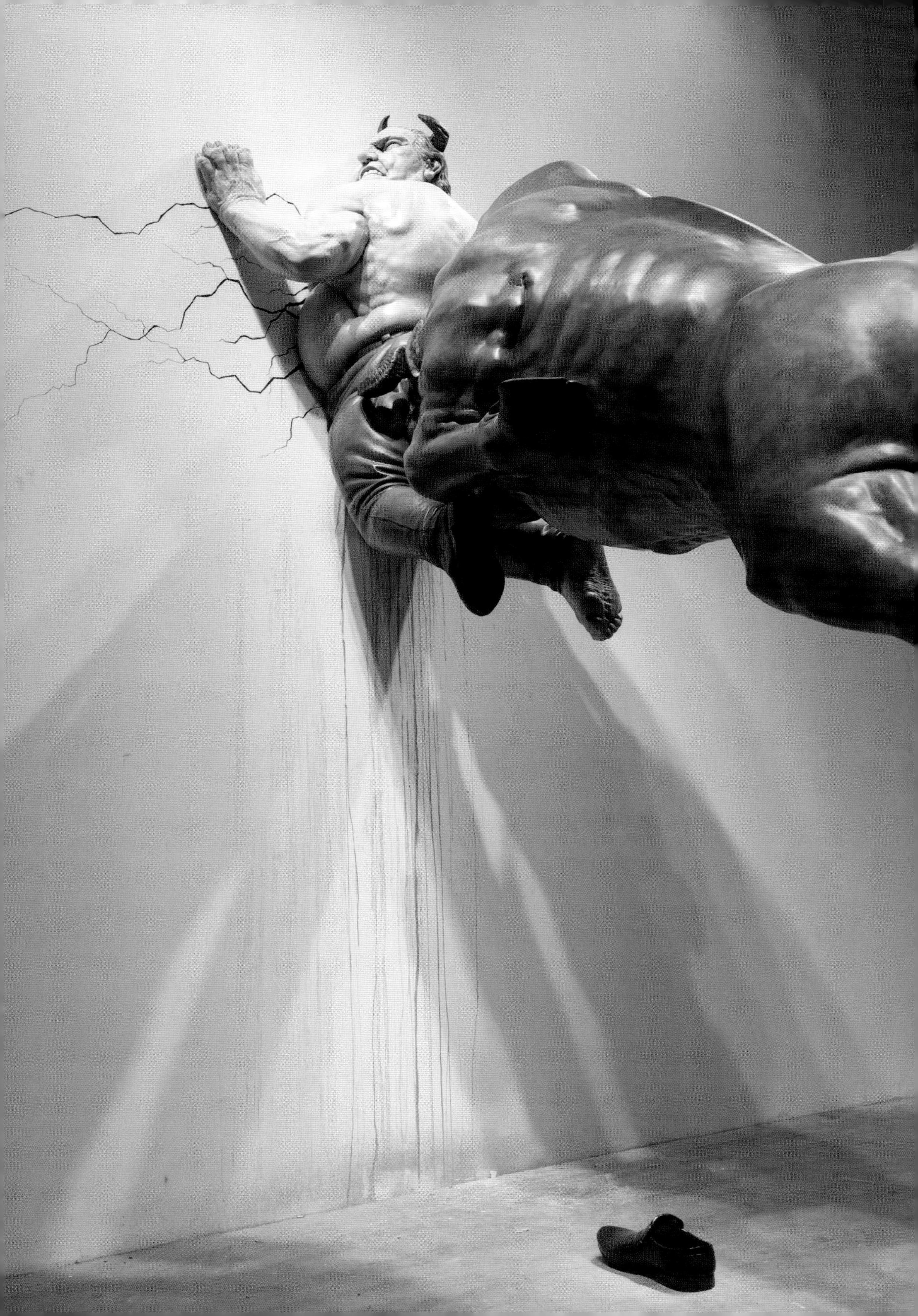

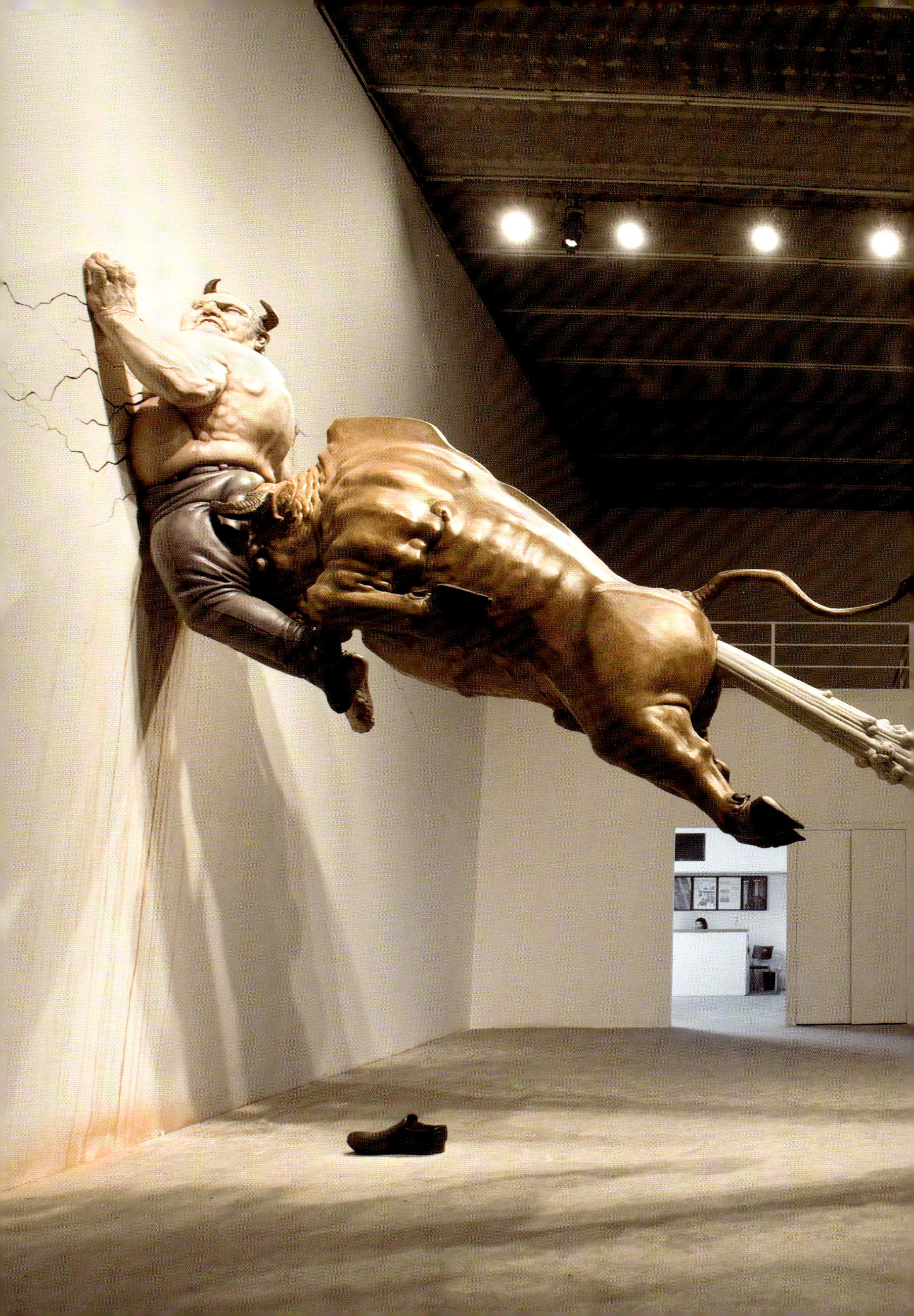

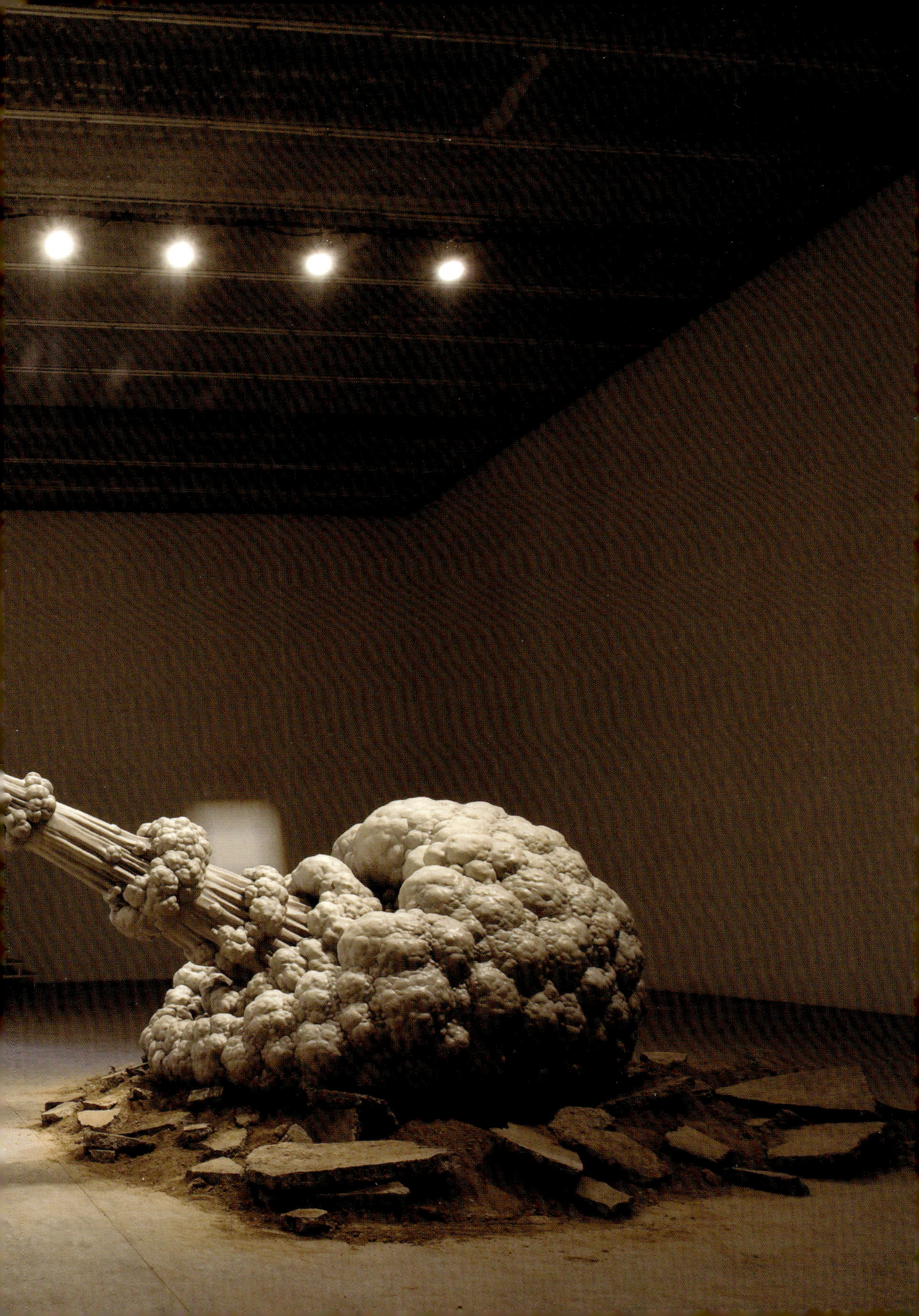

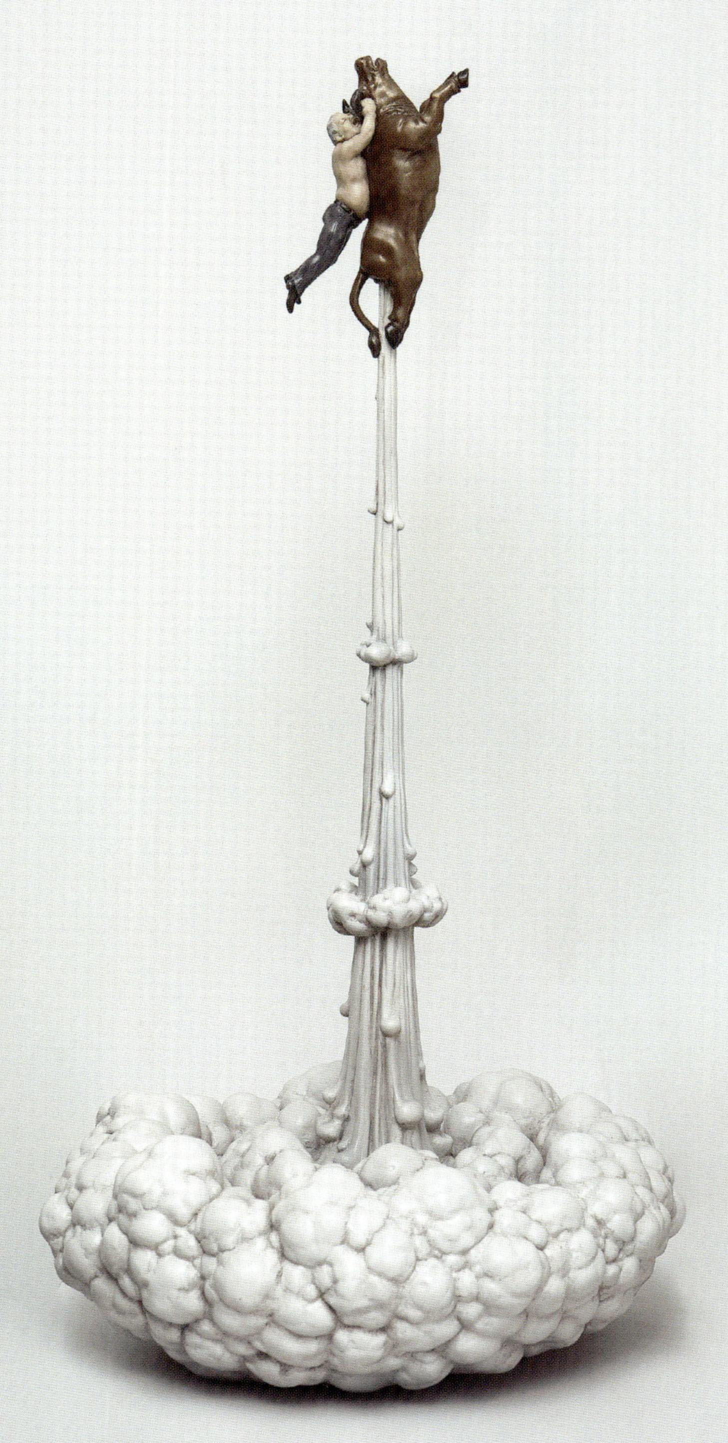

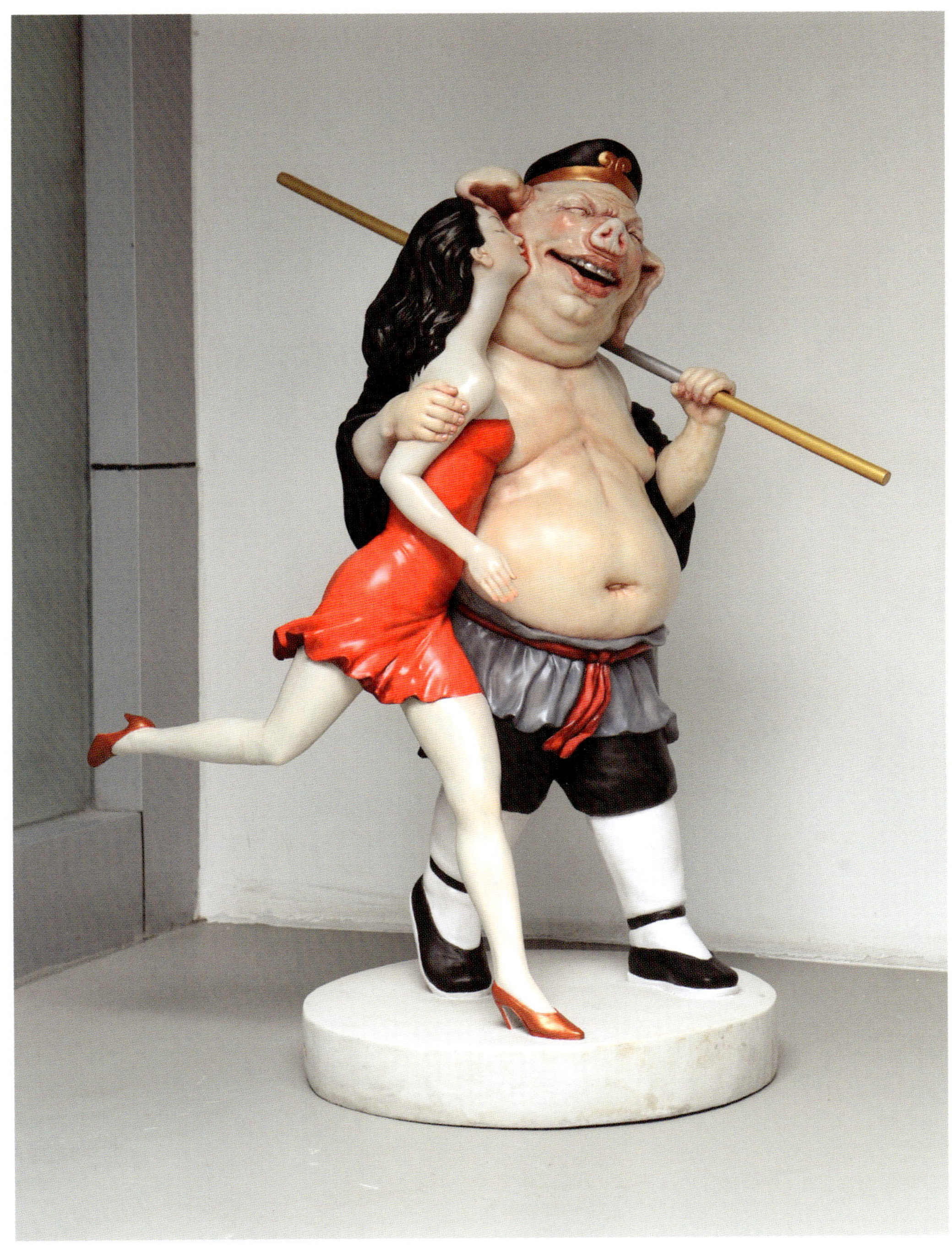

How to Escape / 如何逃离, 2009   *Back from the West* / 西天归来, 2009

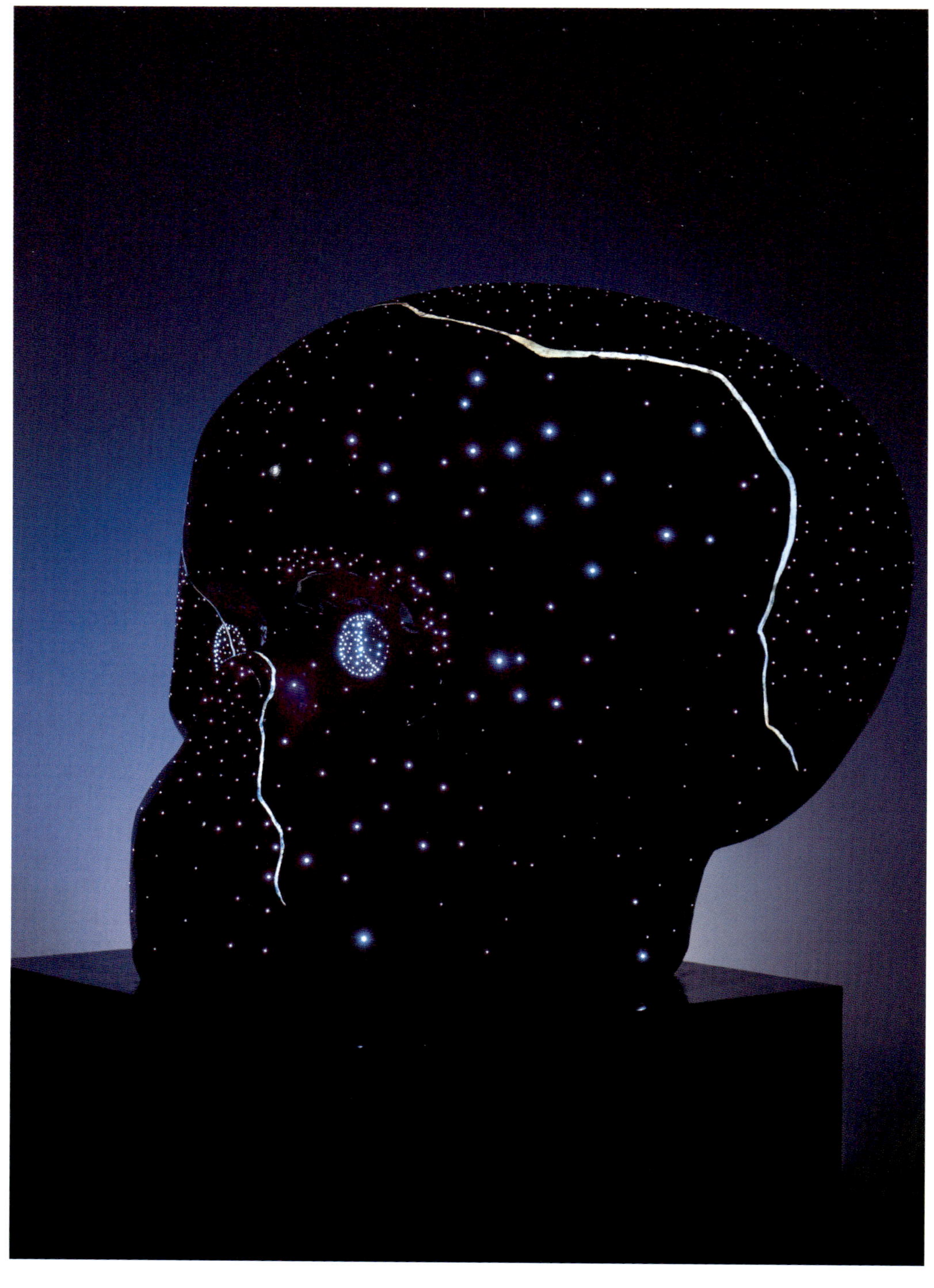

5.12NO.2 12th May No.2, 2009

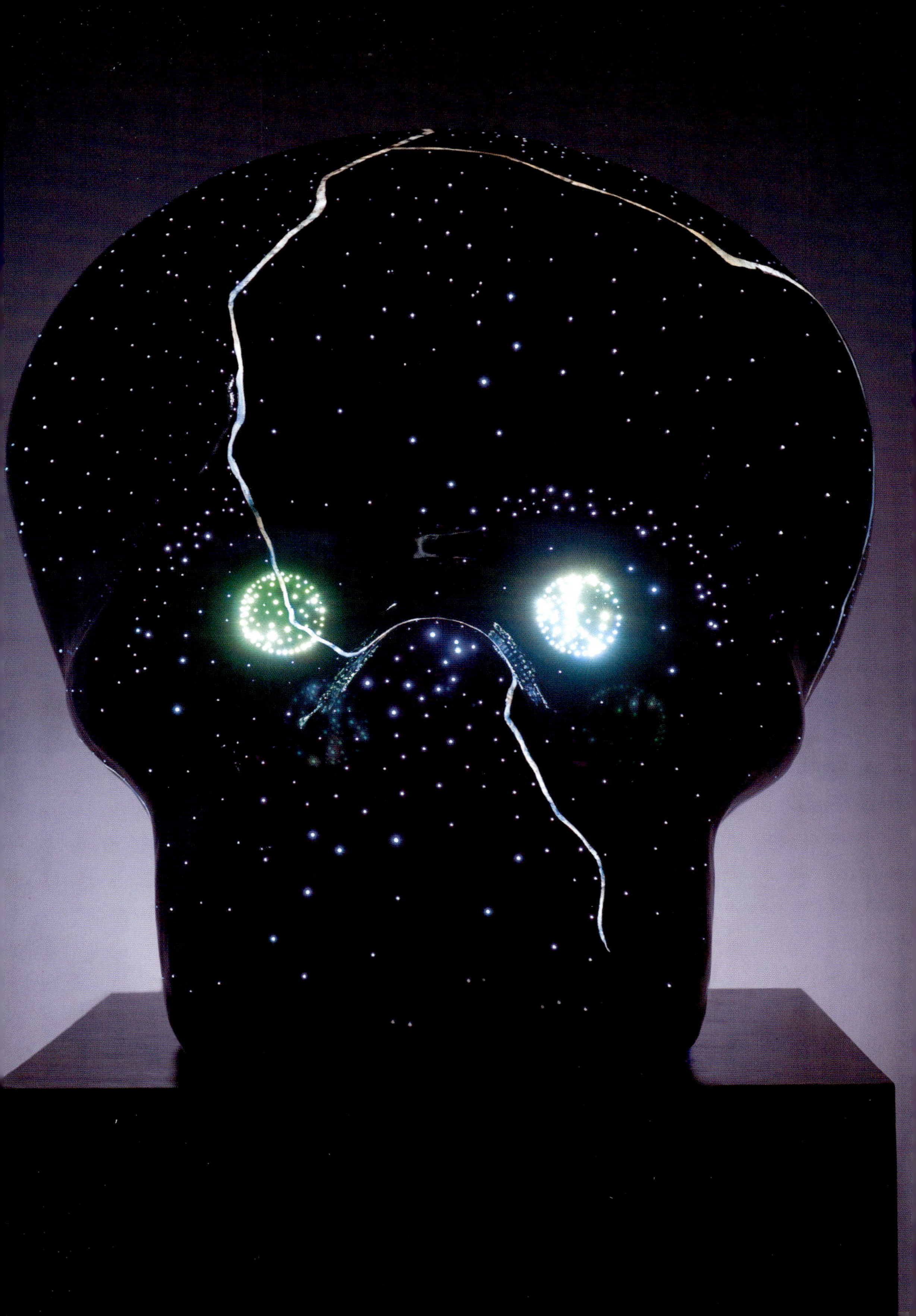

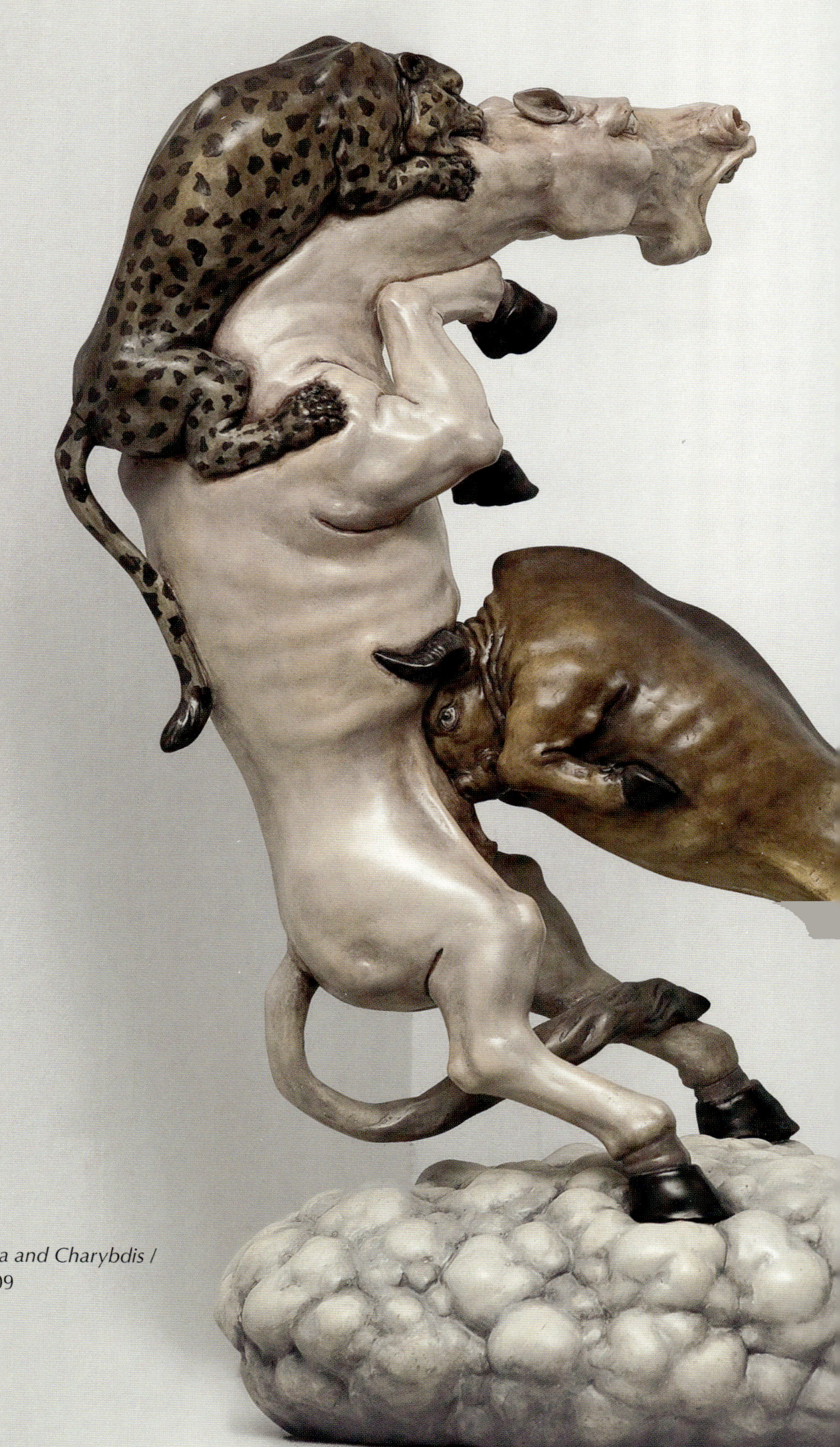

Between Scylla and Charybdis /
腹背受敌, 2009

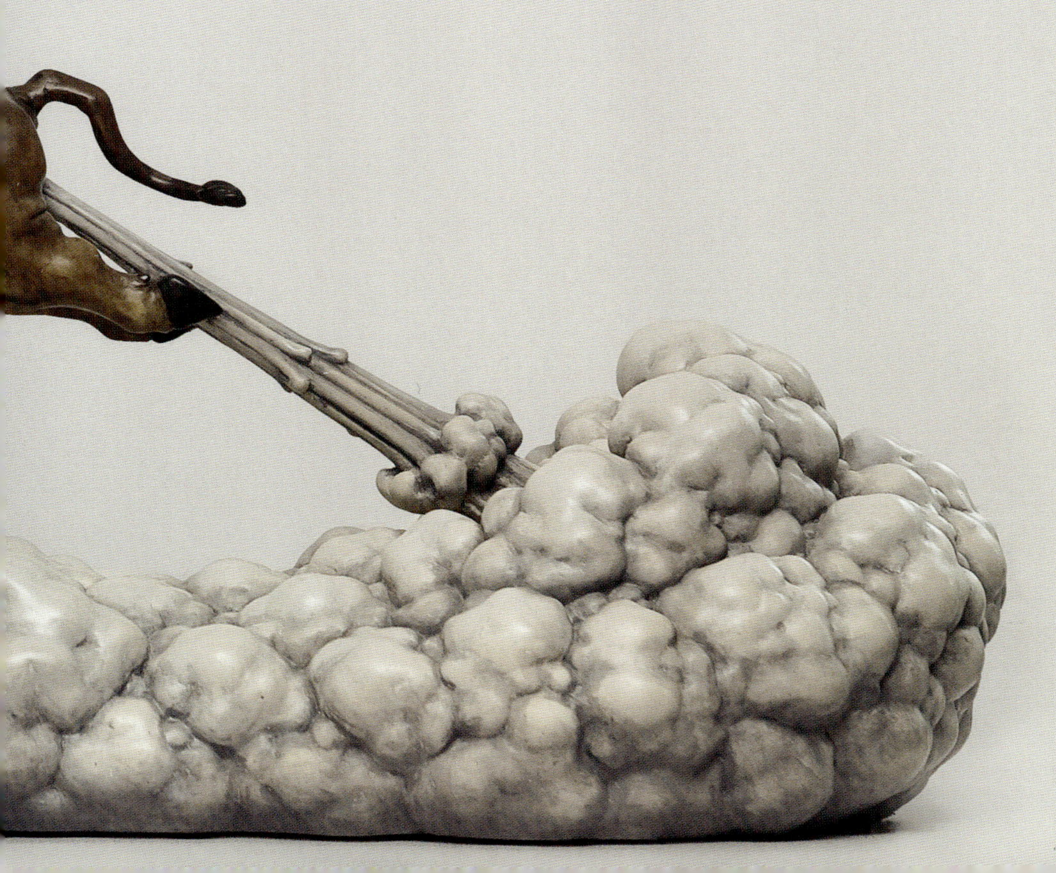

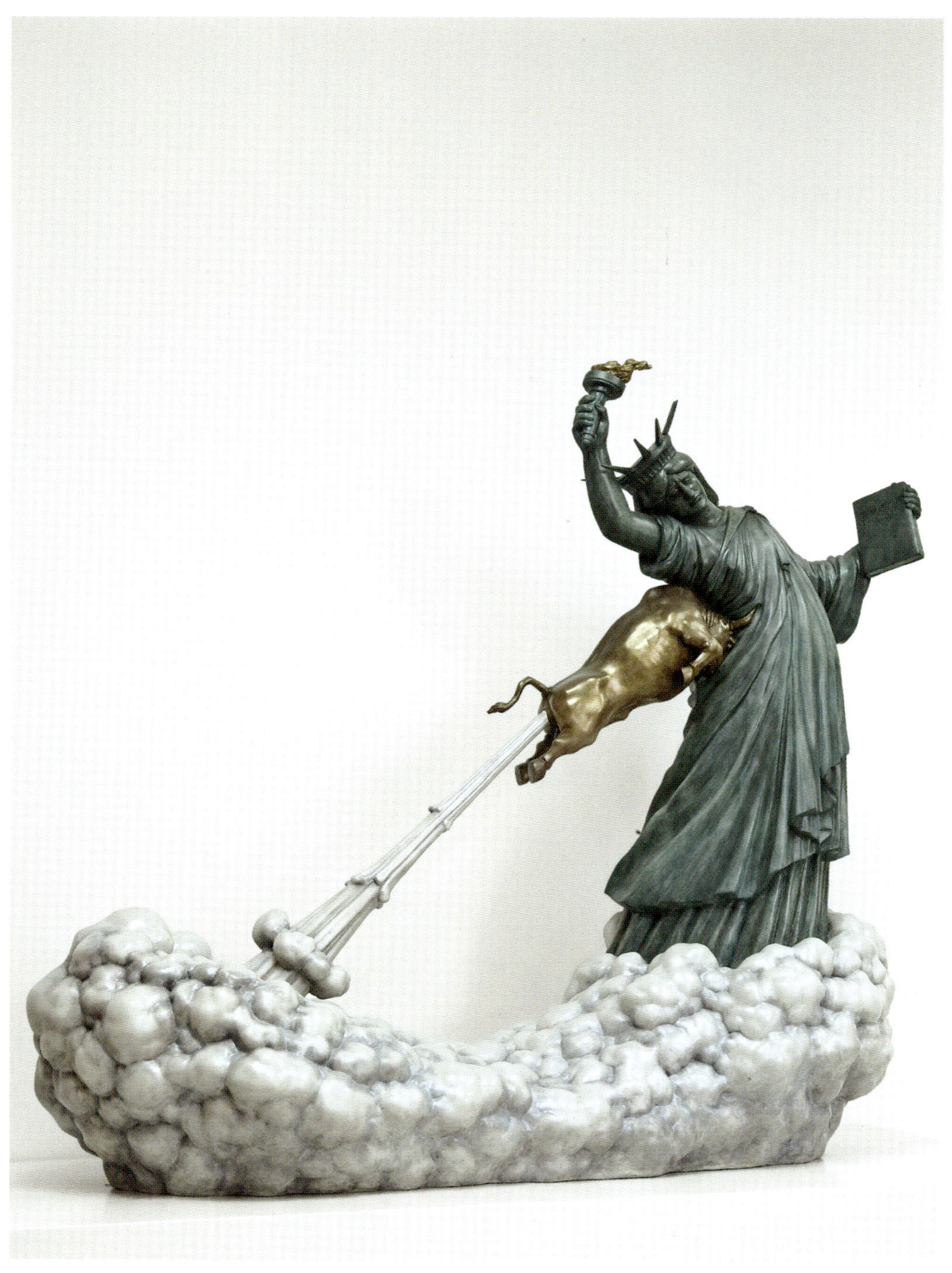

Statue of Liberty and the Golden Bull /
自由女神与金牛, 2009

The Fall of a Noble Steed /
一只行高之马的陨落, 2010

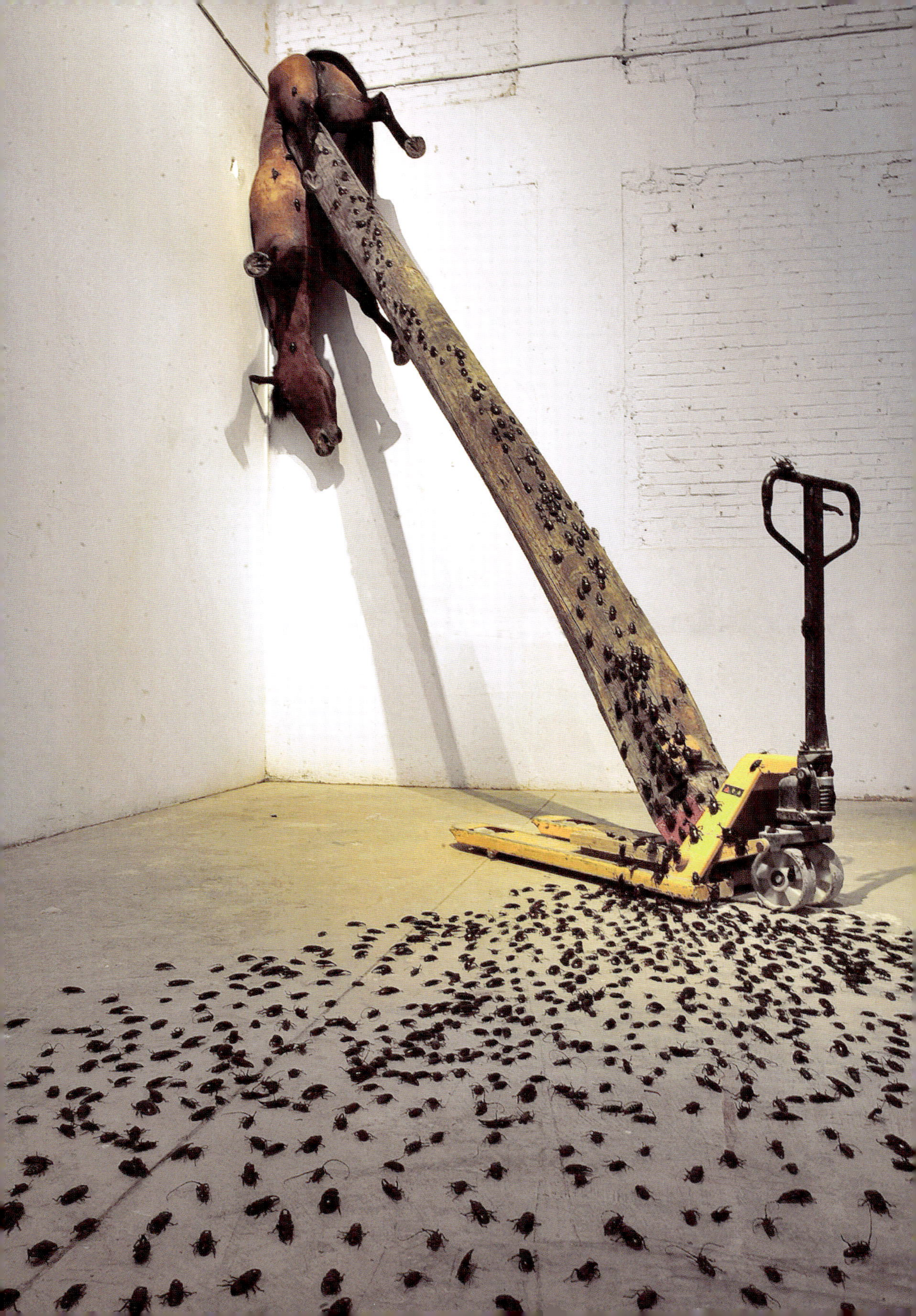

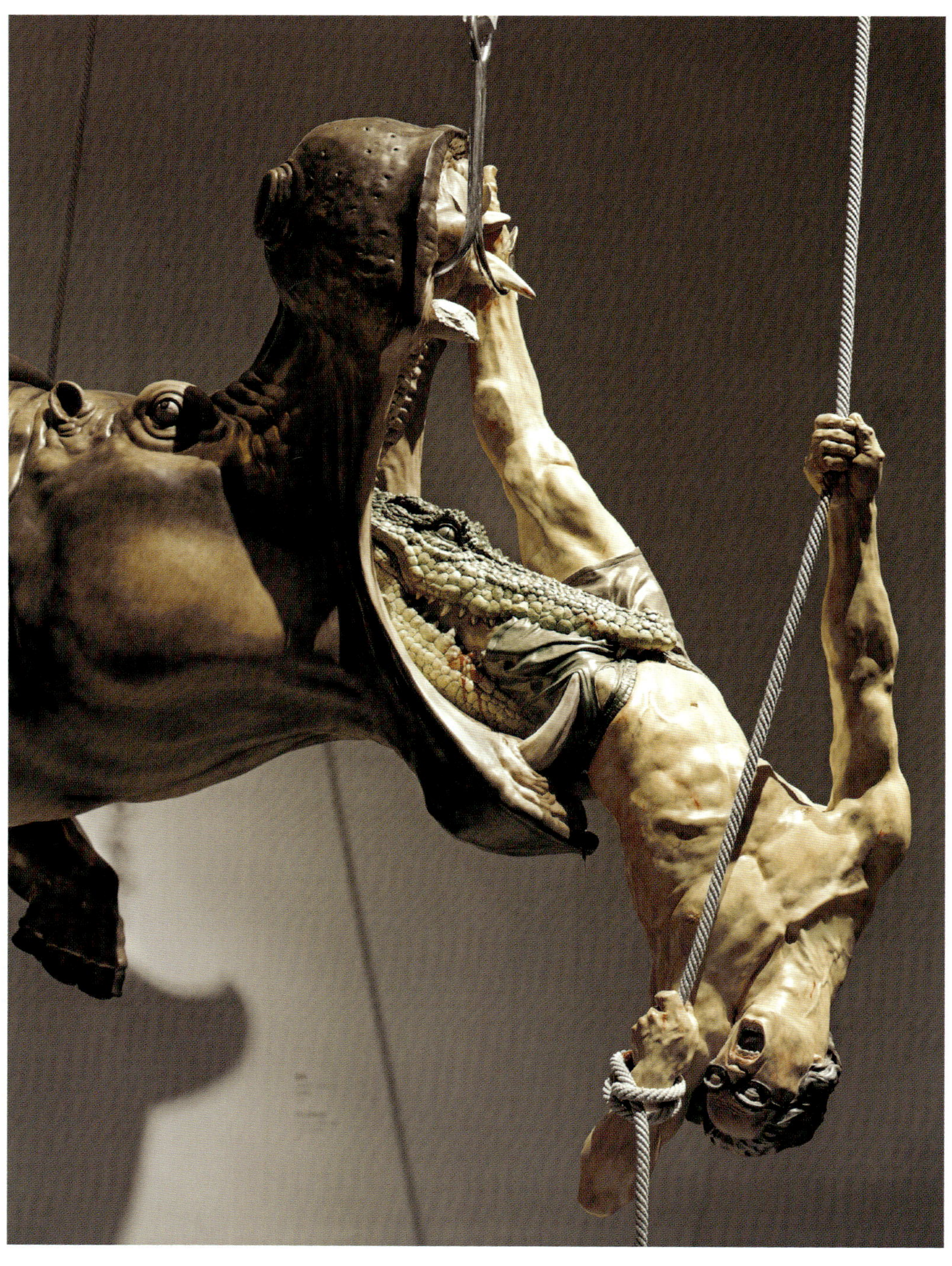

The Suspense Part / 悬案局部, 2010

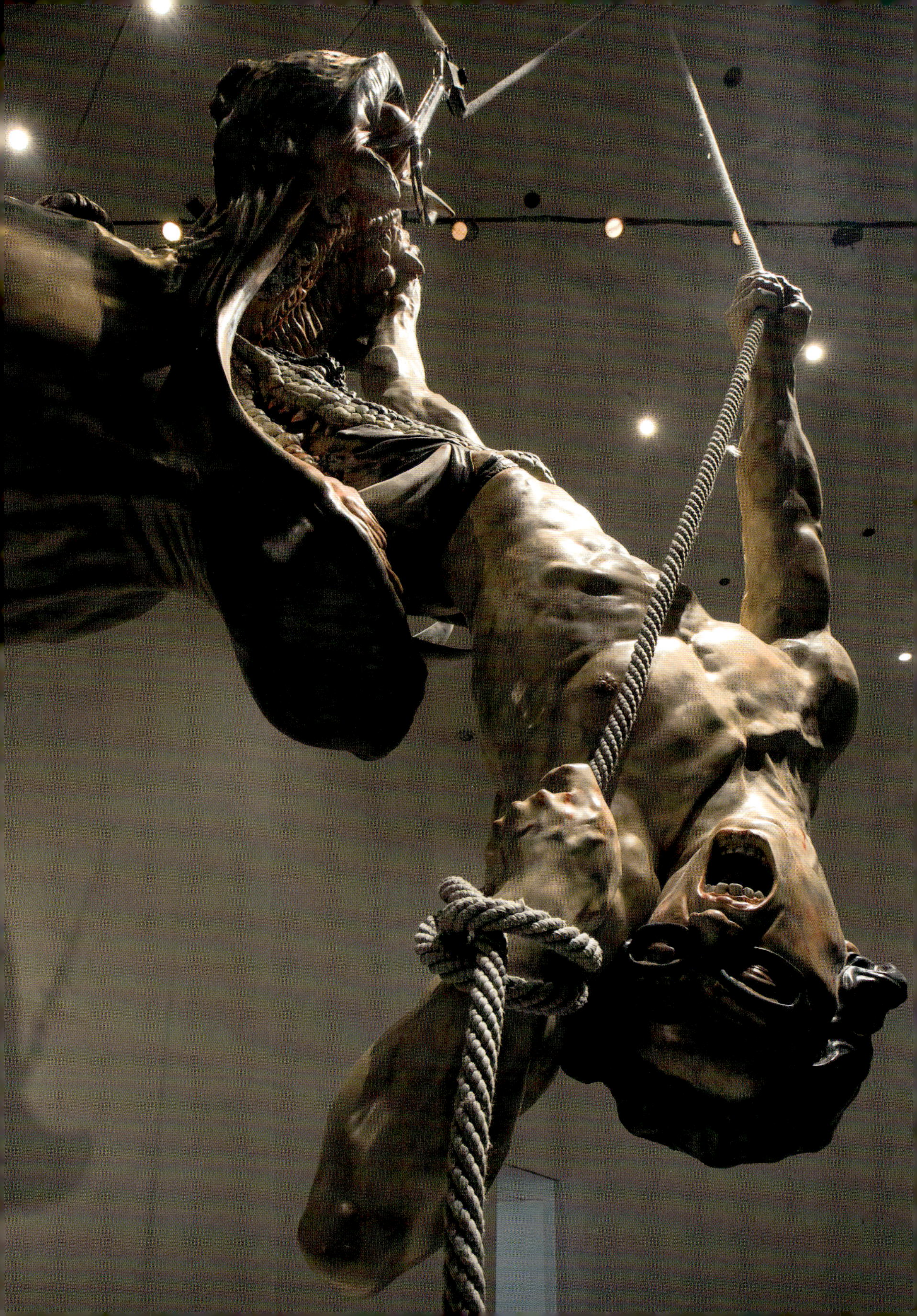

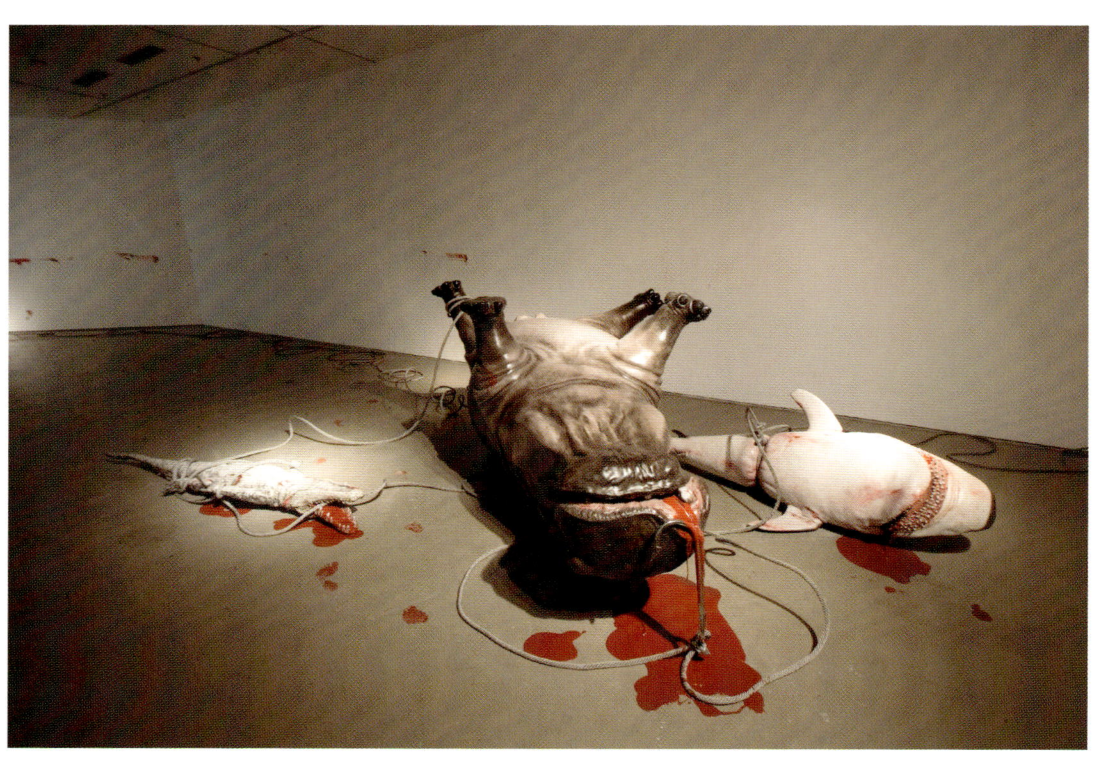

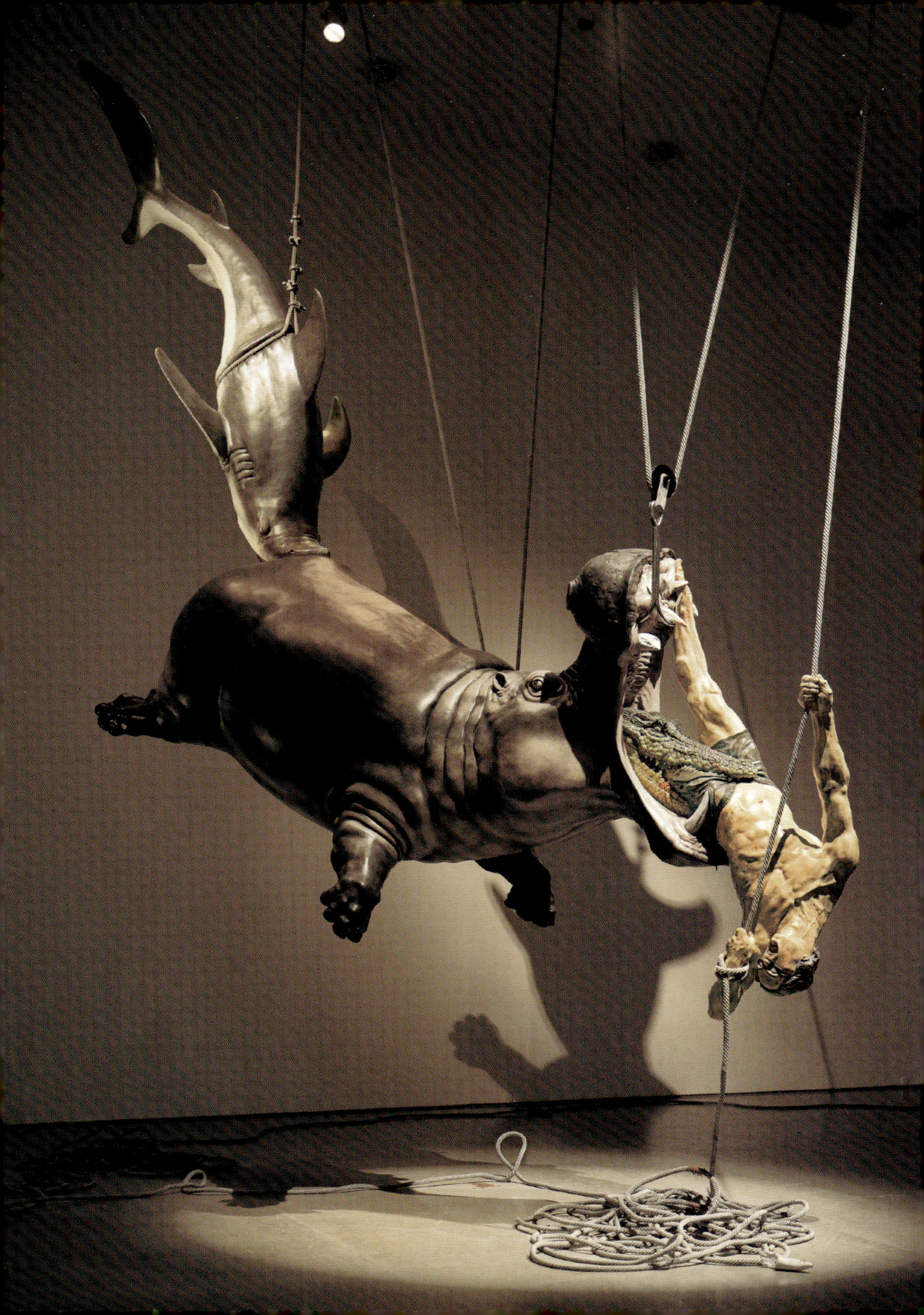

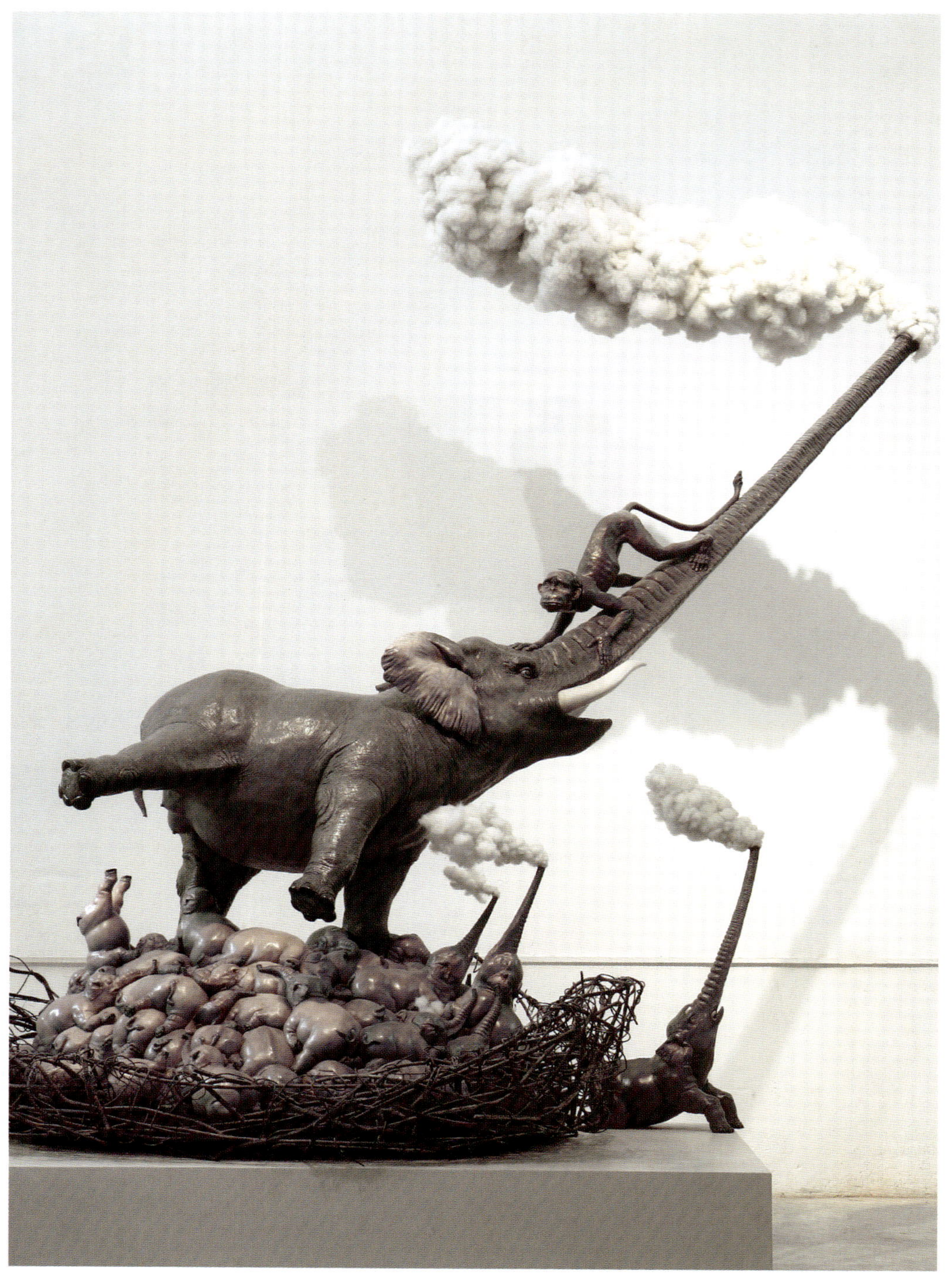

This Is Not An Elephant / 这不是大象, 2010

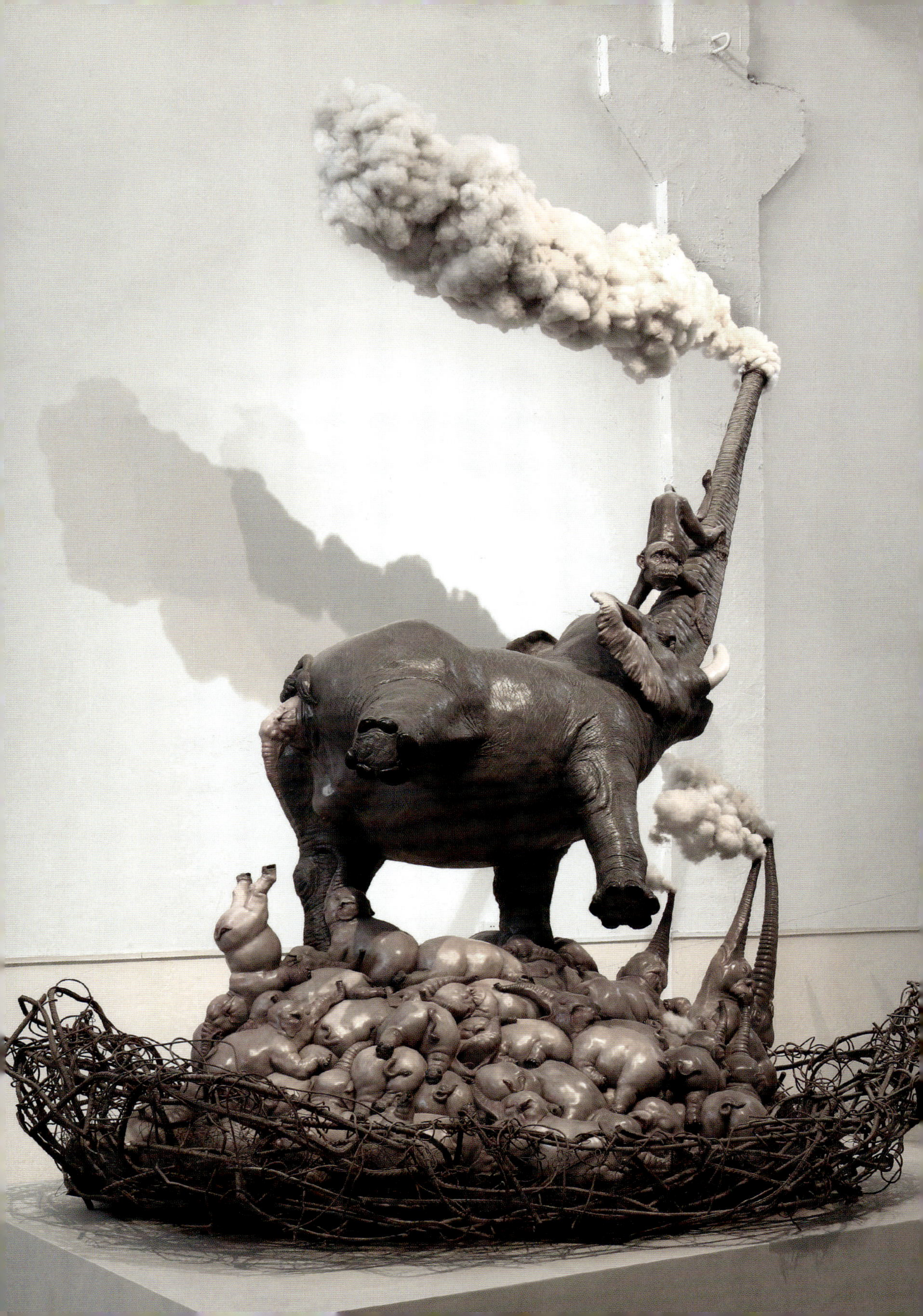

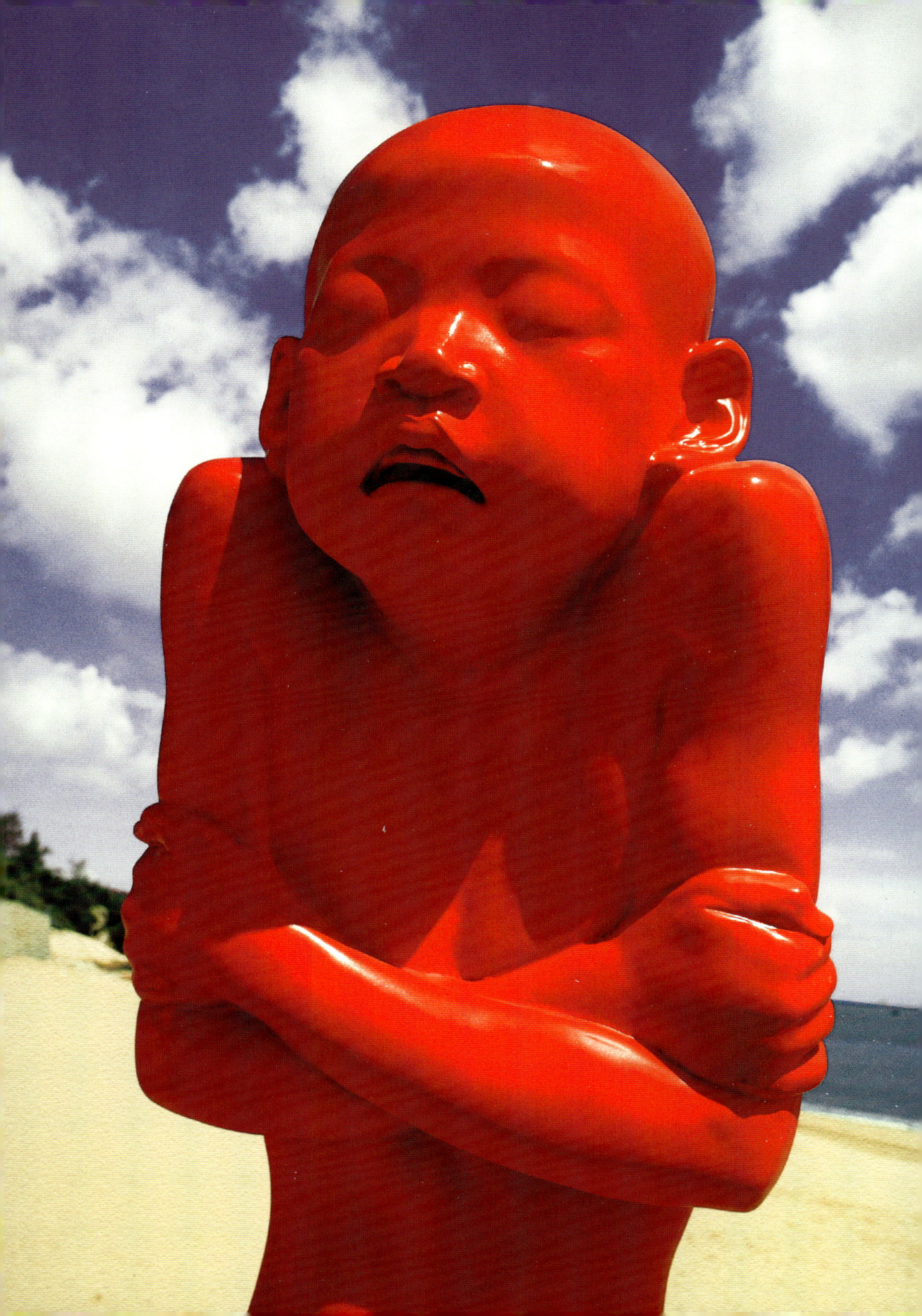

The Red Boy Is Having His Moment

Peng De

The red boy's body from Wenling Chen's *Red Memory* is consumed in red like a raging fire. Red is the color of 2003, from the South Korean "Red Devils" fans to the elusive crimson team uniforms of European football, not to mention all kinds of red Chinese objects; red is everywhere around us. The popularity of the color red has given *Red Memory* its justifiable colorific space. Historically, red has always been an iconic color and the symbol of auspiciousness in southern China. In practice, a red-colored body alters the realistic proportions of the artwork, emphasizes a tendency towards the unreal and expresses the artist's denial of the snobbery, tension, anxiety, fear and cruelty that exist in all adults, yet unexpectedly expounds our common aspiration: cherishing memories of childhood innocence and questioning the precocity of two thousand years of Chinese civilization.

In spring 2002, when Wenling Chen's group of red boys first debuted at Pearl Bay Beach in Macau, it attracted an audience of thousands. By the end of the exhibition, many Macau citizens appealed to the local authorities to keep them in the city permanently. *Red Memory* instantly became a daily topic in the local media. In fall 2002, Chen's *Red Memory* was exhibited in the first Triennial of Chinese Arts Exhibition in Guangzhou. This time, the artwork not only garnered praise from the media and audiences, but also attracted the attention of critics. This group of sculptures, consisting of over a hundred naked boys, was divided into several categories according to their different postures of playing by the water. The sculptures were crafted from blown glass, then sanded, polished and sprayed with red paint, and placed on the beach, on tree trunks, on prows and on top of the lighthouse. 450,000 RMB (US$72,562) was invested to create this installation, the most costly work of all those exhibited. While it is true that the value of an artwork isn't necessarily in direct proportion to the cost of its creation, in this case, the ship certainly has risen with the tide.

There are thousands of solo and group exhibitions in China every year, with only very few works that stand out from the crowd, almost all of which have met one visual need: freshness. Wenling Chen's works belong to a new art form – a combination of sculpture, installation, interactive performance art and a happening. In terms of sculpture, Chen's work is different from both the orthodox classification of academism and the novelty of modernism as well as from the "fat" of Aristide Maillol or the "slim" of Alberto Giacometti. In term of an artwork that combines installation and performance art, Chen's work is also radically distinct – in both artistic perspective and expression – from avant-garde extremes. This group of red boys is neither innocent nor evil, healthy nor sickly. As the public knows, visual art of the late 20th century, whether traditional artwork, movies or 3D animations in video games, is flooded with violence and outcries about imaginary ailments. Wenling Chen's red boys have the character of a lotus, which rises unsullied from mud, and quenches our thirst for a new direction for avant-garde art, whereby art becomes a weapon to criticize humanity and is transformed into a medium on which humanity can be constructed. Whether amateurs or professionals, academics or avant-garde critics, everyone can find their own focus in Chen's work.

Wenling Chen's group of red boys was renamed *Red Memory*. As a piece of contemporary art, its ambiguity demands interpretation. When people look at these boys, they might think of the phrase "red boy"[1], but in less pedantic terms; they might think of the "Red Kid" in the classic novel *The Journey to the West*, but they are not so wicked; they might think of the "red guards" of the Cultural Revolution, but they are not so bloodthirsty. People might also look at Macao as a fortified military stronghold and recall historical wars and battles, but without any traces of fear. For those who know Wenling Chen, they might also associate the red boys with an episode in the artist's personal life. In 1996, *Macao Daily* published an article entitled "Commendable self-defense and self-rescue" about a young couple who were robbed at knifepoint and attacked by the beach. The young man put up a defiant struggle and was stabbed several dozen times. The arteries on both of his wrists were cut while his entire body was soaked in blood. It was the most violent crime in the city's history. The brave young man in the report is the very artist who created the red boys, Wenling Chen, who survived a near-fatal attack. However, there is no hint of vengeance in his work, *Red Memory*.

Contemporary art emphasizes artistic concept and implication, which often leads to artworks that are overloaded with concepts that tire the audience at first glance. Contrary to over-conceptualized artworks, Wenling Chen's installation is modest and earthy, without any deliberate attempts to create concepts. The naked bodies had been stripped of their artificial coverings and what's left is the straightforward connection between man and nature, a direct dialogue between human and society. The moderate exaggeration of facial and body language places the emphasis on these two relationships, and this group of works can be interpreted as a liberation from overloaded concepts, or, a concept trimmed down.

[2002]

---

1. The "red" (赤) here also means "naked" in classical Chinese and was therefore used to describe a newborn baby in classical Chinese texts.

红男孩为什么走红

彭德

陈文令的红男孩，通体鲜红，如火如荼。红色是2002年的流行色；从韩国的红魔拉拉队到欧洲足坛以往罕见的红队服，再到中国各式各样的红色物象，举目四股，处处红色。红色的流行使得红男孩们找到了名正言顺的色彩空间。在历史中，红色是中国南方的标志色和吉祥色。在现实中，红色的人体改变了作品的写实倾向，加强了非现实意图，表达出作者对现实中成人们势利、紧张、焦虑、恐惧、残酷的否定，也不期而然地道出了人们的共同心愿：对童真状态的怀念和对早熟了两千年的中式文明的质疑。

2002年春，当陈文令率领这群红男孩在厦门珍珠湾海滩露面时，立即吸引了成千上万的观众。临近收场时，市民曾向政府呼吁将他们长留厦门。一时间，红孩子成了厦门传媒每天的话题。2002年秋，陈文令的红男孩在广州参加首届"中国艺术三年展"，不仅又一次引进传媒和观众的好评，也引起了美术批评家的关注。这群裸体男孩塑像，总共一百多个，分为几类在水边嬉戏玩耍的姿态。作品用玻璃喷制，打磨，抛光，喷上红漆，放置在沙滩、树干、船头、灯塔上。这组作品投资四十五万，是所有参展作品投资最多的一件。艺术和投资和艺术价值不一定成正比，但陈文令这组作品的确产生了水涨船高的效果。

中国每年数以万计的个展和联展，脱颖而出的作品只是极少数。它们大多能满足一项视觉需要：新鲜。陈文令的作品属于新型的艺术形态，介于写实雕塑、装置、互动式行为艺术和偶发艺术之间。作为雕塑，陈文令的雕塑有别于学院派的正和现代派的奇，有别于马约尔的"肥"和贾柯梅蒂的"瘦"。作为集装置和行为于一体的行为艺术，他的作品同以往走极端的前卫艺术相比，在艺术观和艺术表现上有根本的不同。这群红男孩不是天真的而不是邪恶的，是健康的而不是病态的。众所周知，20世纪晚期的视觉艺术，无论美术还是影视以及电子游戏中的三维动画，充斥着暴力和无病呻吟的作品。陈文令的红男孩有着出淤泥而不染的品格，切合了人们对前卫艺术新流向的渴望，也就是从艺术作为人性批判的武器转变为人性建构的载体。他的作品，使外行和内行、学院派和前卫批评家都能找到自己的看点。

陈文令的这组作品，取名为《红色记忆》。他具有当代艺术见仁见智的多义性。人们面对这群孩子，可能会想到古典文化中的赤子，但却感受不到迂腐。人们可能会想到《西游记》中的红孩儿，但却找不到妖气。人们可能会想到文革中的红小兵，但却看不到杀气。人们可能从厦门这个军事重镇去回忆过去的战火，但却不会造成丝毫的恐惧感。熟悉陈文令的人，还可能会将红男孩同他的一段经历联系在一起：1996年《厦门日报》发表题为"难能可贵的自卫与自救"的文章，说的是一对青年男女在海边被歹徒劫持，男方奋力反抗，身中几十刀，被割开两个手腕的动脉，血染全身，成为当地流血最多的血案。被文章作者描述并视为英雄行为的男青年，就是大难不死的陈文令，不过，在陈文令的《红色记忆》中全然看不到仇恨。

当代艺术强调作品蕴涵的观念，常常派生出观念超载的作风，让人一看就累。陈文令于此相反，显得朴实，没有刻意制造的观念。裸露的躯体剥去了伪装，留下的只是人与自然的直接关联，只是人与社会的直接对话。面部与肢体语言的适度夸张，是对这两种关系的强调，这组作品，可以说是对观念超载的解脱，也可以说是携带着裁减观念的观念。

[2002]

Red memory-Cool / 红色记忆-冷, 2000

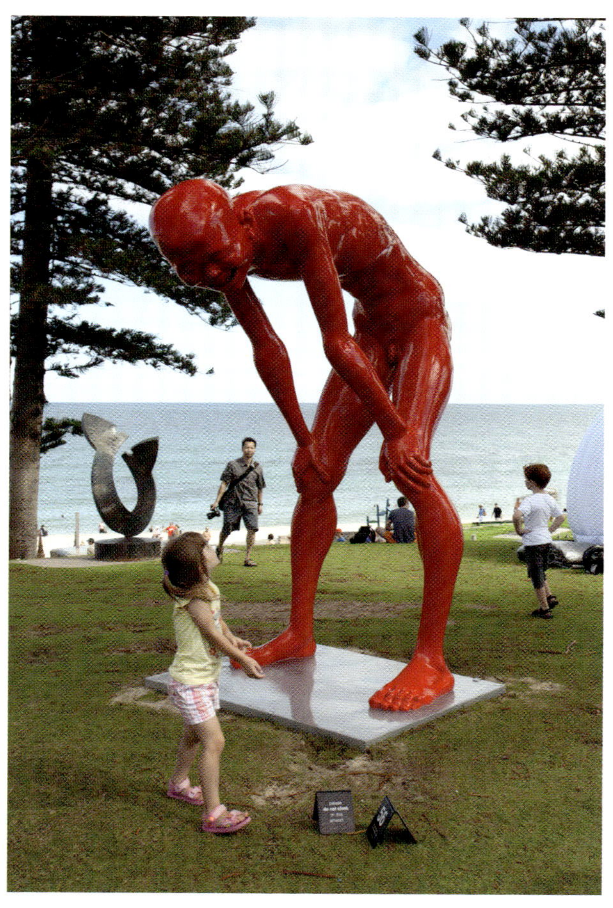

Red memory-Smile in Perth, Australia / 红色记忆-笑在澳洲珀斯, 2011

Page 96–97
Red memory-Cool / 红色记忆-冷, 2000

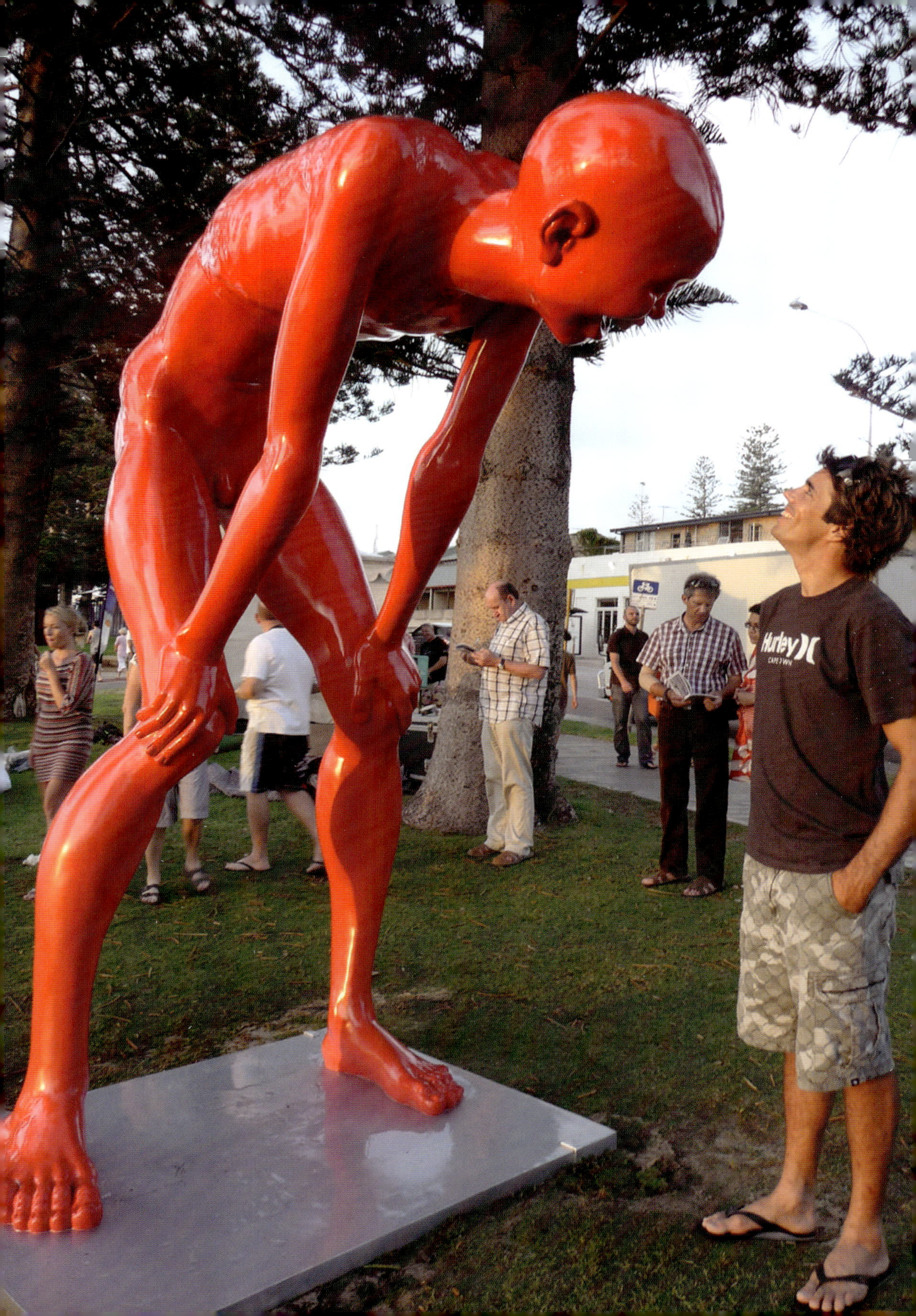

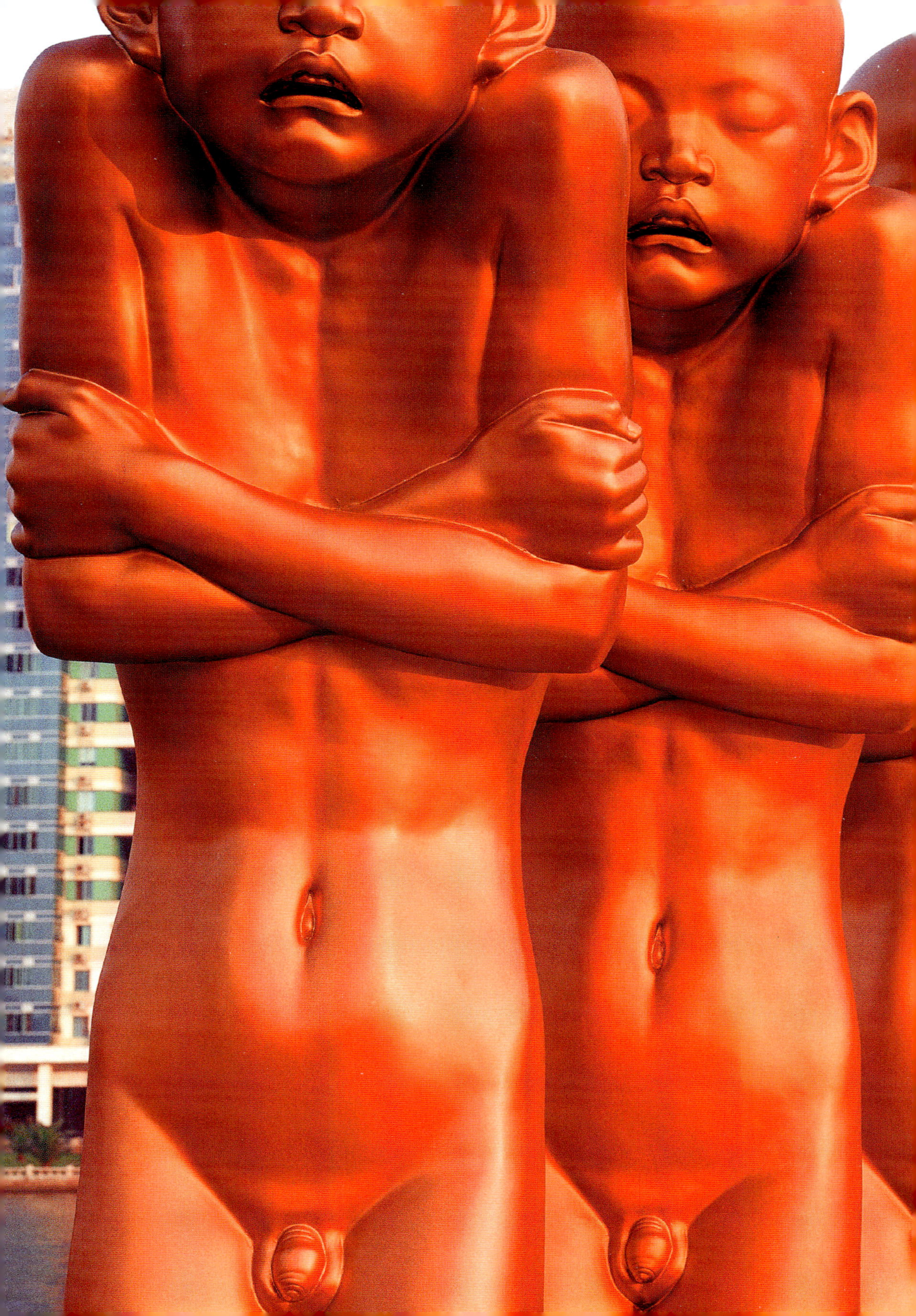

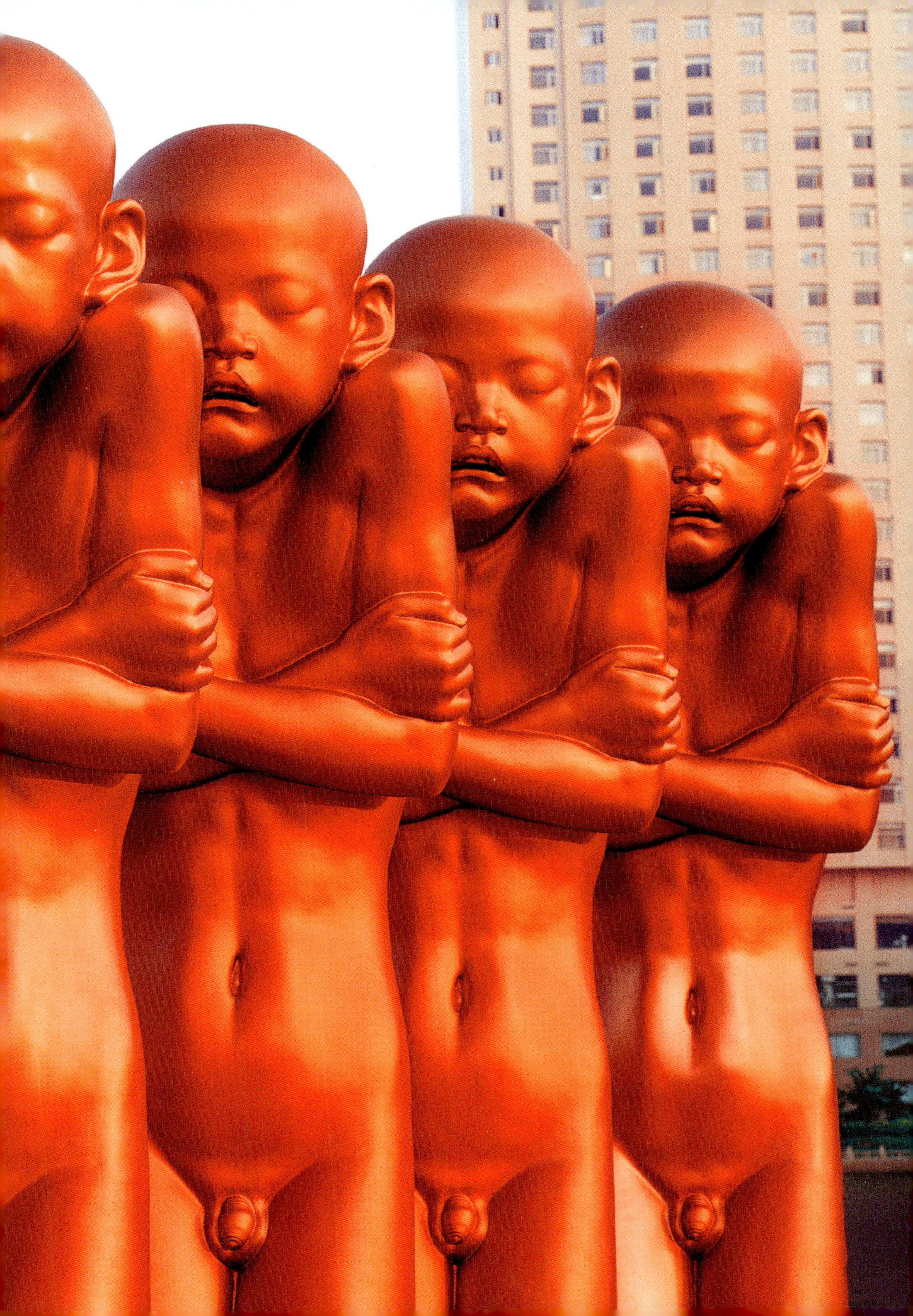

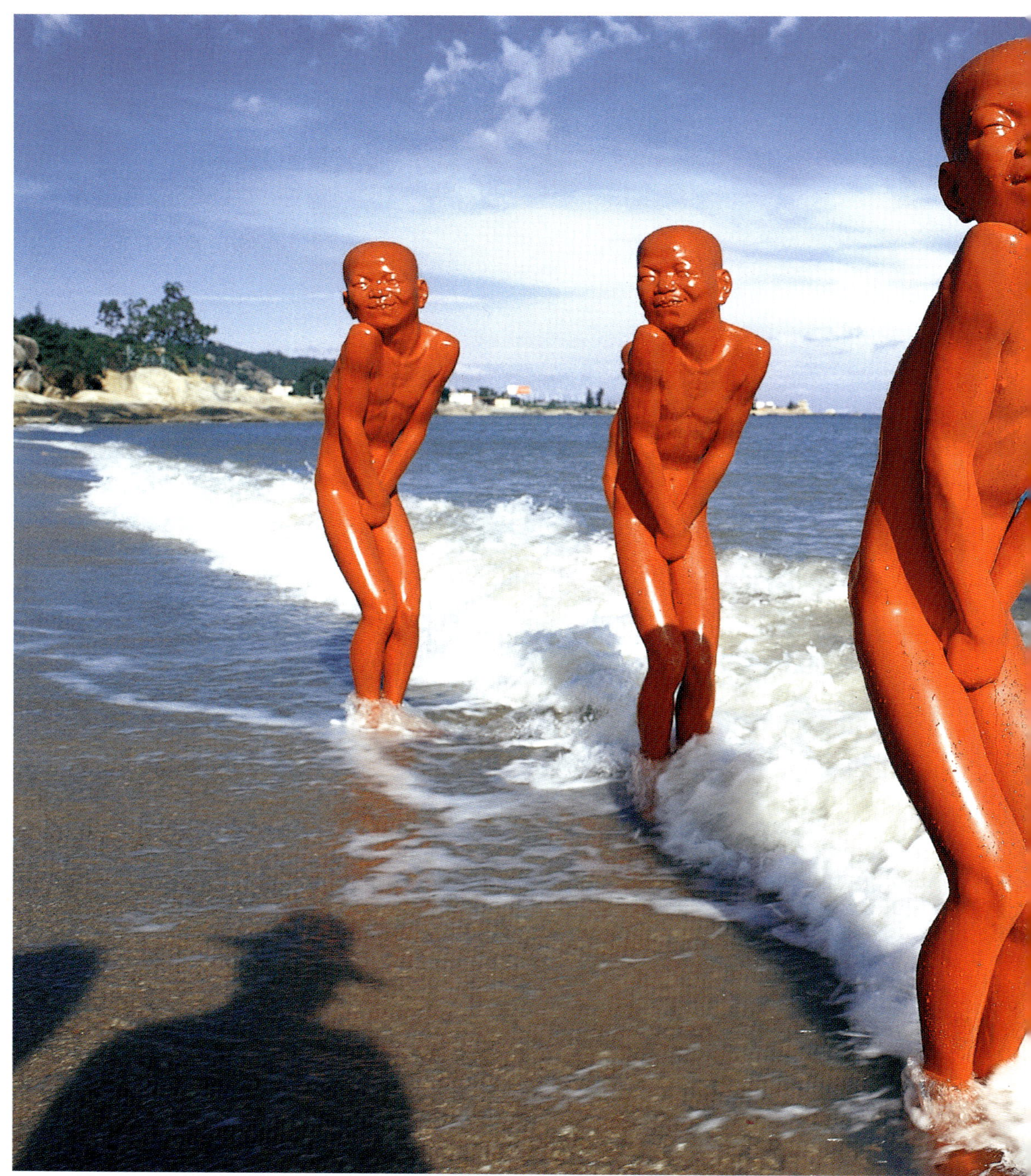

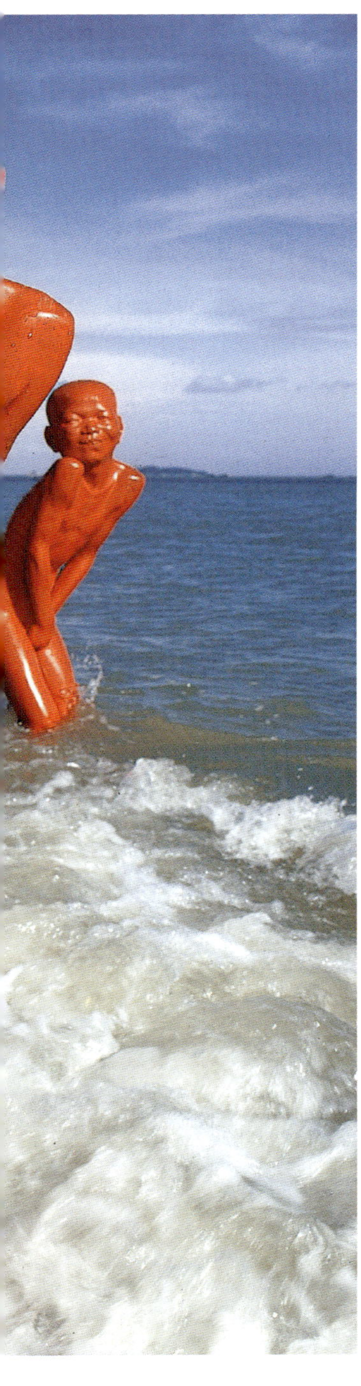

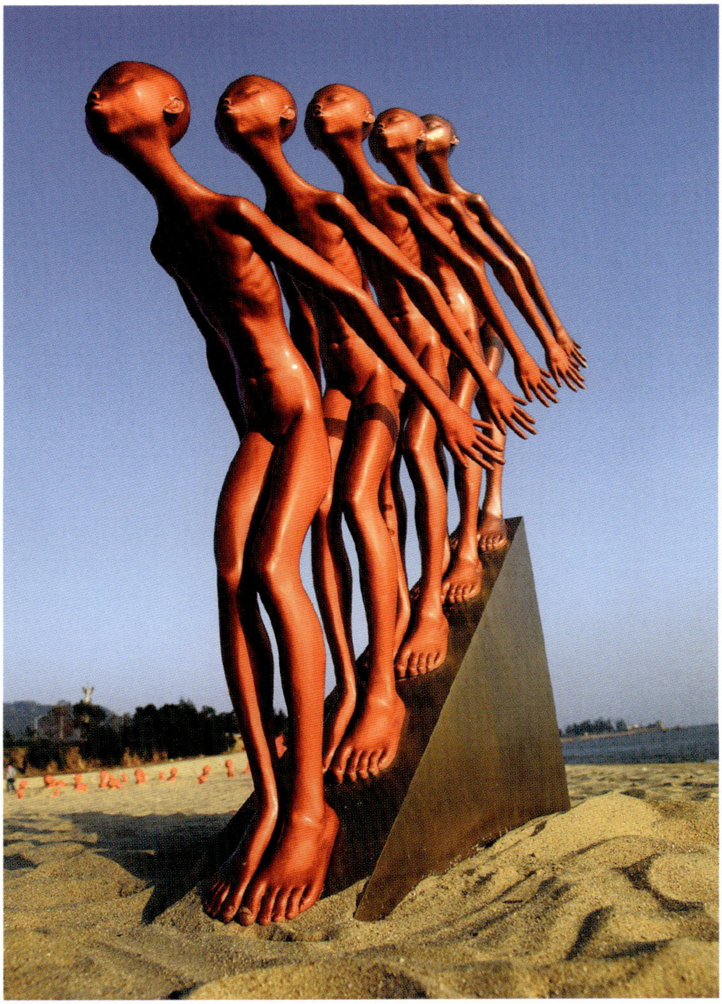

Red memory-Shy boy / 红色记忆-羞童, 2002

Red memory-Dive / 红色记忆-跳水, 2002

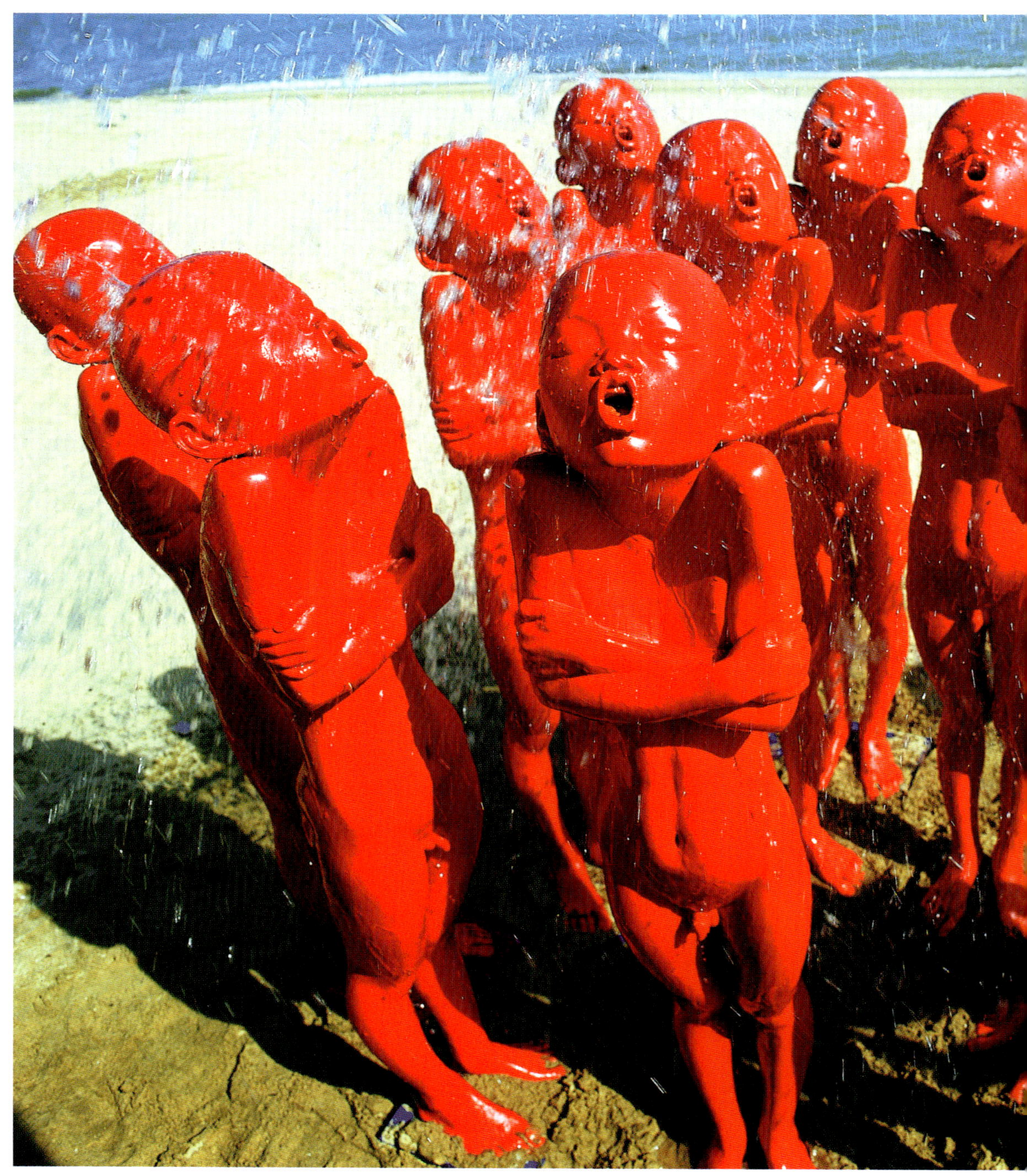

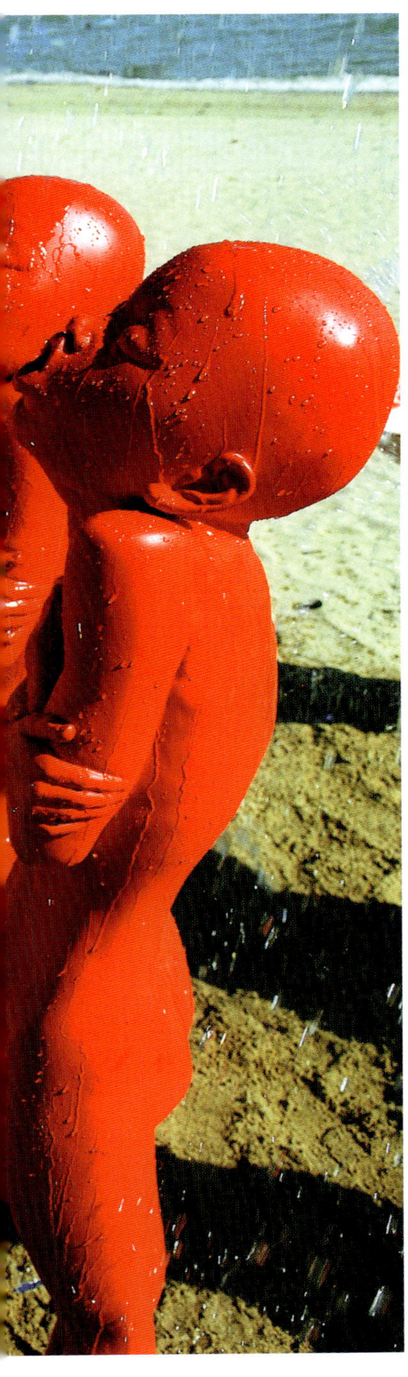

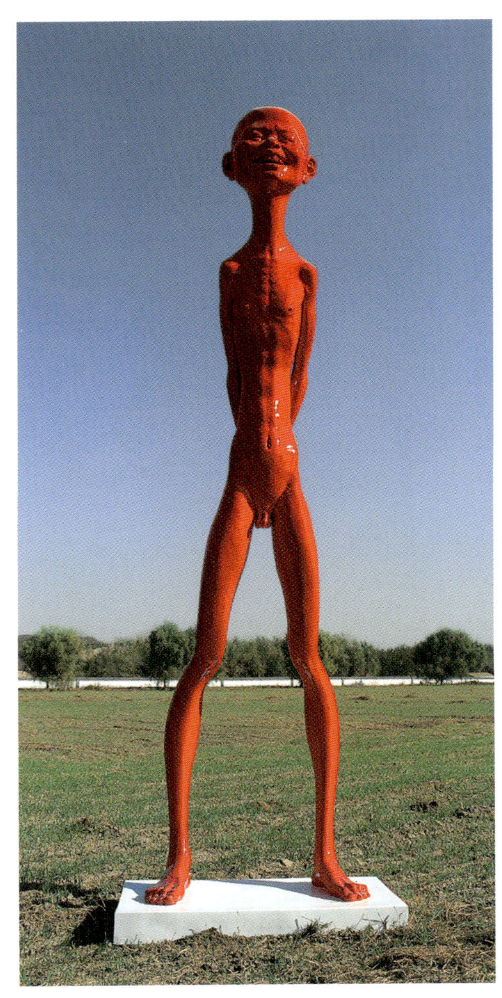

Red memory-Cool in Autumn / 红色记忆-秋凉, 2002

Red memory-Captain / 红色记忆-队长, 2000

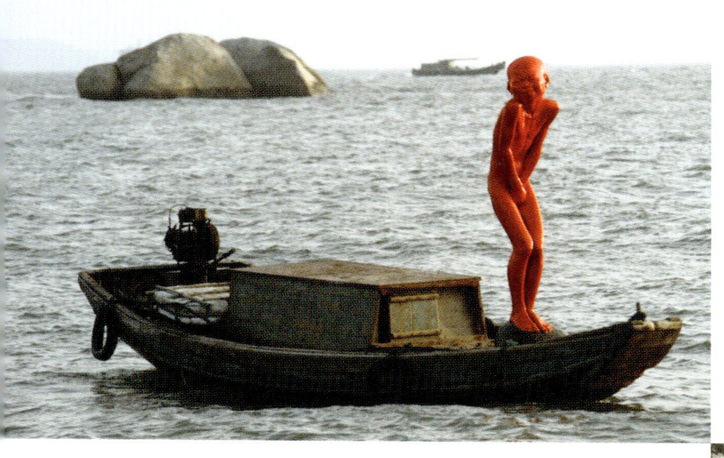

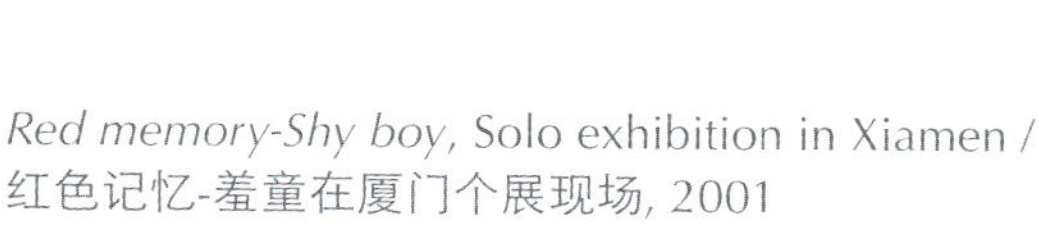

Red memory-Shy boy, Solo exhibition in Xiamen /
红色记忆-羞童在厦门个展现场, 2001

Childhood-Horizon / 童年-海平线, 2010

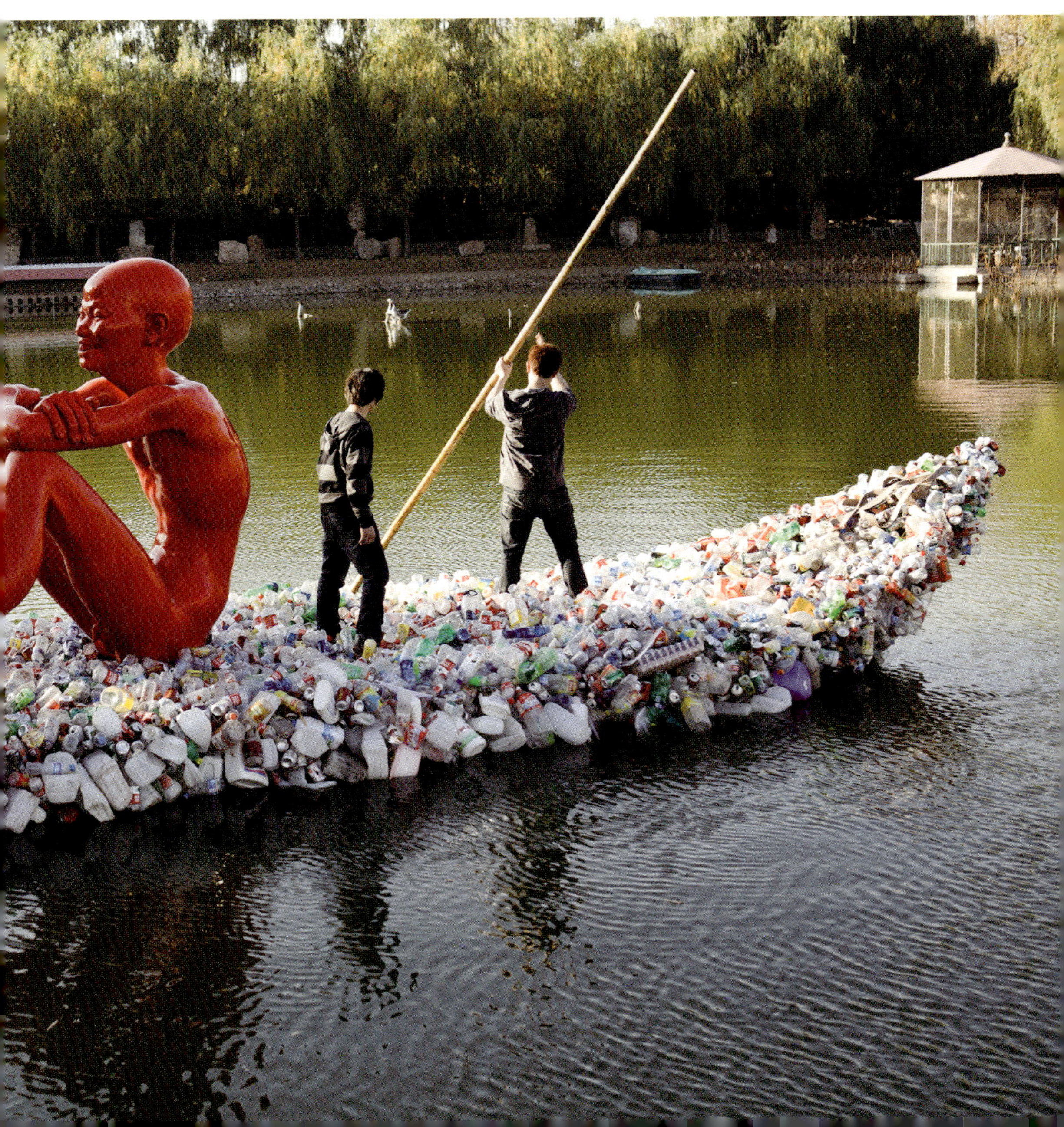

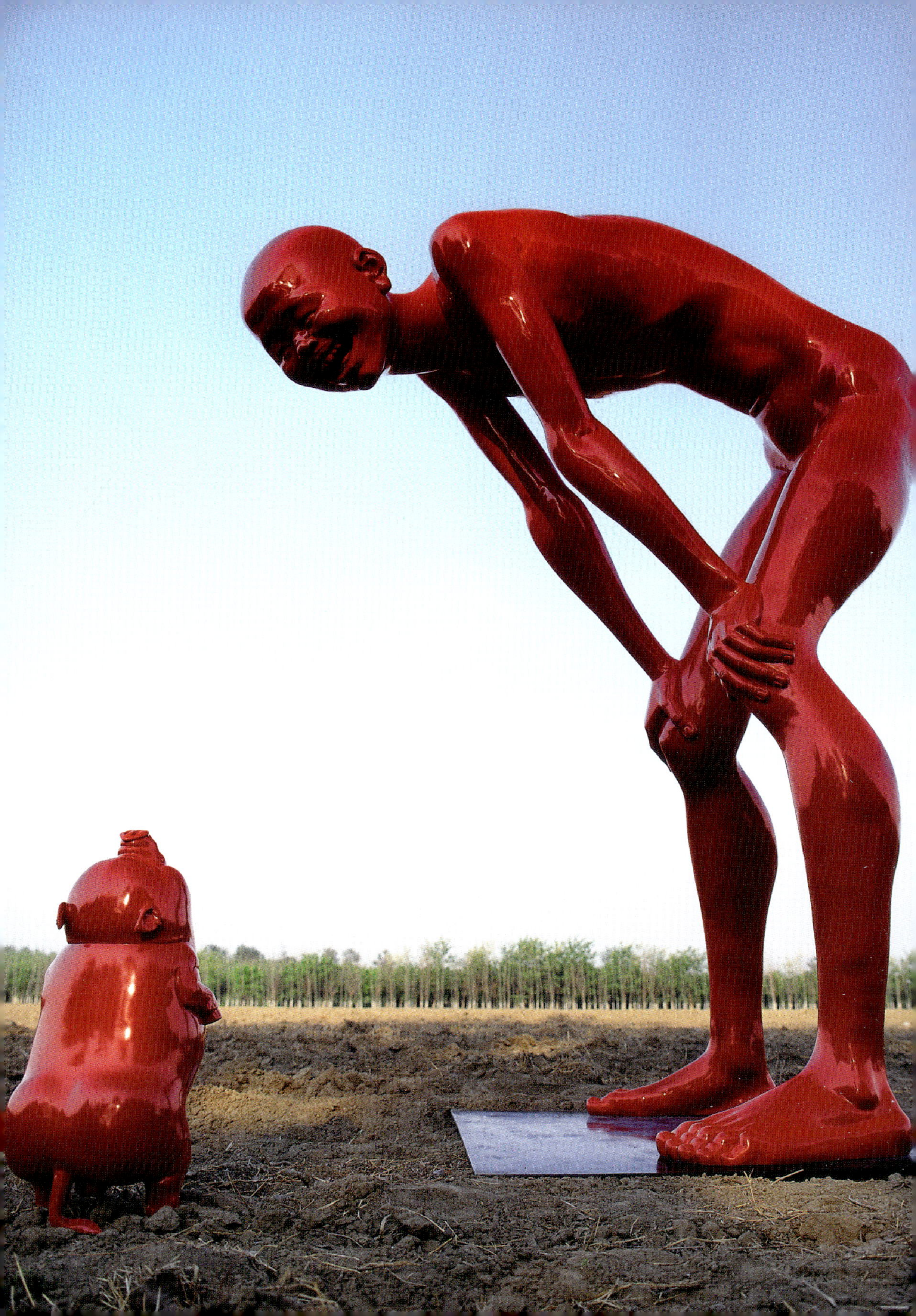

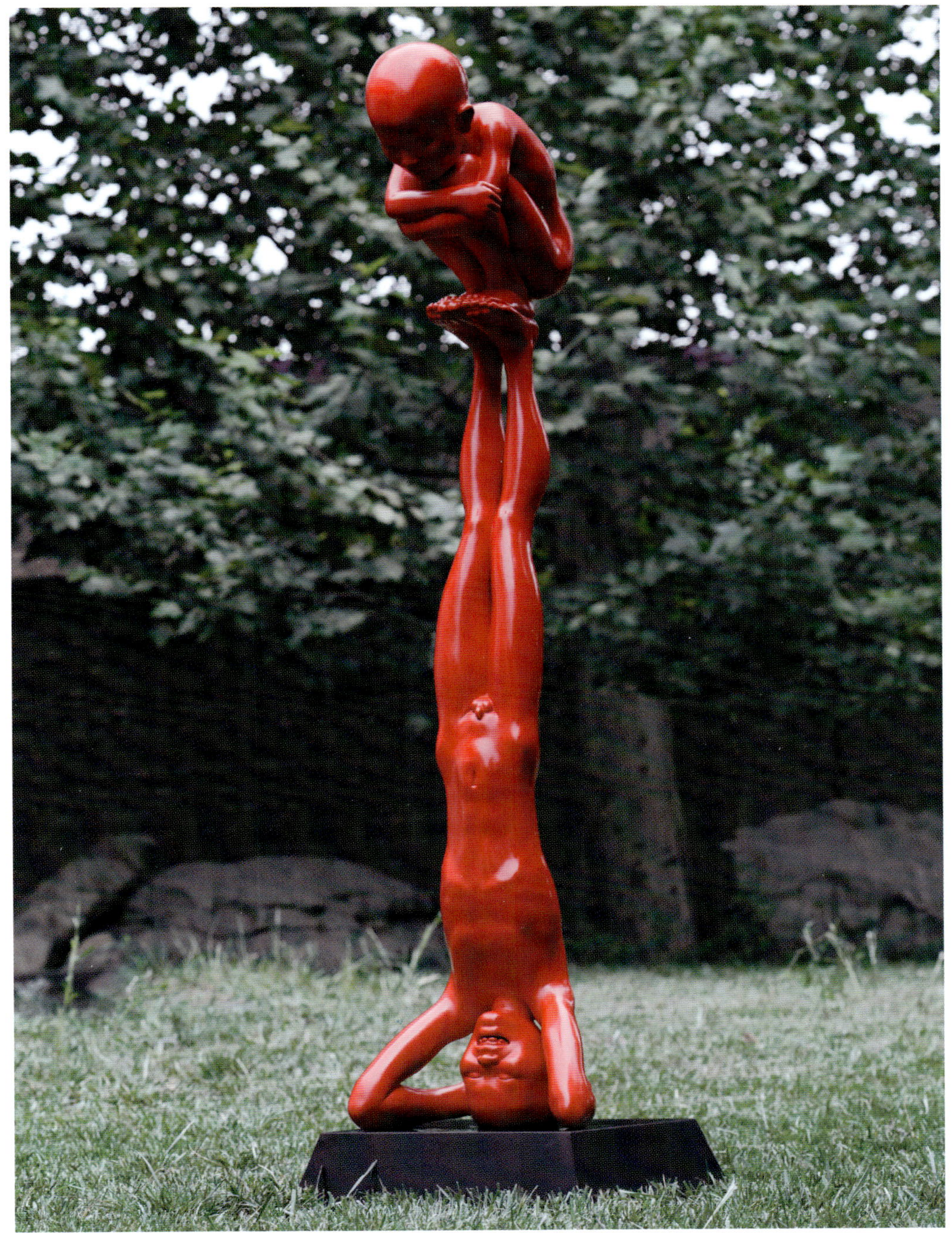

Red memory-Smile / 红色记忆-笑, 2007   *Childhood-Games* / 童年-游戏, 2010

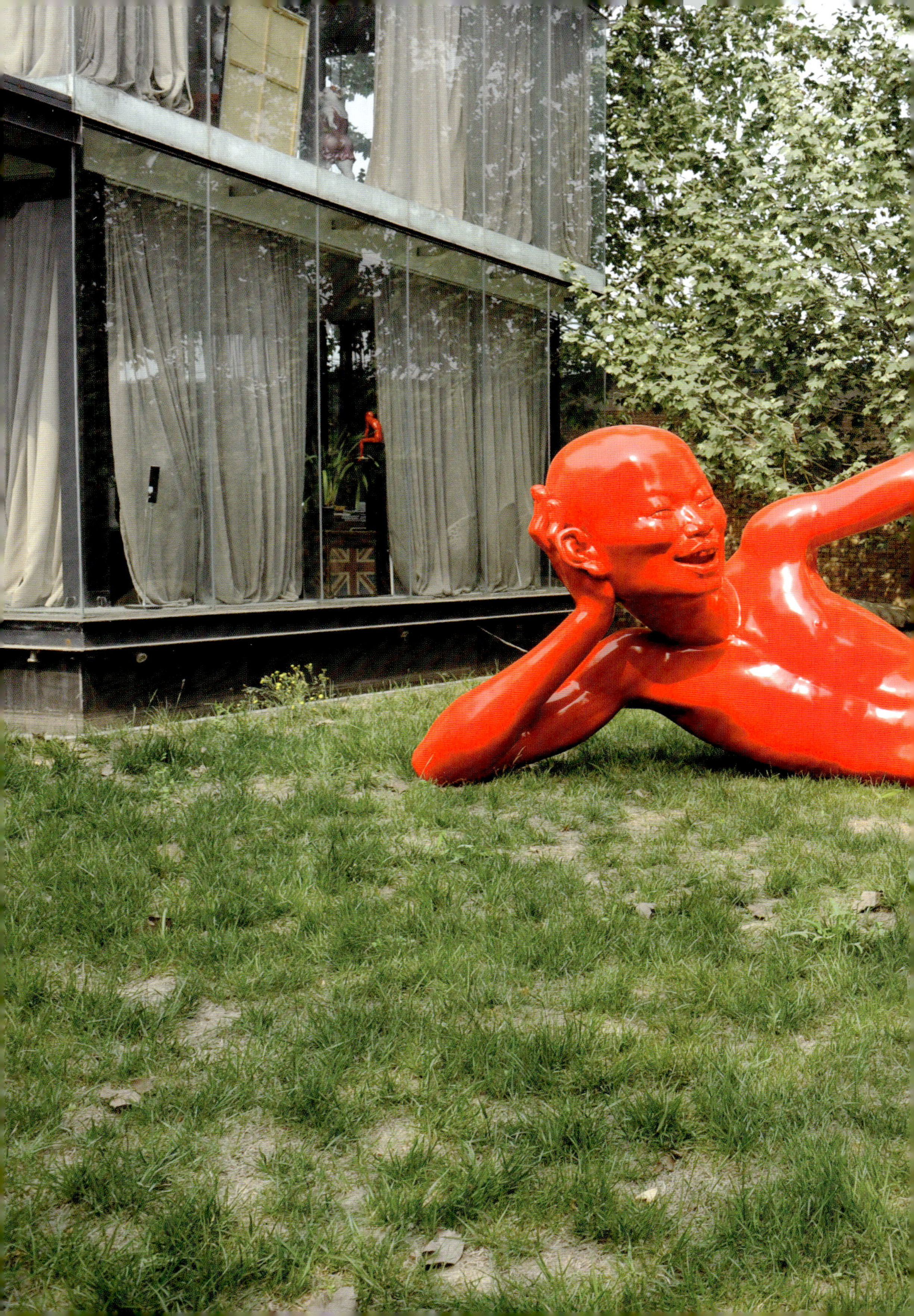

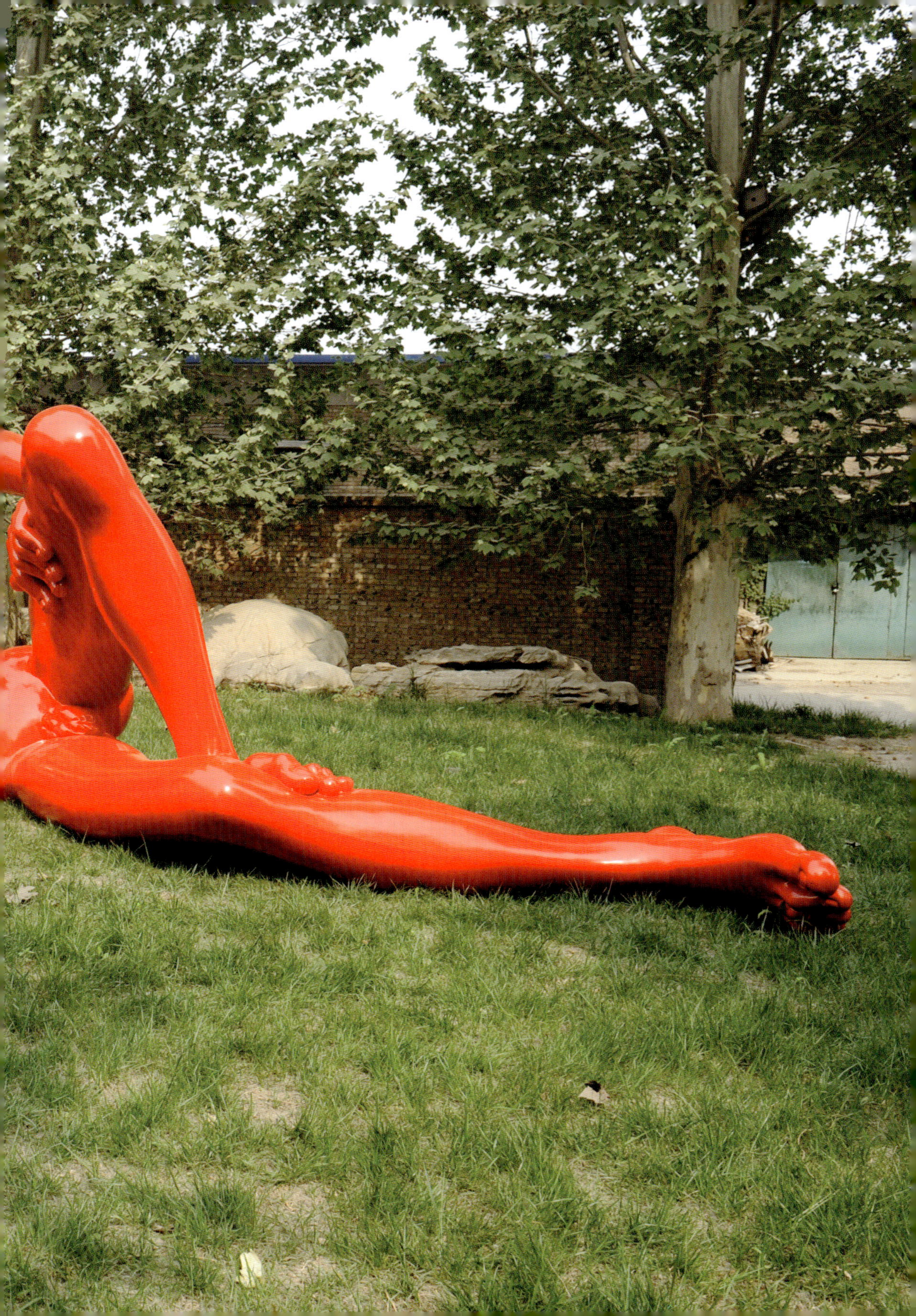

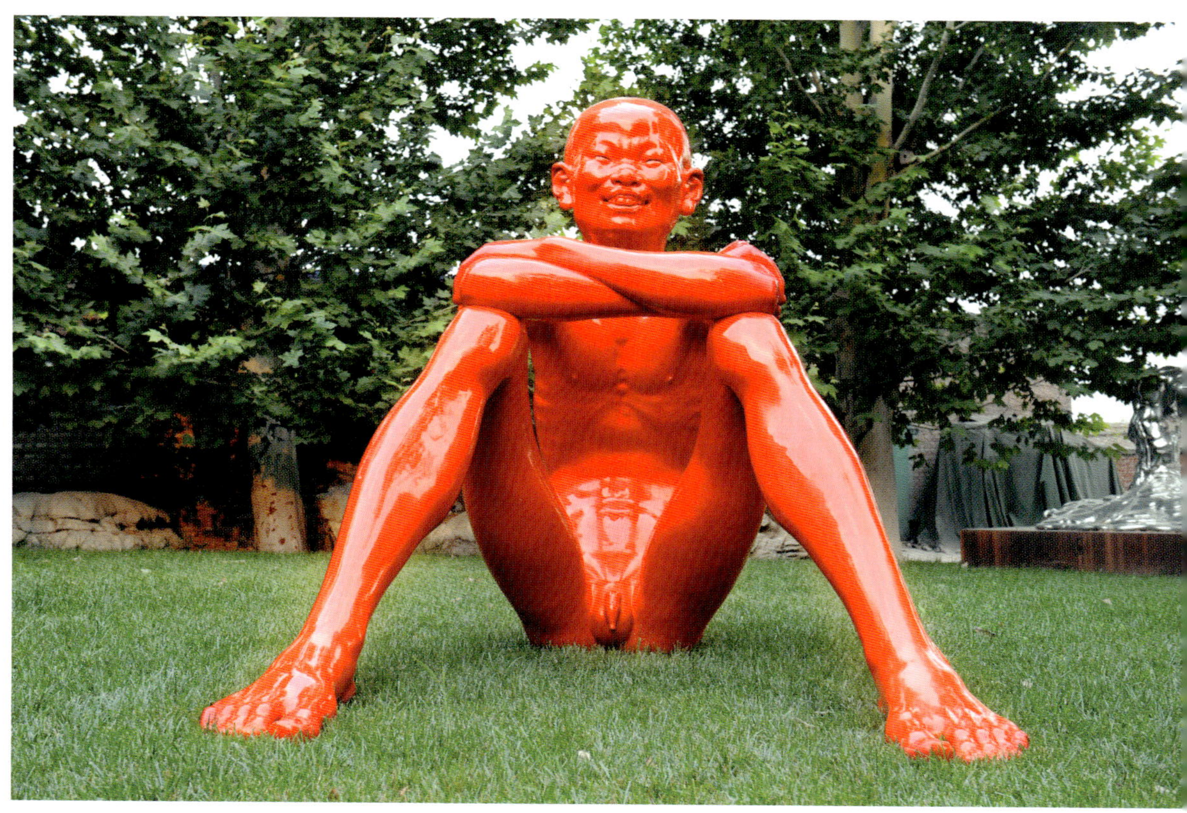

Childhood-Horizon / 童年-海平线, 2010   *Childhood-Aubade* / 童年-晨曲, 2011

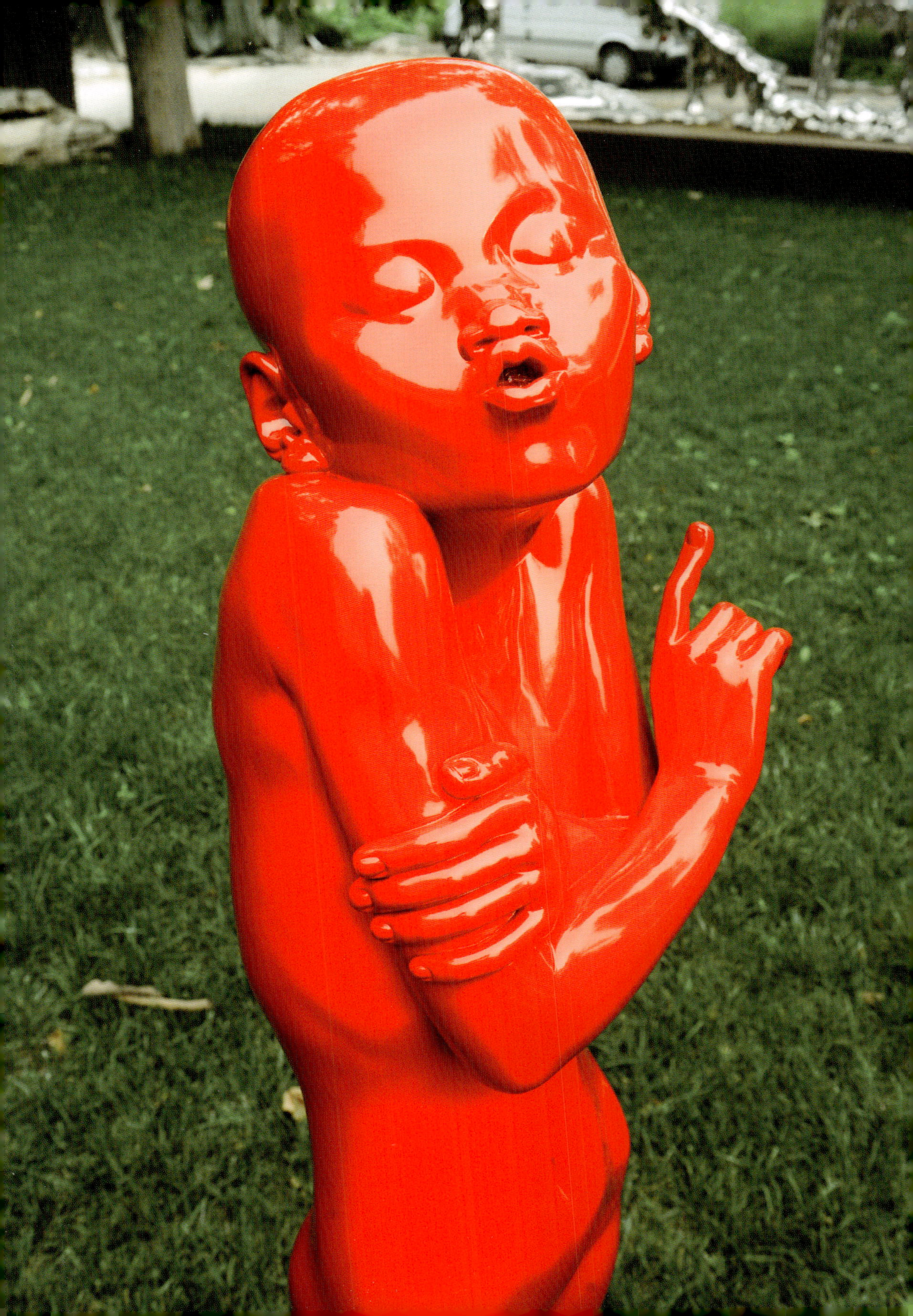

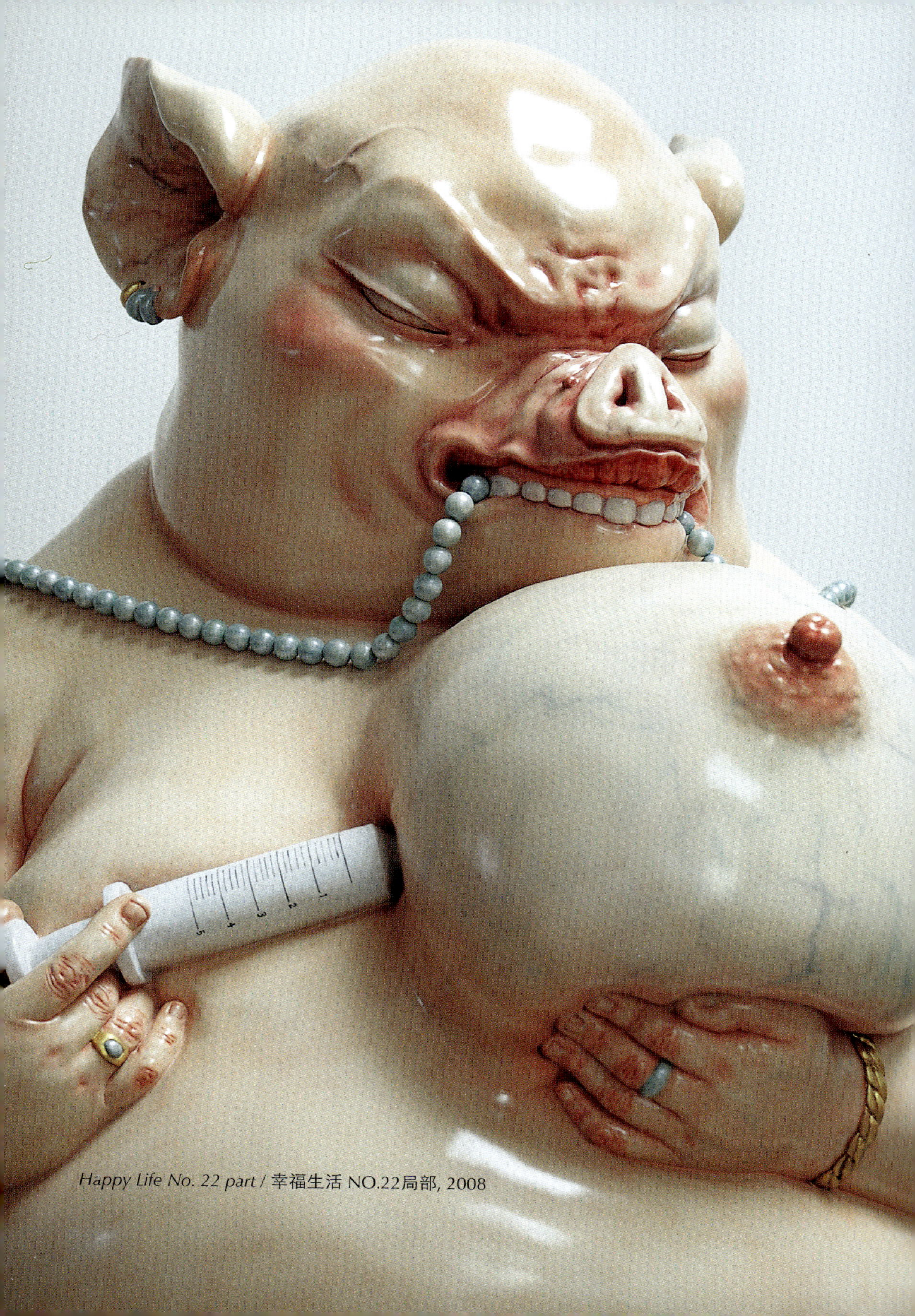

Happy Life No. 22 part / 幸福生活 NO.22局部, 2008

On the Gaudy and Tawdry:
A Double Exposure

Pi Li

In order to understand the work of Chen Wenling, one must first investigate the past twenty to thirty years of change in China's social structure. During the establishment of the "New China," the cultural elegance advocated by the humanistic tradition was taken as the antithesis of mainstream ideology, and was slowly eliminated as a mode of everyday discourse. At the same time, folk culture became a weapon of this same mass ideology, attacking visual culture in general. Styles, languages, and forms borrowed from folk culture were quickly absorbed into mainstream culture across multiple media: the development of oil painting after liberation, political movements in ink painting, and the clay statue-influenced *Rent Collection Yard* all reflect these trends. The movement known as Chinese contemporary art that began in the 1980s was, in reality, a restoration of the language of modern Western art. But as Chinese artists quickly discovered when they began to participate in the international production of semiotic meaning in the 1990s, understanding and imitation of the West would not be enough to achieve the recognition of the international art world. Against this background, the semiotic elements of folk arts and crafts once rejected by contemporary art slowly began to re-enter the visual language of contemporary art production.

In the same way, we cannot ignore the fact that, in terms of everyday life, the material wealth of contemporary life in China only began to be established twenty to thirty years ago. Whereas on the one hand elite ideologies were wiped out of China's cultural sphere by the mainstream, on the other hand material desires were inflated at an unprecedented rate; the irreconcilable gaps between these two levels of social construct have defined the characteristics of China's contemporary visual culture. Gaudy Art, which developed in the mid-1990s, was born out of Political Pop, but in retrospect places much more emphasis on symbols and images from Chinese folk art. It was also created under the unequal conditions of the periphery-center relationship between China and the international art metropoles, so perhaps it may be possible to call it a synthesis between the West and the culture of China's new rich—something simultaneously imagined and constructed. A visual form full of exoticism and sentimentality, it was certainly a product of post-colonialism.

On the other hand, the rich language of Chinese contemporary art cannot be so easily flattened and simplified by Gaudy Art. Generally speaking, the semiotic production of responsible artists manifests itself in experiments of widely ranging styles. If the past serves as any example, the expansion of material wealth and forfeit of cultural modes may be the fundamental contradiction of contemporary Chinese society; many artists have taken this very loss of modes of cultural production as a direction for meditation, analogy, or satire. For example, it could be said that Sui Jianguo, who emerged from the 85 New Wave, uses conceptual art to illuminate the language of social expressionism; it must naturally follow that the new generation of sculptors, who have closed the door on conceptual art, use the linguistic symbols of native folk art to begin a perverse war against mainstream ideologies and Western culture. Zhan Wang uses the popular (and moderately priced) medium of stainless style to reproduce en masse the scholar's rocks that have come to represent refined culture. Liu Jianhua uses the concept of painted porcelain to sarcastically sell his exoticized Qipaos.

Chen Wenling's work belongs to this category, unfolding in the contextual space of art and culture. Studying craftwork and fine arts in Fujian, his work carried very few cultural symbols, and bore no theoretical burden—so unlike Sui Jianguo he holds no attachment to the Western avantgarde, and unlike Zhan Wang and Liu Jianhua he does not linger on the tail of conceptual art. Unlike Gaudy Art in general, folk art does not appear as a symbol in his work; on the contrary, it takes on thematic importance. Chen Wenling rejects the tactics of Gaudy Art, refusing to inspect the pretensions of everyday life with a condescending gaze. Instead, he uses the images and language of folk art to reinterrogate the false elegance of "the Good Life."

On any level, Chen Wenling works in visual art, not conceptual art. In his works, fullness of form takes on a special kind of strength. Countless shapes come together irrationally, forcing the viewer to fall into an unaccountable rapture. Perhaps due to his understanding of Chinese folk culture, his systems of signification are often simple and clear. A pig inevitably symbolizes wealth, comfortable living, and happiness; sex is invariably manifested in large breasts and large buttocks; beauty and taste are demonstrated by red lips and large pearl necklaces. In his latest work, Chen Wenling attempts to develop a system of fairy tales or folk mythology through a series of images of strange animals—a metaphor for contemporary life. Compared with the experiments of China's contemporary conceptual art circle, Chen drifts without roots. He ignored the rationalist implications of conceptualism, but expressed interest in the irrational tendencies of expressionism. Compared with the Gaudy Art inspired by post-colonialism, Chen Wenling is honest and transparent; he never mockingly looks down on his subject matter and puts forth poor imitations of life; often, what he wants to express is even more insane than real life.

Visually, the strong points of Chen Wenling's work lie in their insanity and strength. His images feel rounded, heavy, fleshy, and inelegant. Conceptually, this type of simplicity and directness is born out of the folk culture of an agricultural civilization; these subjects are uncomfortable to look at, overly vulgar and unrefined. And this is precisely the artist's goal—to use this vulgar "peasant flavor" to expose the primal impulses of urban China, despite their veneer of elegance. The fish that represents love, beauty, and innocence in Andersen's fairy tales is appropriated by Chen Wenling and turned into a fat and formless shape dressed up in jewels and finery and placed on a large, vulgar, and tacky man's bed. Here, the artist attempts to express a sort of "low level" point of view, using filth and vulgarity to undermine elegance, or using primitive human impulses to resist contemporary affect and aesthetics.

These works, with their flamboyant colors and fleshy forms, should be considered a dissection and analysis of contemporary life from the perspective of folk culture. They certainly reflect the extreme experience of a society that has undergone a massive accumulation of wealth in a very short period of time; from another perspective, Chen Wenling engages in an ironic response to the lack of cultural life in the space between the pursuit of wealth and the realization of material desires. Just as the 16th- century Dutch painter Pieter Bruegel used folk mythology to satirically reveal the emptiness of Christian culture, Chen Wenling emphasizes and takes full advantage of the power of aesthetic vulgarity, forcing the viewer to gaze nakedly upon that which contemporary life tries to conceal.   [2008]

对媚俗与媚雅的双重戳穿

皮力

要了解陈文令的作品，我们就必须清醒当代中国社会在过去20 – 30年间的转型。随着新中国的建立，提倡优雅的文人传统被主流意识形态视为对立物，而逐渐被清除出日常生活的话语范畴。与此同时，民间的通俗文化，成为主流意识形态标榜文化特性的武器，对视觉文化的生产形成新的冲击。无论的是解放后期的油画民族化讨论，还是水墨画中的新年画运动，抑或是中国雕塑向民间泥塑学习产生的"收租院"这样的雕塑，在不同媒介的艺术创作中，追求带有民间通俗文化意味的语言和形态迅速成为主流。80年代开始的中国当代艺术运动，事实上是中国艺术学习西方现当代艺术的语言复兴。但是当中国当代艺术在90年代开始进入国际当代艺术的意义生产时，作为边缘的中国当代艺术很快发现，对于西方的了解和模仿，并不能带来国际艺术对于中国当代艺术的认同。在这种背景下，曾经被当代艺术否决的民俗与民族语言因素开始进入到当代艺术的语言创造中来。

同样，我们也必须注意到，在日常生活层面中，中国当代生活的财富是在过去20 – 30年代间建立起来的。一方面是文化层面中的精英意识被主流意识形态的清除，另一方面是物质财富和欲望在中国以前所未有的速度的叠加，二者之间无法弥补的鸿沟，造成了当代中国视觉文化的特性。诞生于90年代中期的艳俗艺术虽然脱胎于政治波普，但是相比后者在视觉趣味上却更宣扬中国的民俗符号。但是艳俗艺术产生于中国当代艺术于国际艺术市场之间边缘与中心的不平衡状态，从某种意义上说，它更多是迎合西方对于中国的"暴发户"文化想像而自我建构，充满异国情调的视觉样式，是后殖民文化的产物。

然而，中国当代艺术语言的丰富性并不是艳俗艺术所能"简单化"的。更多的试验在那些富有责任感的艺术家的语言创造中以不同的方式试验着。如前所述，财富的叠加与文化趣味的丧失是中国当代社会的根本矛盾，对于社会文化趣味的反省、嘲讽和比拟也成了很多艺术家试验的方向。如果说脱胎于85新潮的隋建国用观念艺术来重新阐释社会现实主义的语言的话，那么新一代的雕塑家则开始有意识的彻底摒弃了观念艺术的有效性，用本土民俗化的语言符号同时向社会主流意识形态和西方文化偏见开战。展望用流行而廉价的不锈钢批量复制代表高雅文化的"假山石"，刘建华则是套用陶瓷中彩塑的概念，反讽地贩卖着"异国情调的旗袍"。

陈文令的作品就是在这样的文化和艺术的上下文中展开的。在福建学习工艺美术的陈文令并没有太多文化符号和理论的负担，所以相比上述隋建国，他对于西方当代艺术的先进性完全没有依恋，相比展望和刘建华，他也不留观念艺术的尾巴。相比艳俗艺术，民俗艺术并非是一个符号，相反是他创作的主题。陈文令并非像艳俗艺术那样，在用鄙夷的眼光审视故作清高的审视着当下的日常生活。相反，他是用民间符号和语言来重新诠释那些故作高雅的"幸福生活"。

　　从某种层面上说，陈文令创造的是真正"视觉艺术"而不是观念艺术。在他的作品中，饱满的造型总是充满特殊的力量感，无数形体的非理性组合，使得面对他作品陷入到莫名奇妙的狂喜之中。同样，也可能与他对中国民间文化的了解有关，在他的作品中，符号系统往往是简单而明确的。猪必然象征着财富和衣食无忧和生活的快乐，而对于性感的呈现，则是胸大屁股大；美丽和品味则体现为血红的嘴唇和硕大的珍珠项链。 在最新的创作中，陈文令试图发展出一种与民间神话相关的寓言风格，创造出各种奇怪的动物形象，以比拟当代生活。相比中国当代艺术体系的观念艺术试验，陈文令是个十足的草根：他并非关注观念的理性推演，相反对现实的非理性化有着浓厚的兴趣；相比那些后殖民激发的艳俗艺术，陈文令则是真诚得近乎透明：从气质上说，他从不居高临下地嘲讽，拙劣的模仿，往往，他要表现比现实更加疯狂。

　　从视觉上看，陈文令的作品的绝妙之处在于他的疯狂和力量感。他的作品中所有的造型都是圆形趣味，体量丰硕，充满肉欲而毫无优雅可言。从趣味上说，这种简单直接的造型脱胎于耕种文明的民间文化，相比当代社会而言，他们多少有点不堪如目，过于粗鄙而不登当代都市生活的大雅之堂。但是，草根出生的陈文令的文化目的恰恰是要用这种粗鄙的"农民趣味"来呈现当代都市文化被高雅所遮蔽的原始冲动。安徒生童话中，象征着对爱情忠贞的美人鱼，被陈文令用肥硕的形体呈现，用珠光宝气打扮，并编排到充满粗鄙的胖男人的床上。在这里，艺术家所试图传达的是一种"下层"的眼光，他同庸俗来消解高雅，用原始冲动来消解当代的情感与趣味。

　　被艳丽的色彩和肉欲的造型所包裹着的这些作品，其实是民间眼光对于当代生活的一次有力剖析。它们是对一个在短期内积聚巨大财富的社会的生活趣味的极端体验，但是从另一个角度看，陈文令作品的真正指向是反讽地反应出在追求财富与欲望实现过程某些重要文化环节的缺失。就像16世纪尼德兰画派中的博鲁盖尔用民间寓言反讽基督教文化的虚伪一样，相比那些高雅的当代艺术而言，陈文令难以置信的将庸俗作为一种力量发挥到及至，让我们赤裸裸的面对我们在当代生活中试图掩盖的东西。

[2008]

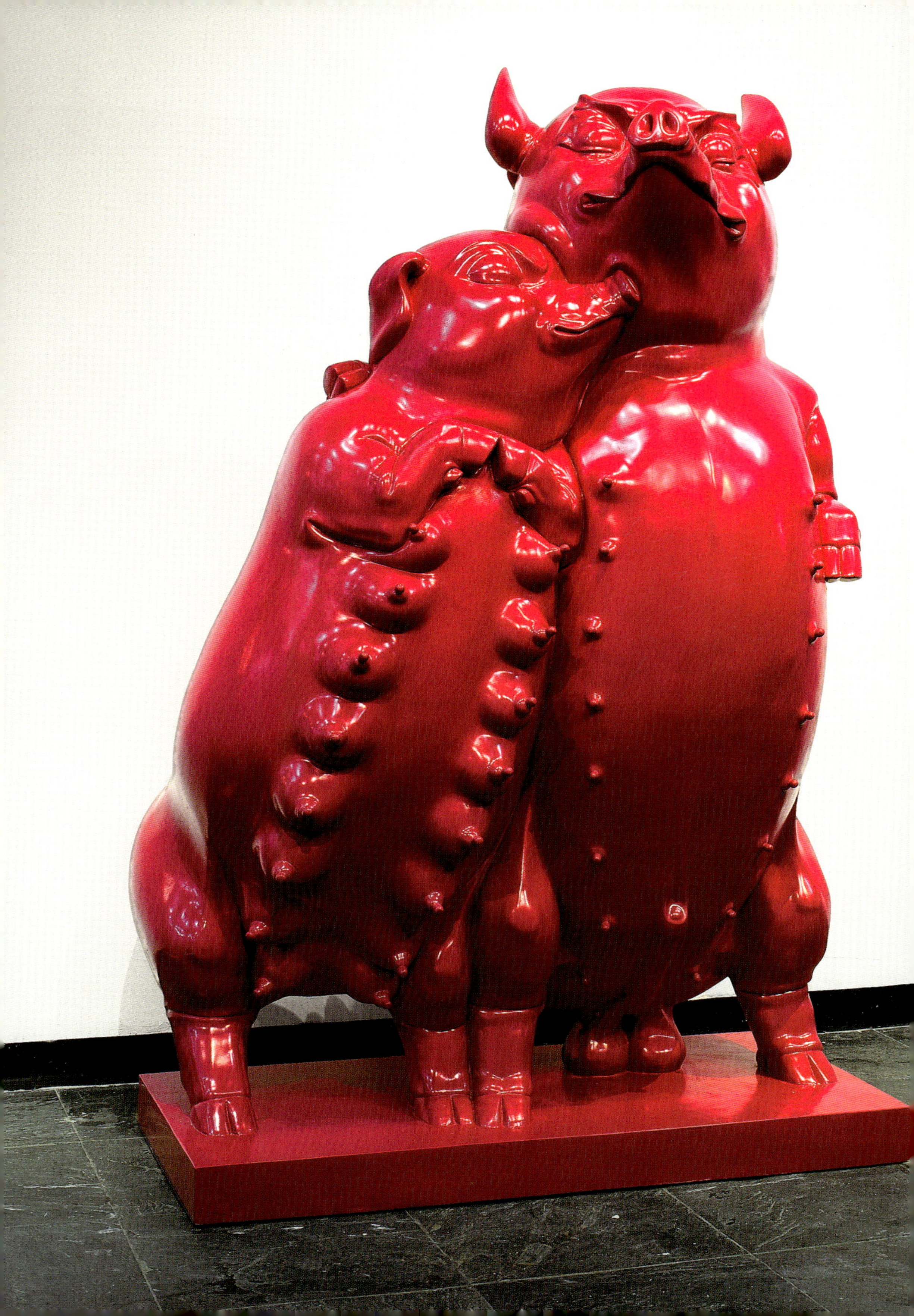

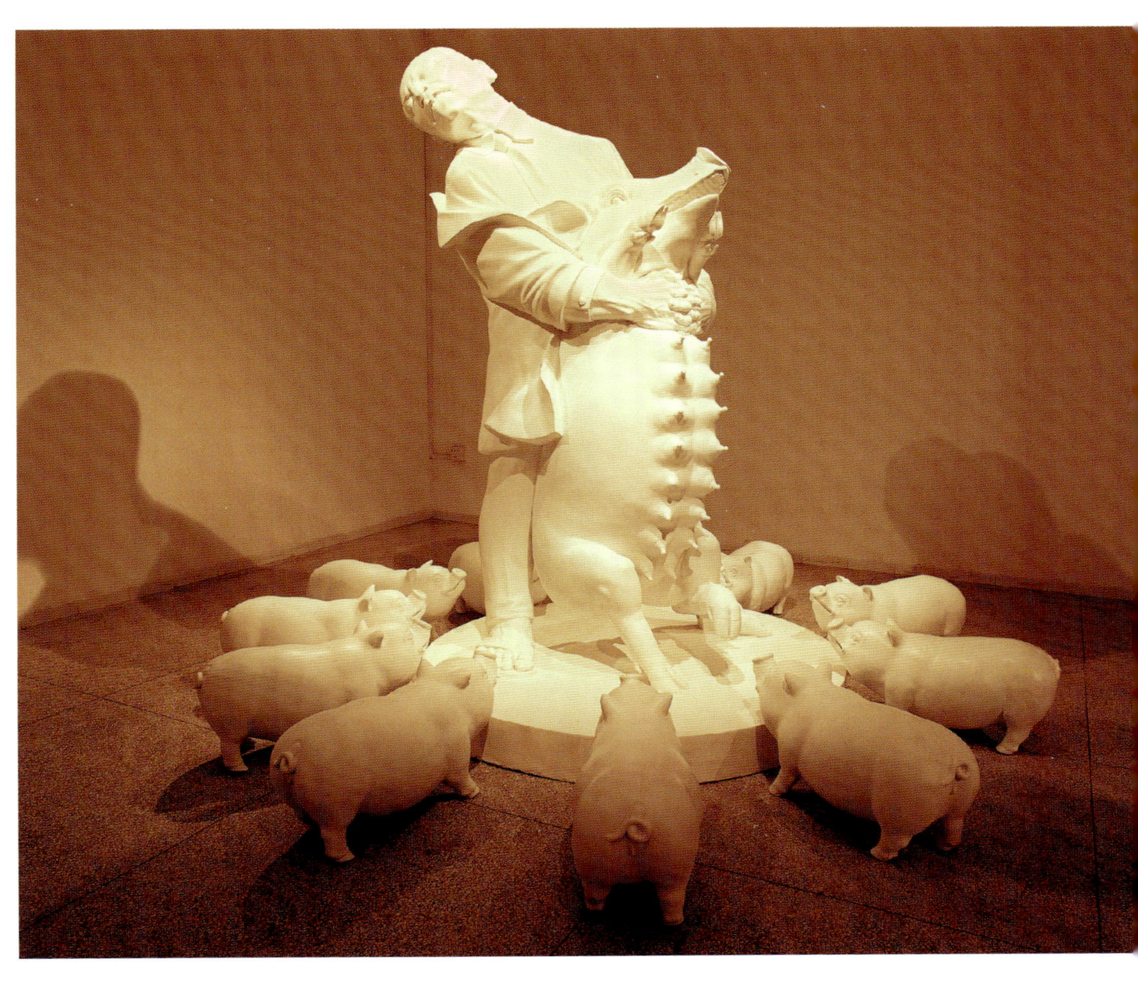

Happy Life No. 6 / 幸福生活NO.6, 2003

Happy Life No. 1 / 幸福生活NO.1, 2005

Page 118
Happy Life No. 22 /
幸福生活 NO.22, 2008

Page 119
Happy Life exhibition site /
幸福生活系列展出现场, 2005

Page 119
Happy Life No. 2 / 幸福生活NO.2, 2005

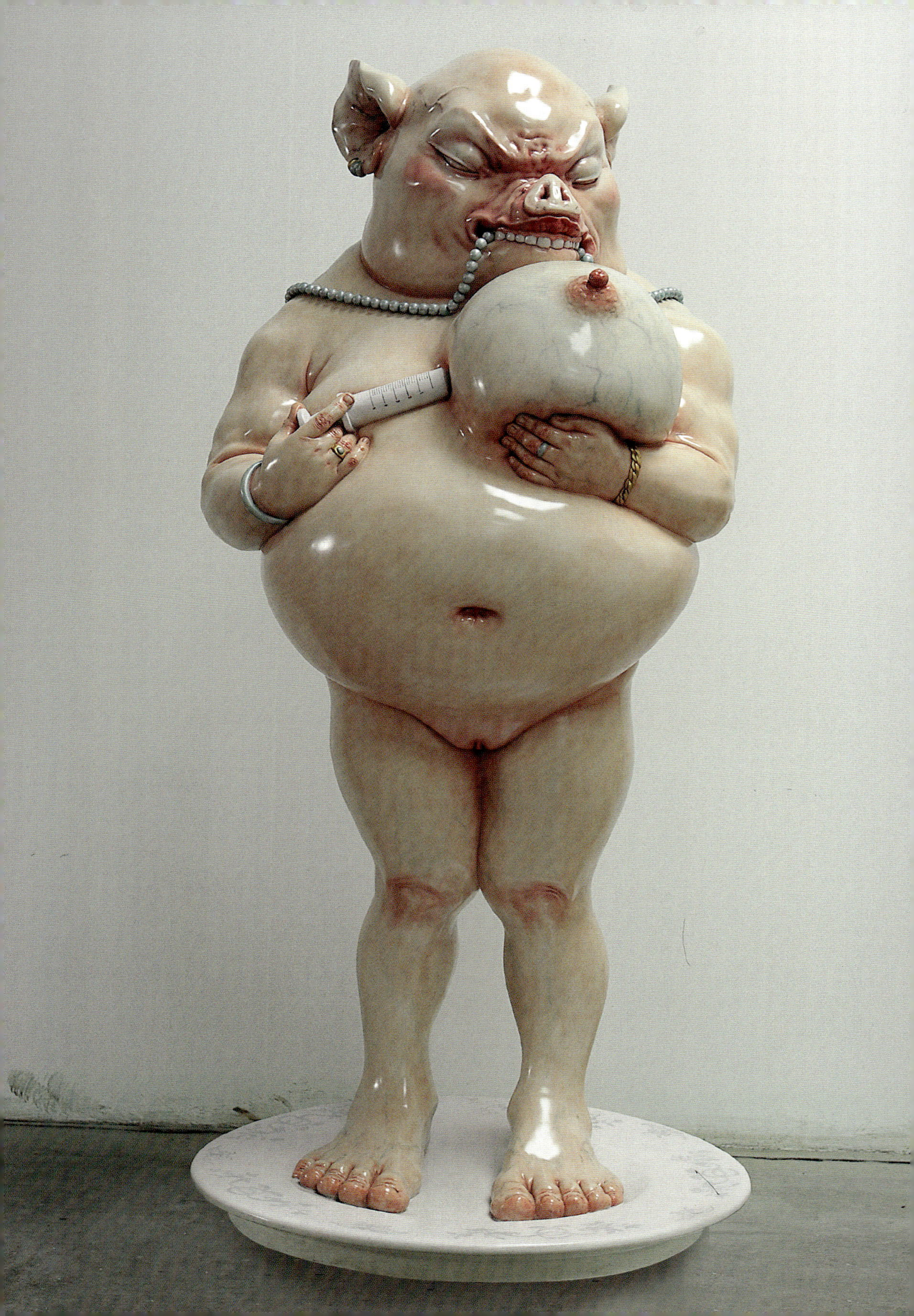

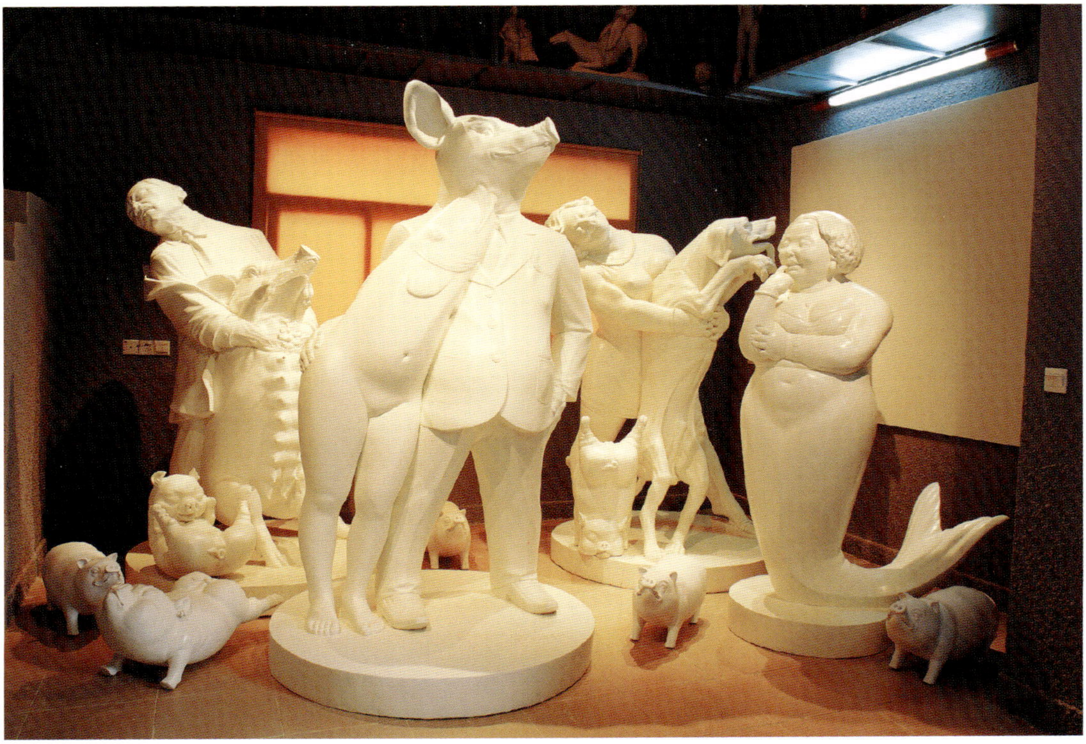

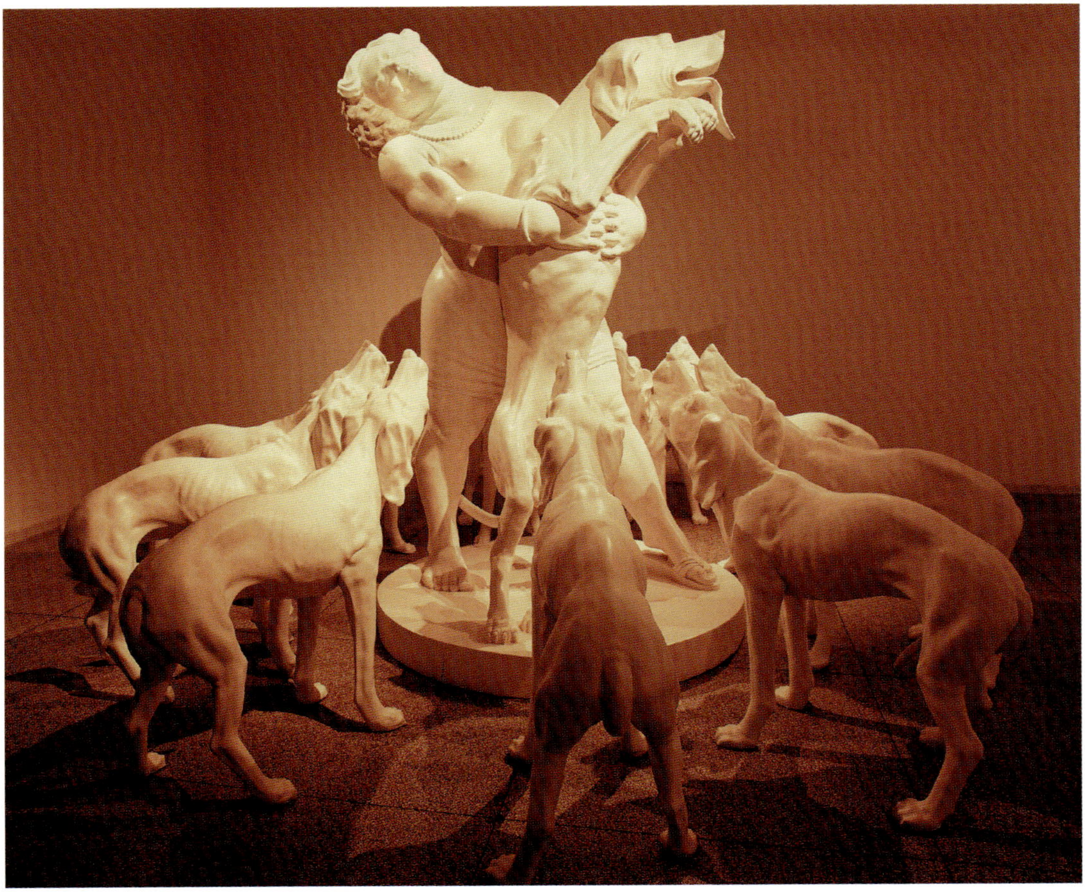

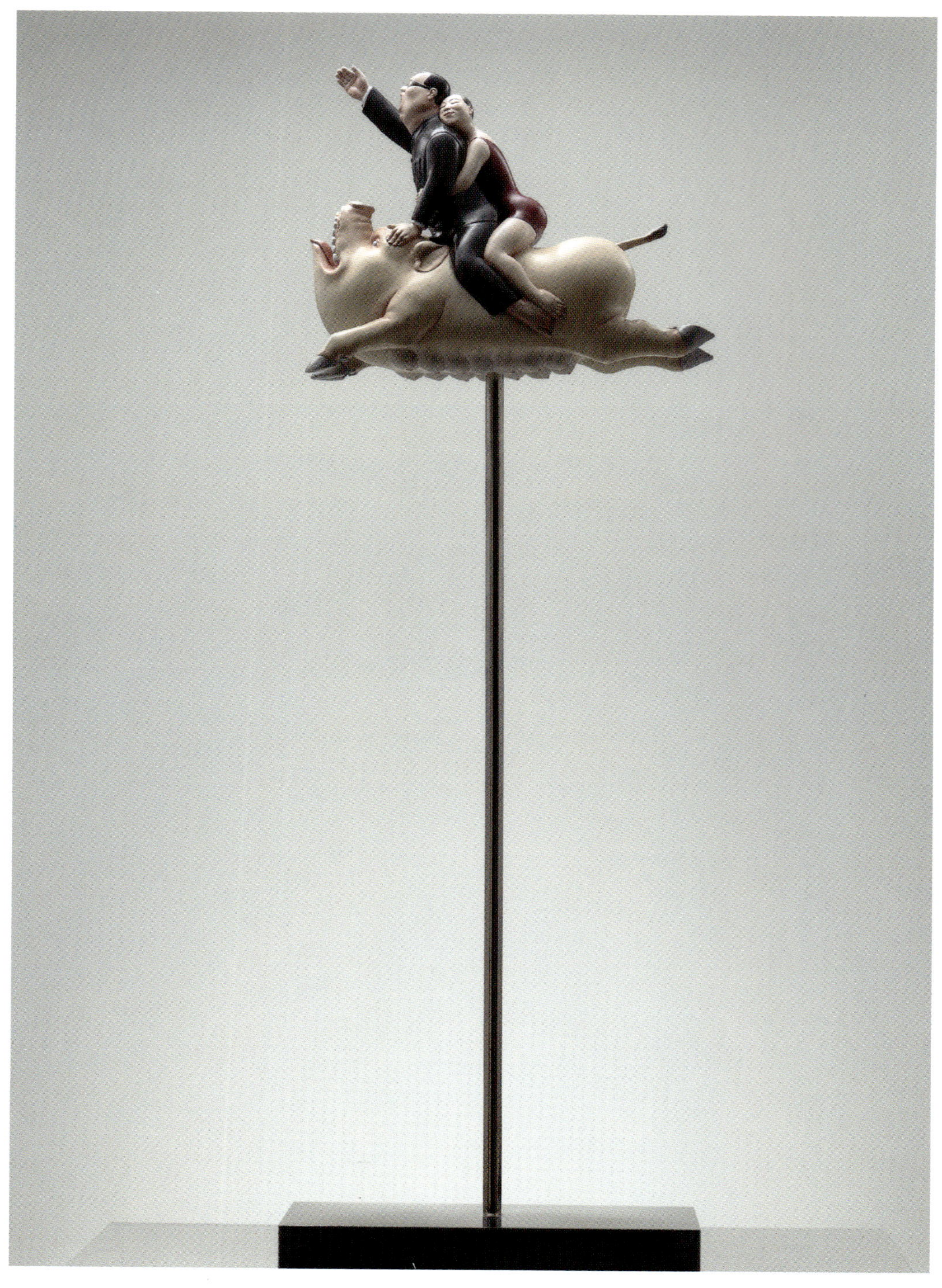

Happy Life No. 12 / 幸福生活NO.12, 2005   *Happy Life No. 21* / 幸福生活NO.21, 2008

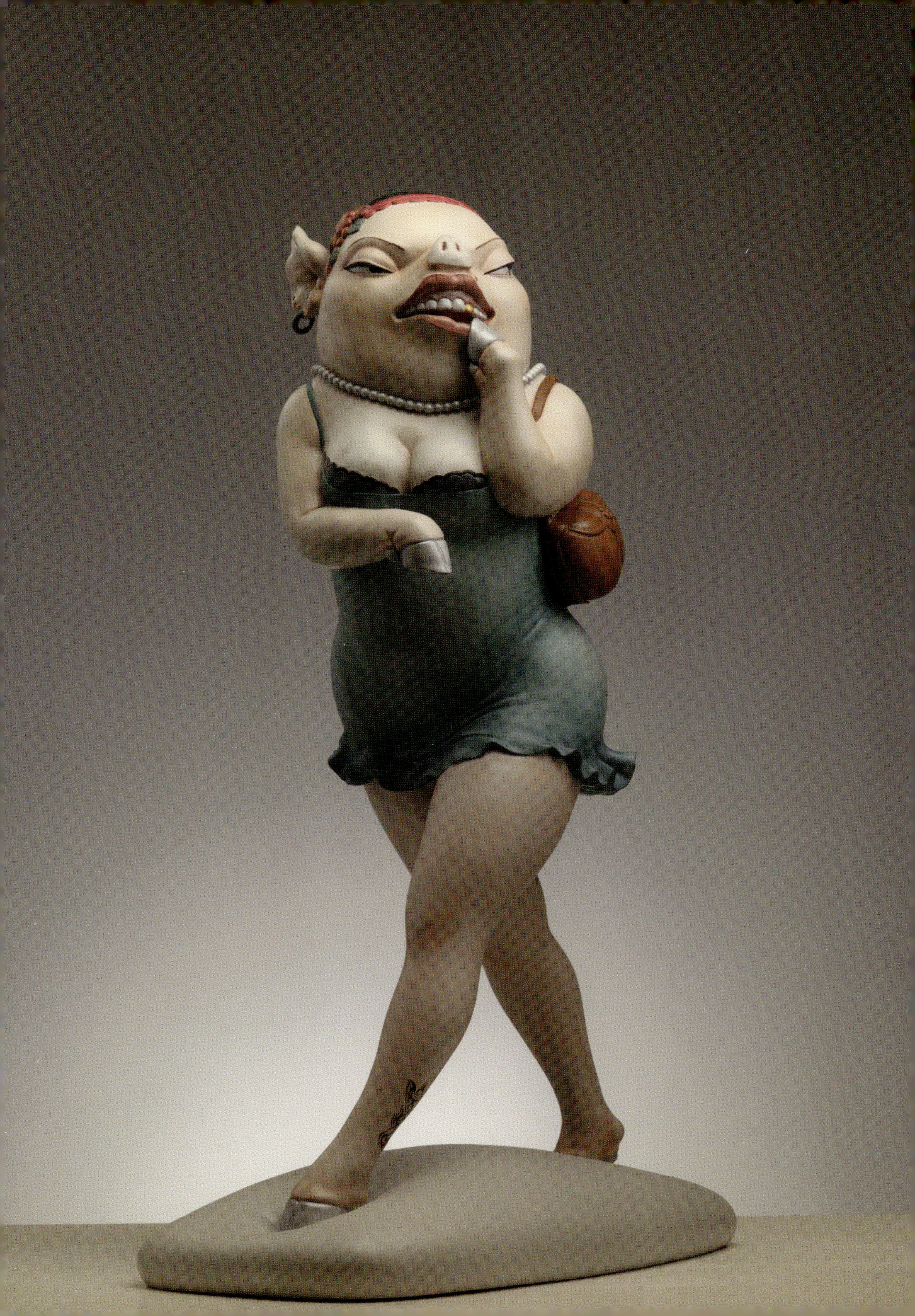

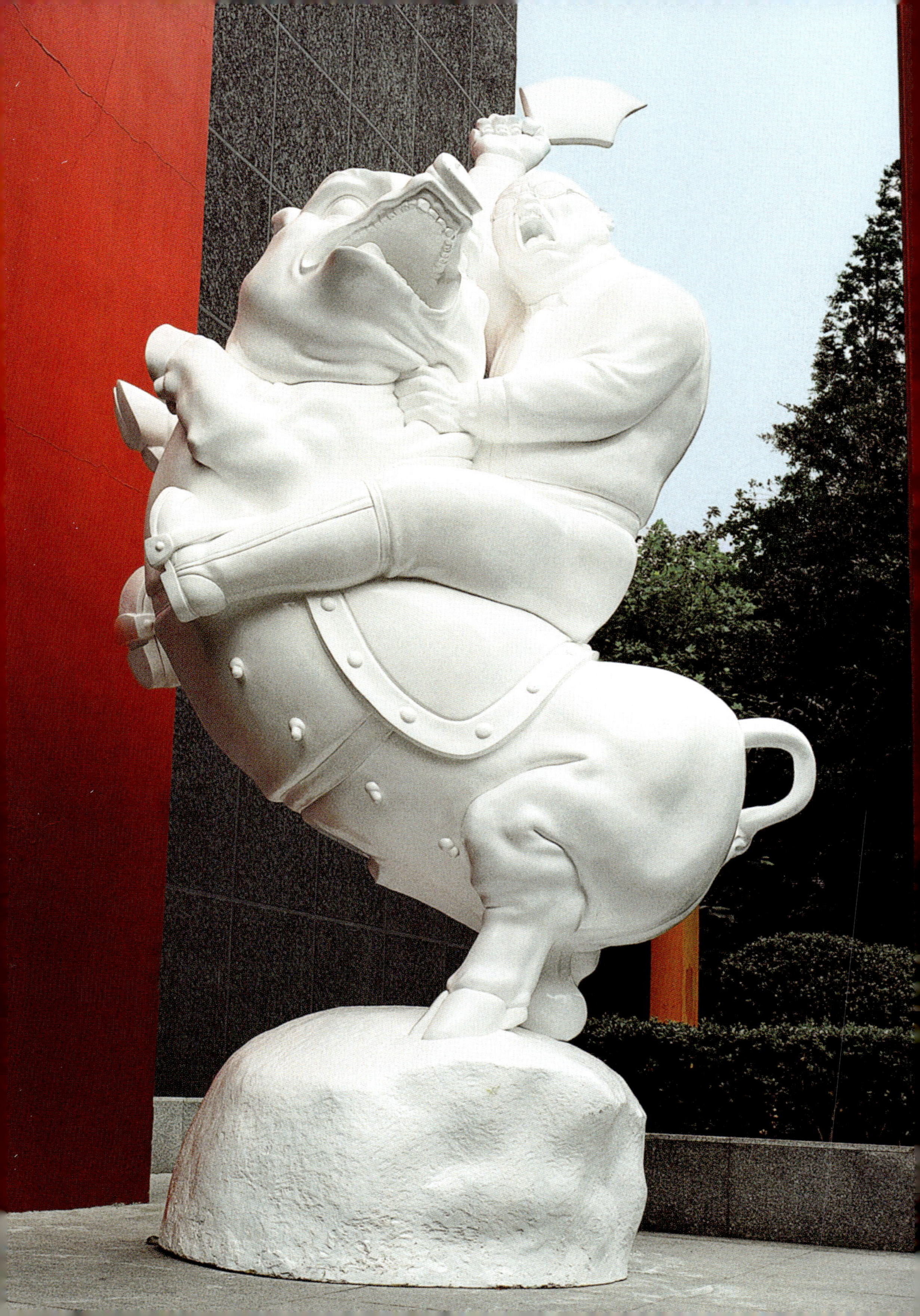

Living Organisms:
Chen Wenling's Open Sculpture

Gary G. Xu

In 1962, the Italian critic and novelist Umberto Eco published an influential book, *The Open Work*. This book could not have appeared at a better time. Europe had gradually clawed itself out of the post-war slump, the Civil Rights movement was sweeping across the US, and the Cold War had started to escalate. There was a general consensus among artists to call for more tolerance, plurality, and multiplicity. Eco's book was part of the consensus, but it also preceded its time: many of the book's ideas about art's openness were only later developed. By "openness," Eco refers to the incompleteness or ambiguities of certain artworks, which leave it to the audience to complete the work, or allow the work to be interpreted from multiple perspectives. He summarizes four open possibilities: disorder, chance, mobility, and indeterminacy.[1]

Chen Wenling's recent sculptures are open works. For some, it seems redundant to say that a contemporary work of art is an open work. It's almost a given that all works of art are plural, mobile, indeterminate, and open at the age of plurality. This presumption, however, is not always accurate, because it only describes the situation in the post-industrial world, that is, Euro-America. For works from other parts of the world, they are usually seen as representations of shared group identities: nation, culture, tradition, and so on. As such, these works are "closed" because their meanings, no matter how ambiguous, multilayered, or incomplete, are subject to definitive readings related to the larger frameworks of national culture. These nation's artists face everyday reality by experiencing oppression against which personal identities and individualism can only be secondary issues. Chen Wenling's earlier works, represented by the red man series, are indeed reflections of the artist's own individual vision pitted against forces larger than the self. The humor, the humble and humiliated expressions, the disproportionally elongated bodies, the twisted body postures – these should all be seen in the wider context of individual expression vs. an overwhelmingly collective culture.

What has changed in Chen Wenling's recent works is that he has acquired a universal sculptural language along the direction of openness. The meaning of his works is not only filled with the classical implications of openness as defined by Eco: disorder, chance, mobility, and indeterminacy, but also expands on openness by being interactive, whimsical, self-reflective, and imaginative. This new openness is relevant to China's changing social and economic environments. We know that China is in the midst of the largest urbanization project in human history: villages are being annexed into megacities, high-rises are being erected everywhere, interesting buildings designed by world-class architects are popping up here and there despite the lack of an overall urban planning scheme in most Chinese cities. These developments, however, have not left much room for public spaces. There are limited public spaces, and rarely can public art be seen. Chen Wenling is ambitious, and aims to reverse the lack of public art by making his large-scale sculptures specifically with urban residents in mind. These works are designed to be interactive, to be touched, played with, and fantasized about. Only with the participation of the new urban residents do the meanings of these works become complete.

Take, for instance, *Noah's Ark* (2012). Measuring five meters high, three meters wide, and seven meters long, this sculpture is designed to allow people to play inside and underneath. On the double decks, there are several hundreds of small animal figurines. What is interesting about this sculpture is not only its interactivity, but also the fact that it is more of a living creature or organism than an inanimate boat. Inside the main cabin, a sound device is installed to play beats emulating pulses; lights go on and off to the rhythm of the pulse. Under the boat, support is provided by limbs that resemble octopus tentacles and tree roots. The Biblical boat is supposed to float when the flood comes; Chen Wenling's boat takes root in the ground and can grow on its own. As a living organism, this boat is more like an object from a Dr. Seuss book, in which everything has a life in the wildest and most whimsical of imaginations. Many factors contribute to Dr. Seuss's enormous popularity; his rich imagination is one of them. This imagination, however, is not simply about combining otherwise incompatible elements. Dr. Seuss uses a hodgepodge of different ingredients to construct a spatiality that is more psychological than physical, more for harboring intense emotions than for hiding from realities.

Chen Wenling's living organisms are also spatial constructions. This is evident in his work *A Heterogeneous Space* (2012). The largest ball seems to be the mother cell, with several flagella growing out of it. These tentacle-like flagella constantly give birth to smaller cells, and continue to sprawl around like sensory organelles, to explore new territories. This creature can be likened to a living, breathing octopus, or to a submarine. But more importantly, it allows us the possibility of constructing a "heterogeneous space," which does not belong to any of the known dimensions. It is not three-dimensional, nor even four-dimensional, but rather supra-dimensional in the sense that it inspires imaginations of an individualized and highly differentiated space. Given the giant size of the sculpture, this space allows for playful and participatory interactions. All the openings are not only symbolic, they are actually functional, serving as entrances and exits in a giant labyrinth.

The Illusory Realm (2012) is smaller in scale than *Noah's Ark* or *A Heterogeneous Space*, but no less interactive. In the alcove, under the lotus petal beneath the meditating figure, is a basin designed to be filled with water. The stainless surface of the sculpture is already highly reflective; adding water not only enhances the reflections from multiple angles, but also creates a ripple effect that destabilizes the stainless surface. The artist also plans to place koi in the water so that the ripples are constantly stirred up. The ripples are precisely the manifestation of the mind of the meditator, who needs to complete the impossible task of calming the ripples down. The artist has entitled this sculpture *The Illusory Realm* in reference to the fantastic nature of the scene, which is supposed to exist only in our imagination. "Disorder" and "chance" play crucial roles in the completion of this work.

We should note that Chen Wenling's openness and fantastic imagination are not simply inspired by pluralism or biochemical discoveries in the West. *The Illusory Realm* has Buddhist implications; and his living organisms are particularly relevant to Taoism, which teaches us to follow the natural course of things. If a lotus petal or a flat pumpkin are large enough to float, why don't we send them floating on a lake (*The Floating Chamber of Desire*, 2012)? And if a gourd is too big to be made into a spoon, why can't we make a pavilion out of it so that travelers or urban residents can enjoy the shade it provides (*The Gourd Pavilion*, 2012)? The last example clearly pays homage to *Zhuang Zi*, in which Zhuang Zi once responds to Hui Zi's complaint about a gourd too big to be useful: "Why can't you make a boat out of the giant gourd and float on rivers and lakes?" All things have their own purposes and uses; we only need to find out what these purposes are. Chen Wenling makes us re-think the use and nature of sculptures. Sizes are all relative. Big or small, all depends on perspectives and purposes. Because of this hint of Taoist relativism and of the natural course of things, his new sculptures made for the new urban public spaces are both functional and meta-sculptural. They are sculptures that respond to questions about this ancient and yet constantly renewed form of art.

[2012]

1. Umberto Eco, *The Open Work*. Trans. Anna Cancogni. Cambridge: Harvard University Press, 1989.

活生生的生物机制：陈文令的开放的雕塑

徐钢

1962年，意大利批评家安伯托·艾柯出版了一本深具影响力的书《开放的作品》。这本书出版得恰逢其时：欧洲渐渐从战后的消沉中艰难走出，人权运动正在横扫美国，冷战在逐步升级。艺术家在呼唤宽容、多元化与多样性上达成了普遍共识。艾柯的书正是这共识的一部分，但它仍然是超前的。书中许多关于艺术开放性的观点后来才慢慢兴起。通过"开放性"一词，艾柯指出了特定艺术作品的不完整性或含糊性，这样就可以让观众来完成作品，或允许作品在多重视角下被解读。他总结了四个开放的可能：无序性，机会性，流动性和不确定性。

　　陈文令最新的雕塑都是开放的作品。很多人会认为，说一个当代的艺术品是开放的显得多余，鉴于我们本来就处在一个多元化的时代，所有的艺术作品都是多元的、变化的、不定的并且开放的。然而，这个假设并不总是准确，因为它只描述了后工业社会的情况，就是欧美的情况。对于世界其它地方的作品来说，他们通常被看作是共有的集体特征的代表：国家，文化，传统等等。一旦跟这些宏大的国族叙事挂钩，这些作品的意义就被封闭起来了。不管这些作品起初的意思是多么含糊、多层次或是不完整，都受制于与更大的国族文化相关的明确解读。非欧美国家的艺术家，因为每天都要面对残酷现实中的种种政治压力，身份认同和个人主义只能被放在第二位。陈文令早期以小红人系列为代表的作品，的确是艺术家个人想象与那些大大超于个体的势力的对抗的反映。滑稽、自卑或羞愧的表情、被拉长的不成比例的身体、扭曲的身姿——这些都应该在一个更大的语境中理解，也就是在个人表达和强势的集体文化之间的矛盾。

　　陈文令最近作品的变化是越来越开放，有了一种很流畅的跨文化的雕塑语言。他的作品不仅仅是有着被艾柯定义的经典的开放性的含义：无序性、机会性、流动性和不确定性，而且通过互动作用、异想奇思、自我反照和充满想象力的行为进一步延伸了开放性的可能。这种新的开放性和中国正在变化的社会经济环境息息相关。我们知道中国正处在人类历史上最大的都市化进程中：乡村被越来越大的都市吞并，到处都耸立着高楼大厦，那些由世界级的建筑大师设计的各种有趣的建筑在各个角落冒出来，虽然中国的绝大多数城市都缺乏整体规划方案。这些发展并没有给公共空间留下多少余地。公共的空间十分有限，也几乎看不到公共艺术。陈文令有着庞大的计划，梦想着扭转这种缺乏公众艺术的趋势，在创作他的大型雕塑的过程中时时不忘新都市居民的需要。这些作品被设计成能够互动的、可以触摸的、可以与之玩耍或是促成幻想的。只有当新的都市居民参与进来，作品才实现了意义的完整。

　　以他的作品《诺亚方舟》（2012）为例。5米高，3米宽，7米长的雕塑，目的是为了让人们可以在内部和底部玩耍。在双层甲板上，有几百个小动物塑像。这个雕塑有趣的地方不只是它的互动作用，而是相较于无生命的船，它更像是个活生生的生物或有机体的事实。在主舱里，安装了一个声音装置来模仿脉搏的跳动；根据脉搏跳动的节奏灯光随之明灭。最有意思的是，在船下面，支撑重量的是既像章鱼触角又像树根的肢体。《圣经》中的诺亚方舟在洪水到来时可以漂浮起来，为生灵万物留下生存的种子，而陈文令的船却植根于地面并可以自己生长—它本身就是一个种子。作为一个活的有机体，这艘船更像一个从苏斯博士的书中走出来的结构，在最大胆和最异想天开的想象力下，每个事物都有生命。苏斯博士的超级流行是很多因素造成的，异想天开便是最重要的。异想天开的背后却不是乱七八糟地将各种不相容的东西混搭在一起，而是通过这些东西制造出一种空间感。这种空间感与其说是物理上的，不如说是心理上的；与其说是躲避现实的，不如说是包容多种复杂而强烈的情感的。

　　陈文令的活生生的生物机制如苏斯博士的幻想一般，是为了空间的构成。在《异度空间》中，底座最大的球状体就好比是一个催生一起生命的母体细胞，而从中伸出的长长的东西便是生物学上所说的鞭毛。这些像章鱼触角的鞭毛，不断延伸，在延伸的过程中生出新的细胞繁殖机制，再通过对外界的感知不断拓展母体的空间范围。我们可以将整个物体想象成一个大章鱼或者一艘潜水艇，但是"异度空间"这个题目让我们明白这个空间不属于已知的任何一维：既不是二维、三维，也不是四维的，而是超出维度的范围的空间，属于高度个人化、独特化的空间。因为作品的尺寸巨大，这个个人化的空间允许参与性的、游戏性的互动，所有的开口处不仅仅有象征的意味，而且有了实际的功能，变成这个大迷宫的出口和进口。

　　另一件作品，《幻界》（2012），虽然比《诺亚方舟》和《异度空间》的规模小，却丝毫没有减少作品的互动性。壁龛中，在莲花花瓣下，冥想的小人的下方的是一个设计好来装满水的大盆。雕塑不锈钢的表面已经是高度反光的了；再加水将不只从多个角度加强反光，也会产生涟漪，从而破坏不锈钢表面的稳定。艺术家还计划着把锦鲤放进去，涟漪就会不断地被激起。涟漪恰好是打坐者的心思的显现，因为他需要心里的涟漪平静下来，而这几乎是不可能的。艺术家将雕塑命名为《幻界》，指涉这幅图景奇异幻想的特点，它原本应该只存在于我们的想象中。"混乱性"和"机会性"在这幅作品的完成中起到了关键作用。

《幻界》这样的作品提醒我们，陈文令的开放性和狂放的想象跟西方的多元主义或者生物化学等学科最新的发现没多大关系，而是从中国传统中原本就内在的开放性中找到启发。《幻界》有很深的禅意，而陈文令的活生生的生物机制跟道家的"天地生万物"、"道法自然"的说法息息相关。如果一个荷花叶抑或是一个大南瓜有足够的浮力，为什么我们不放其在湖上漂浮呢？这是《漂流欲室》背后的道理。如果一个葫芦大而无当，做水瓢都嫌太大太重，那为什么不干脆拿它做个凉亭，为行路者或城市居民提供阴凉呢？这是《葫芦亭》背后的道理。说到大葫芦，我们不由不想起《庄子》中，惠施对庄子抱怨的无用的葫芦。庄子回答说："今子有五石之瓠，何不虑以为大樽而浮于江湖，而忧其瓠落无所容。"所有的事物都各有其用，无用的东西只不过是因为用的人不明其理罢了。陈文令用这个道理来我们重新思考雕塑的作用和性质。大或者小，现实主义或抽象，纯观赏的或允许互动的，都取决于视角。因为这样的对思考的启发，陈文令为新的城市空间制作的新雕塑既是有功能性的，也是"元雕塑"—关于雕塑的雕塑。

陈文令的开放，是将视觉的领域完全开放，并邀请观看者从多个角度参与进来。在他绝妙的视觉想象中，所有的形状和物体都拥有了生命，变成活生生的呼吸着的有机体。这种神奇可能会改变中国死气沉沉的城市景观。

[2012]

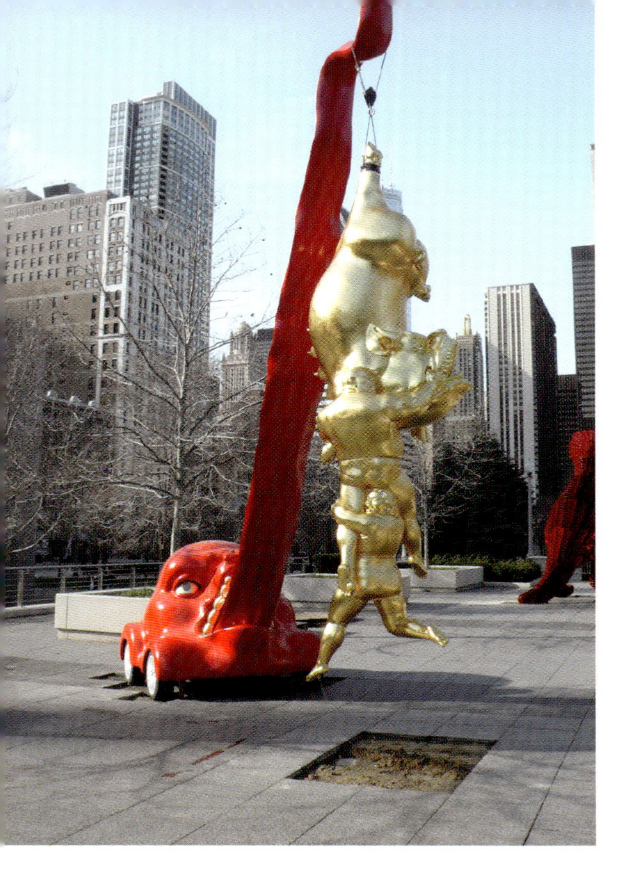

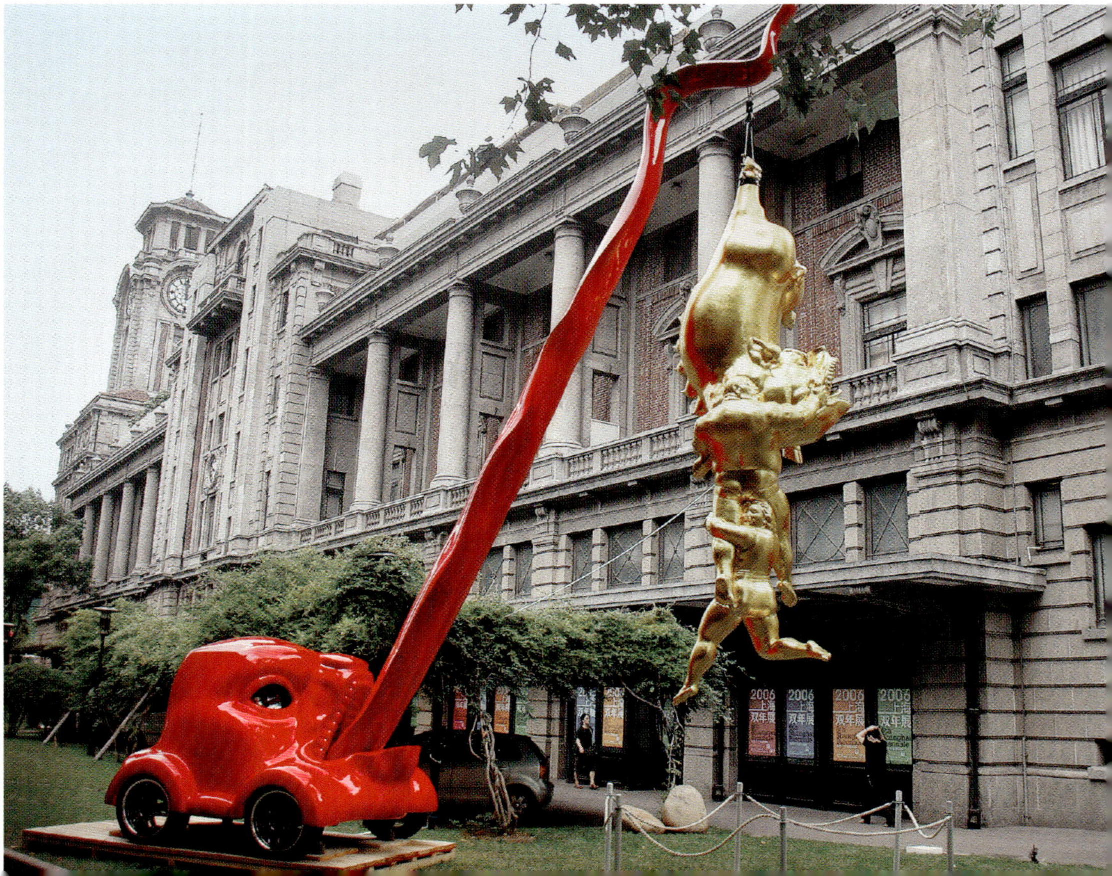

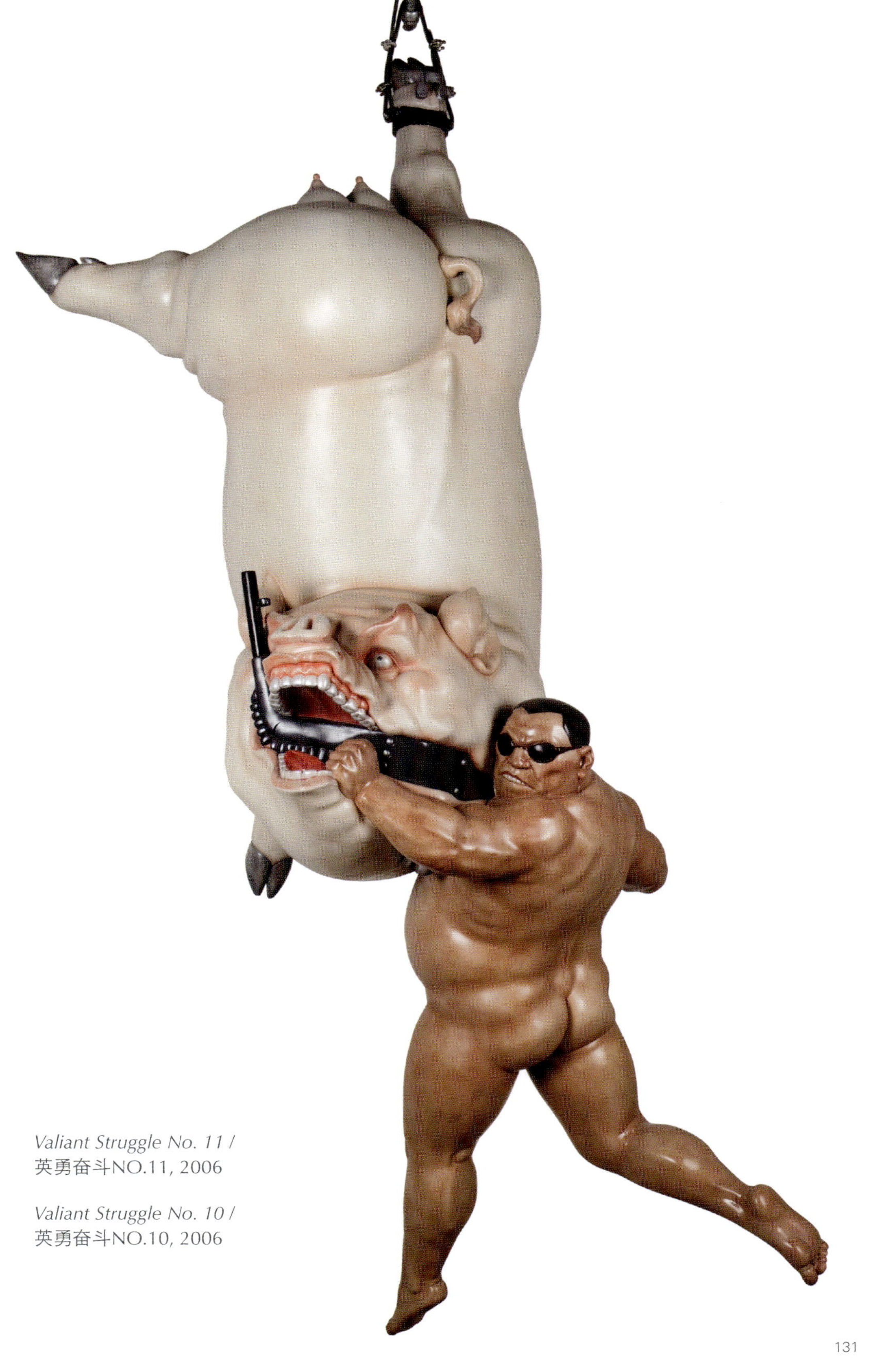

Valiant Struggle No. 11 /
英勇奋斗NO.11, 2006

Valiant Struggle No. 10 /
英勇奋斗NO.10, 2006

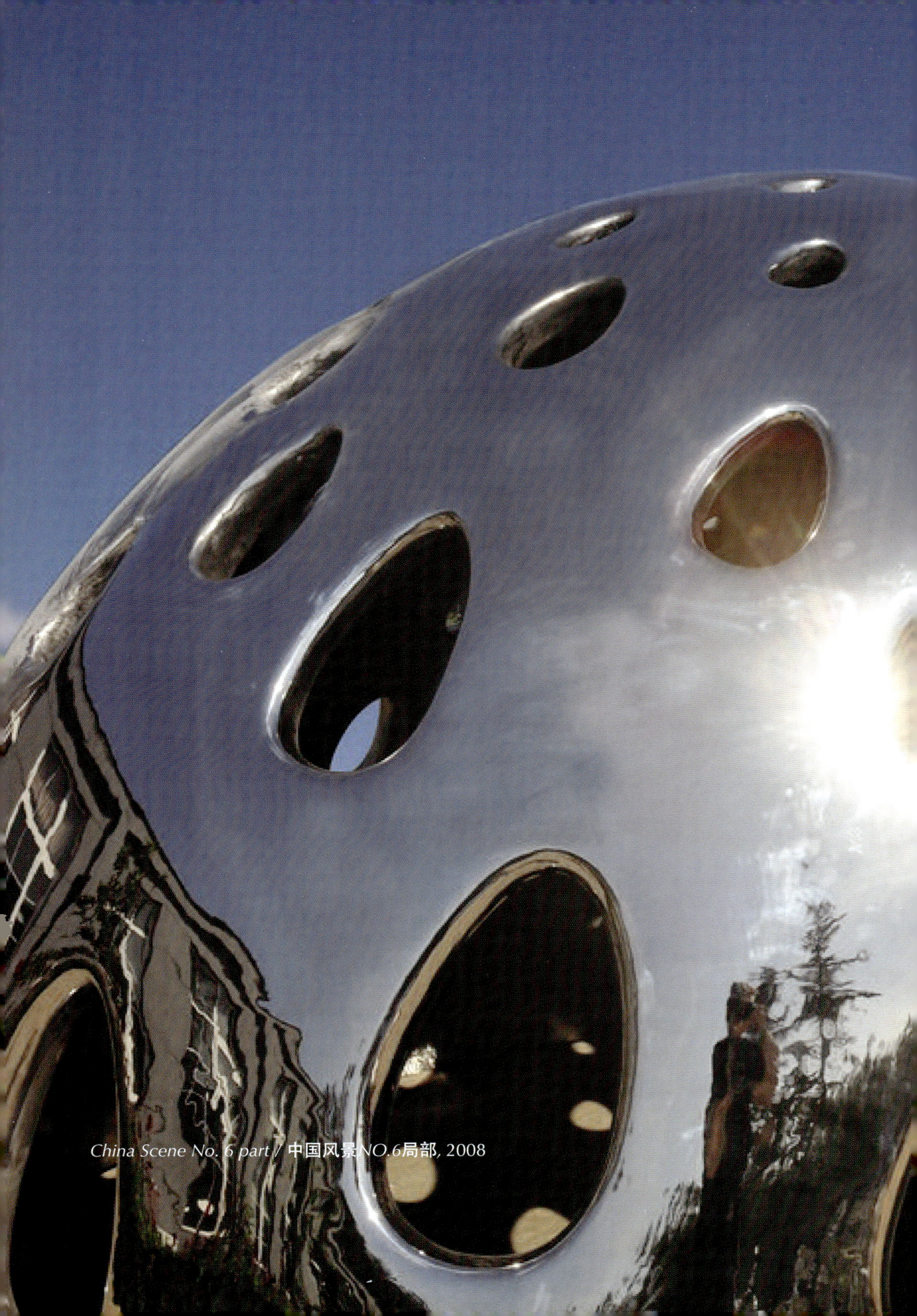

China Scene No. 6 part / 中国风景NO.6局部, 2008

I Don't Even Know How I Grew Up: Chen Wenling's Original Landscapes

Chiba Shigeo

1. That Would Be . . .

Chen Wenling's works (from *Red Memory, Happy Life*, and *Terrestrial Subterranean*, and all the way to *Fetish*, together with the works in his *Emergency Exit* exhibition) reveal that his creative activities have been relentless. In content, his subject matter is extensive, reflecting subjects as diverse as the Chinese people today, the economic crisis on Wall Street, and Noah's Ark. His modes of expression range from individual sculptural works to installation art, and he has never been confined to a single form. That has all been widely acknowledged, but I have long been pondering where the foundations of these works of his lie. What does he ultimately want to express?

If we take his *Red Memory* series as a starting point, then works from his 2009 show (*Emergency Exit*) to the present group of exhibited works together suggest that his development has taken him over a comparatively great distance. However, ultimately where do the roots of his oeuvre lie?

2. The Core of Expression

In 2009, I was highly appreciative of what I saw at *Emergency Exit*, but I was not surprised, because the technique and content of the works were logically set out. At the same time, in this venue filled with "works of artistic excellence," my mind settled on the images that emerged from the *Red Memory* series, and it was at that time that I began to wonder "Why?"

Could that possibly be because the *Red Memory* series and the works in the *Emergency Exit* exhibition were diametrically opposed? The axis of the former series was subject matter related to the individual, the latter works related to society and not simply themes drawn from Chinese society. So, as

I understood it, Chen Wenling could essentially be explained as two artists working at opposite poles, and his future work should open up somewhere between these two extremes.

Of course opposites attract, which is in itself also a paradox. Of course this is no easy task, but because of this, we can say that the pain of this contradiction enriches his work.

Regarding two of the works shown in the *Emergency Exit* show (*What You See is Not Necessarily True* and *How to Escape*) the former attracted wide attention and became a topic of conversation. But the latter was shown in a very small space with its six sides painted black, and I felt that this work also hinted at the inner recesses of the artist's mind. The expression of the blackness implicitly or explicitly suggested that the mind had justification for wanting to escape from confined conditions. In this sense, I felt that the mood or mindscape of the works of the *Red Memory* series was also latent in this work.

Needless to say, this is not to suggest that the *Red Memory* series had already revealed his entire oeuvre, because expansion also brought new inspiration for the artist. At the same time, in terms of potential meaning, I did feel that perhaps all his latent potential could be found in the *Red Memory* works.

A writer strives to open up and reveal the latent self that has been concealed. However, a good artist, however much he opens up, must still hold back his "expressive core."

Artists might say that they themselves do not care, but they are consciously or unconsciously compelled to preserve this "expressive core." An artist can never really leave this core, and this inability to leave can become the starting point for a true artist. Generally speaking, an artist constantly pursues freedom of expression but freedom is impossible for his own "expressive core."

The moment he abandons it or loses it, he ceases to be an artist. This is because what we call "expression" must spring from this core.

3. Parched Homesickness

The catalog of the exhibition *Emergency Exit* contained two very interesting interviews with Chen Wenling, and from them we acquire a general understanding of how he grew up and how his spiritual world took shape.

Chen Wenling was born in 1969 in Jingu Village, Anxi County, Fujian Province, and was the descendant of a village "landlord." His home was located in a small valley among fertile mountains. Although he was a stutterer as a child, he grew up as a lively child surrounded by rice paddies and green fields. From a very young age, he played creative games, making pictures in sand and fashioning objects from clay. These hobbies opened his mind to possibilities and gradually led him towards the road travelled by artists.

In 1991, he completed his studies in Xiamen, and then began studying sculpture at Beijing's Central Academy of Fine Arts in 1993. In the following year, he set up a studio in Xiamen and began formal creative activities. It was at that time that the policy of the socialist market economy was declared (1992) following the implementation of the reform and opening-up policy in 1978.

Subsequently, in 1998, he began creating his *Red Memory* series, and the group of works he created over three years was exhibited in 2002 at a seaside exhibition in Xiamen. This was his first solo exhibition.

Although I did not see the open-air exhibition in Xiamen in 2002, one can see that the "child" in the *Red Memory* series is a self-portrait of Chen Wenling, and there would seem to be no other possibility. When he began formal creative activities, he most wanted to express past joy and suffering, the various thoughts that spring to mind at the end of a happy childhood and memories of the "environment" in which he grew up. These are condensed in his work. His images of children derive from his own memories, experiences, and feelings: shy children, laughing children, children turning cartwheels, children covering their chests with sand, and children waving their arms in the air.

But it is worth noting that in creating works that evoke the ideas conceived in a beautiful past he is by no means simply beautifying his own boyhood. Although this might be his basic departure point, his completed works clearly turn the self into an image and objectify it. In other words, the "self" is extended to "society." By turning the self into an objectified object, his created works reflect the contemporary society. However, it is not a leap out of the self to a higher level from which to observe society, but placing oneself in the midst of an "objectified = objective" society.

Another very important thing is that, although he developed an "objectified = objective" approach, and even though the good old days had elapsed, those many mixed feelings were never lost from the mind of the artist. If one only sees the "sociality" in his *Red Memory* series of works then one's interpretation of his oeuvre will be incorrect, because I feel that the

Red Memory series of works necessarily reflects the "homesickness" of the artist. This "homesickness" is not strong but is lightly sealed up in memory, but despite this it is nevertheless "homesickness."

Thus, treading between extremes, the poles are far apart but he is without fear; this method, which he prefers to describe as attitude, Chen Wenling has successfully attained.

4. Other Things: Pop Art

If we try dividing art into the art used for self-expression and the art used to express social conditions, the mainstream of modern art in China is mostly the latter. (Before modern Chinese art began, art had in the main completed a cycle, and the mainstream of art in the artistically advanced countries of Europe and the United States was mostly art of the former type.) Art of the latter variety based on social themes is called "pop art," and most of China's modern art is basically "pop art."

Pop art takes social conditions as its themes, and these can be simplistically divided into the following two extremes: one is a criticism and negation of social conditions; the other is affirmation and praise. Criticism and negation are not absolutes, and between the poles of criticism and negation on the one hand and affirmation and praise on the other there is much intermediate ground and there are relative positions with no hard and fast categories. Pop art must necessarily only be relative. But in the pre-reform period of "socialism" this was not the case, and at that time only unqualified affirmation and praise was permissible.

So if pop art can be relative rather than absolute, then this is especially true of pop art in modern China.

5. Expanding into One's Own Depths

Chen Wenling's works, overall, can be described as pop art. In retrospect, it seems that in the *Emergency Exit* show the work titled *What You See is Not Necessarily True* is the most like quintessential pop art. In contrast, his most recent works, *Noah's Ark* and *Urban Bulls,* are slightly different from works previously exhibited.

Of Chen Wenling's latest group of works, I have only seen the photographs he sent me; but *Noah's Ark,* in addition to containing various species of animals, has a shape that could not exist in reality, and it is not typical pop art. The things resembling large roots jutting out from the ship look particularly incredible. This is a completely imagined work of fantasy. *Urban Bulls* seen from a distance does resemble a bull in shape, though it is 14 m long, but the viewer is not so much seeing a "bull" as being integrated into the feeling or sense of a "bull." In this way, it is not so much pop art, and is more appropriately explained in the terms of "environment" as that term is used in modern Western art history. Elements of "environment" also adhere to installation art.

Regarding the meaning expressed by the work, *Noah's Ark* draws on social themes that have the scale of humanity, and the stretching roots and the wonderful shape of the ark have great imaginative power. I find myself riding among the animals in the ark and rather than talking about pop art, this is seeing the tenderness of Chen Wenling. Like the clay shaped by Chen Wenling as a child, elements from his past bring a touch of softness to the fantasy of this work.

Urban Bulls, for example, feels like a large plastic model (typical pop art), but in contrast how can this be appropriate for his new work *Cultural Landscape*? The feeling is like some kind of flow. Visually, a line of stainless steel and steel elements gives the viewer the sense of transmitted heritage. This "tradition" is transmitted by creatures, mountains and rivers, heaven and earth, as naturally symbiotic transmitters of "heritage," and the natural world and the human world move forward together, allowing us to ponder and feel the heritage of life.

In terms of the connotation of the works' expression, *Noah's Ark* and *Urban Bulls* both express this illusoriness and the heritage of life, something seen for the first time in his work.

The Illusory Realm and *The Floating Chamber of Desire* are works that basically leave pop art behind, and the feeling is exactly the opposite in that the works moves in the direction of the interior of the individual. Because the central figure in *The Illusory Realm* is not just sitting cross-legged but in the lotus position, we can speculate that this so-called *The Illusory Realm* refers to the religious significance of "illusory worlds." Moreover, at the center of *The Floating Chamber of Desire* we see children watching goldfish swimming, and although the color is not red, it is obvious that these children come from *Red Memory*. *The Illusory Realm* and *The Floating Chamber of Desire* are an extension beyond the color red from the creative sources embodied in *Red Memory*. It is a work that is a fresh affirmation of his "roots" as well as the beginning of a movement in a new

direction. The former moves towards religious and philosophical serious-
ness; the latter confronts his happy childhood and the deepest of his roots.
The former is a rational direction, recognizing the existence of the direction
of "bitterness"; the latter is the direction of feeling and the direction of the
taste of happiness.

So it is in fact very difficult to categorize Chen Wenling's actual experiments as belonging to mainstream modern Chinese pop art. Even when
selecting social subject matter, the core of his experiments is in the deep recesses of *Red Memory* to which he is unconsciously drawn. This is different
from the gravity, but however far he travels he will be drawn back. No, perhaps the farther he travels, the stronger is the force drawing him back.
Brought from his childhood to the present, his feeling for art comes from
the inner recesses of the heart of *Red Memory*.

6. Other Extraneous Thoughts: Distorted Historical Trends, the Distorted Self

In expanding the depths of the self, I feel, as a Japanese, that the situation
of modern Chinese society and the Chinese modern art world might not
necessarily allow Chinese artists to move simply in this direction. Modern
Chinese society is determined by history and the current situation of modern Chinese society, as Chinese modern art is also determined by the history
and the current situation of Chinese modern art. This situation is certainly
different from the history and current situation of art in artistically developed areas. In Japan, the development of modern art has nothing to do with
geography, and it is located on the fringes and corners of those countries in
which art is developed, and having been born and raised here, I can clearly
determine that. Chen Wenling, having been born and raised in Jingu County,
Anxi County, Fujian Province, can obviously also feel this. Art and global-
ization are not necessarily congenial companions.

Nevertheless, the expressive forms of art are very interesting, and
whether it is flat painting or solid sculpture, since the birth of civilization
human forms and manifestations of expression have been shared. What is
different is the "inner meaning" of the expression.

Although Chinese modern art is determined by the history and current situation of Chinese modern art, after the reform and opening-up, society as a whole experienced "modernization" (as well as Westernization),
and this also inevitably meant being affected by the developed areas of

Western art. For example, the content and quantity of modern Chinese "consumer behavior" have undergone huge and rapid advances, and there is even evidence of excessive "modernization" (Westernization). What do people living in modern China really need? Needless to say, Chen Wenling is concerned about this question.

7. Original Scenery

Chen Wenling is, however, essentially a passionate person. There is an interview with him published under the title "I do not know how I grew up." In modern China, being a sincere person is a face-to-face experience, and Chen Wenling often returns to the horizon of feeling. There, although the country is still very poor, in a certain sense this does not limit the freedom of childhood being extended to the horizon. It is now spreading beyond the horizon to those who have gradually become rich but are beset by various contradictions. He is of course torn apart and rocked by this, and this situation is also reflected in his artistic expression. Even so, he chooses to actively accept these contradictions, and walk between the two extremes. What supports him in this are, of course, his happy childhood memories, and so he depicts the buildings of the village, with a variety of materials to create a variety of things of childhood memory. Human beings are shaped by memory, and survive in memory.

But it is not simply for these reasons because the young Chen Wenling also studied Chinese traditional painting, and he is really able to understand the importance of the traditional forms of expression for learning the new techniques of expression that he must inherit. Although tradition signifies history, no doubt in the process of human growth "place" also becomes living memory. Here I cannot but think of his work *Cultural Landscape* which I mentioned in passing before. It is like a painting, a landscape painting. It is 4 m long, 1 m high, and 70 cm wide, and is a three-dimensional work. Seen close up, the bull in the work *Urban Bulls* comprises objects stuffed together, but from a greater distance, the work resembles a city landscape, and from a fair distance the work looks like a natural landscape.

Cultural Landscape should be constituted by the human world (people, creatures, buildings, etc.) on behalf of the elements of nature (mountains, water, trees, etc.) as elements of scenery (*shanshui*). It also refers to the human world that resembles such a landscape. The various interconnected elements just mentioned, like those in *Urban Bulls* and *Calabatine* (Gourd

Pavilion), are however independent of the existence of these works. He has a vision of the human world as scenery (*shanshui*).

In turning various things of the human world into his works, he separates these things from their own identities. Thus, he is sometimes critical of society, sometimes humorous, and sometimes typical pop art. But in *Cultural Landscape*, we do not feel this, nor do we feel he is separate from his own identity. In this work, we can say that there are no obstructions between the work and its creator.

Cultural Landscape is probably Chen Wenling's original landscape. The childhood home in that small mountain village and the environment in which he was raised are fully expressed in the determination to use art to express art hopes in his exhibition *Art and the Search for Origins*. I mentioned earlier that those elements that constitute *Red Memory* are the same. In the fifteen or so years since he completed those works, he has changed and further developed *Red Memory* in the new works before us. This "return" is not retrogression, but a rise up a spiral, and this is the path of expansion Chen Wenling has followed. This spiral axis is his "original landscape."

I also do not know how I grew up, but this is not a problem, and it is just fine. He feels there is nothing wrong. But I hope that as he ascends the spiral staircase to a higher level, he will not leave his inner heart behind, but will examine it even more closely. Looking at *Cultural Landscape*, I firmly believe this is happening.

[2012]

我也不知道自己是如何成长的
－陈文令的原风景

千叶成夫

1　那是什么

从《红色记忆》和《幸福生活》、《地上地下》一直到《物神》、「紧急出口」展，再加上本次展览会的作品群，陈文令的创作活动一直没有停歇过。在内容上，从反映现代中国人的面貌到表现华尔街的经济危机、诺亚方舟等，题材非常广泛。在表现手法上，从个体的雕刻到装置艺术，从不拘泥于一种形式。以上这些虽然已经被很多人所认同，但是我一直在思索的是他的这些作品其根基在哪里？究竟要表达的是什么呢？

如果把《红色记忆》系列作为出发点，2009年的「紧急出口」展到本次展览会的作品群可以说从出发点向相当远的地方一路发展过来。但是，他们的根基到底是什么呢？

2　表现的核心

2009年，在「紧急出口」展上看到的时候我就非常欣赏，但是并不感到吃惊。因为无论是从技法上还是从内容上，都是理所当然的展开。与此同时，在「卓越艺术」会场，我的脑海中不由得浮现出《红色记忆》系列作品的影像，就是在那时"为什么呢？"我开始思考。

大概因为《红色记忆》和「紧急出口」展是所谓的完全相反的作品吧？前者的轴心是个人的题材，后者是社会，是不仅仅包括中国的社会的题材。于是，我是这样理解的－陈文令本质上是表现这两个极端的美术家，今后的作品也应该会在这两极中展开吧。

被完全相反的两极所吸引，也正是本身矛盾的体现。这并不是见容易的事，但正因为此，可以说这种矛盾的痛苦丰富了他的作品。

在「紧急出口」展上展示的两幅作品《What You See is Not Necessarily True》和《How to Escape》，前者广受瞩目并成为话题。但是，后者被展示的很小的空间中六面被涂成黑色，我觉得这也暗示着美术家的内心深处。那个黑暗的表现是有理由的，暗示或明示从闭塞状况下逃出的意图也是有理由的。从这个意义上，我想《

红色记忆》作品的意境也是潜在其中的。

毋庸置疑，不是说在《红色记忆》系列中已经展现了他的全部，而是扩展为美术家带来了新的灵感。与此同时，从潜在的意义上，感觉他的全部都潜在于《红色记忆》中。

作家活动就是将自己自身潜在的东西扩展并表现出来。但是，作为一名优秀的美术家，无论如何扩展都会保持"表现的核心"。

美术家就是比方说即使自己完全没有在意，可无论是否刻意都会保持"表现的核心"这种东西的人。他无法从这种核心真正离开，就是这种不能离开，是使其能够成为一名真正的美术家的出发点。一般来说艺术家终究是追求表现上的自由的，可是唯独自身的"表现的核心"是不可能有自由的。

一旦放弃它或者失去它，也就不成其为艺术家了。为什么呢？是因为所谓"表现"一定是从"表现的核心"中诞生出来的。

3　干涸的乡愁

「紧急出口」展的图录中刊载着陈文令的两篇很有意思的访谈。从中可以大致了解他的成长和精神世界形成的概略。

陈文令于1969年出生于福建省安溪县金谷村，是"地主"的后代。他的家乡位于富饶山间的一块小盆地。虽然小时候口吃，但是在稻田和绿野的环抱中，作为一名活泼的孩子渐渐长大。从很小的时候开始，他就喜欢在沙子上作画，用粘土捏东西这种创造性的游戏。这些爱好打开他的心扉，引导他逐渐走向成为美术家的道路。

1991年，他完成在厦门的学业，93年在北京中央美术学院学习雕刻，翌年在厦门成立了工作室，开始了正式的创作活动。那时正是1978年开始执行"改革开放政策"后宣布进入"社会主义市场经济政策"的阶段（1992年）。

然后，1998年开始创作《红色记忆》系列作品，用3年时间创作的作品群于2002年在厦门的海边进行了展示，可以说这实际上是他最初的个人展。

我虽然没有在现场看过2002年厦门的展示，但从照片资料中可以看出《红色记忆》的"儿童"们就是陈文令的自画像，可以说除此以外不可能是他人。当正式的创作活动开始的时候，他最想表现的是过去既有欢乐也有辛酸，可结局是幸福的少年时代的自己的样子，心中、脑海里涌现的各种思绪以及自己生长的"环境"。

这些都凝缩在他的作品中。害羞的孩子，开怀大笑的孩子，倒立的孩子，把沙子埋到胸口的孩子，向天空高举手臂的孩子，这些都来自于他自身的记忆，体验和感觉。

但是值得注意的是，怀着对已经逝去的美好过去的万千思绪进行创作，他并不仅仅是美化了少年时代的自己。虽然根源是从那里出发，可是完成后的作品显然是把自己对象化、客观化了。换句话说就是把"自己"扩展到了"社会"。由于对自己进行了"对象化＝客观化"，创作出的作品反映了当时的社会。但是，它不是跳出自身从一个更高的角度来观察的社会，而是身居其中表现出的"对象化＝客观化"社会。

还有一件非常重要的事情就是，虽然进行了"对象化＝客观化"，尽管过去的美好时光已经流逝，可作者心中不曾失去那些百感交集的感怀。只看到《红色记忆》系列作品的"社会性"就对其进行解读是错误的，我的看法是《红色记忆》系列作品应该是反映了作者的"乡愁"。这种"乡愁"不是浓烈的而是淡淡地封存在记忆中的，即便如此它也是"乡愁"。

由此，脚踏两极，被两极撕裂而不恐惧，这样的方法，不，与其说是方法不如说是态度，陈文令就在这里获得了。

4　其他－流行□艺术

如果将美术试着分为表现自己和自己内心的美术以及表现社会状况的美术两种作对比，中国现代美术的主流多为后者（参考：
在中国现代美术的开始以前，美术大体上完成了一个循环，作为美术先进国的欧美国家美术的主流，是前者）。后者作为以社会状况为主题的美术被称为"流行□艺术（Pop Art）"。中国的现代美术基本上都属于"流行□艺术（Pop Art）"。
"流行□艺术"以社会状况为主题，可以单纯化地划分以下两个极端：一种是对社会的现状进行批判和否定；另外一种是肯定和赞美。这种分类在上世纪60年代美国出版的「流行□艺术的鼻祖」中得到了证明。在「流行□艺术的鼻祖」中，"批判□否定"并不是绝对的。也就是说是"批判□否定"还是"肯定□赞美"二者之间不是非此即彼的，而是相对的。"流行□艺术"必然也只能是相对的。不过在改革开放以前的"社会主义"时期却不是这样，那时候只可能是"肯定□赞美"的。
所以即使在现代中国"流行□艺术"或者说"流行□艺术"的美术也是相对的而不是绝对的，甚至可以说在现代中国尤为如此。

5　向自身的深处展开

陈文令的作品总体来说是属于"流行□艺术"。现在回想起来，「紧急出口」展的《What You See is Not Necessarily True》是最属于"流行□艺术"的作品。与之相比，最近的《超验的方舟》、《城市公牛》等这些作品则有稍微不同于以往展开。
关于陈文令的最新作品群，我只看了他送来的照片资料，《超验的方舟》中，除了乘船的各种生物外，形状是现实中并不存在的东西，不属于典型的"流行□艺术"。特别是从船上像根一样伸展出去的东西，看上去不可思议。这是完全是想象的，甚至是幻想出来的作品。《城市公牛》从远处看好像是牛的形状，长度有14米，观看者与其说是看到了"牛"不如说像是被融入了"牛"中的感觉。从这个意义上，与其说是"流行□艺术"，不如说用美术发达地区的现代美术史的用语"环境"来解释更为恰当。也就是在装置艺术中加入了"环境"要素。
所要表现的内涵是什么呢？《超验的方舟》选取人类规模的社会主题，伸展出去的像根一样的东西以及方舟本身奇妙的形状等，极具幻想力。我从乘坐方舟的生物中，与其说看到了"流行□艺术"，不如说看到了陈文令的温柔。它们就像是陈文令儿时捏的那些泥塑的延伸，于是这些个过去的元素为这个作品幻想性带来了一丝柔软。《城市公牛》，比方说感觉就像一个大的塑料模型（典型的"流行口艺术"），它的反面，也就是像新作《人文山水》那样的，怎么说合适呢？感觉就像是某种流动。从视觉上，不锈钢口钢铁构成的一行，让观众产生传承的感觉。这种"传承"是生物与山河、天地、自然共生的"传承"，自然的世界与人类世界共同推进，让人联想并且感受到生命的传承。

从表现的内涵来看，从《超验的方舟》、《城市公牛》中看到的这种幻想性和大的"生命传承"的表现，在他的作品中首次出现。

《幻界》、《漂流欲室》这些作品基本上脱离了"流行口艺术"，并且感觉是向个人的内部这种完全相反的方向脱离。因为《幻界》的中心人物不仅仅是盘腿坐着，而是結跏趺坐，所以可以推测所谓"幻界"是指宗教意义上的"幻界"的意思。还有，《漂流欲室》的中央那个看着周围游曳着的金鱼的孩子，虽然颜色不是红色，但是明显的是来自于《红色记忆》。《幻界》、《漂流欲室》是他《红色记忆》中所体现的创作根源向红色以外的方向的延伸。是一部一面对"根"进行再次确认，一面向新的方向展开的作品。前者是向宗教、思想的严肃性方向，后者是向幸福的童年时代，也就是他的根的最深处。前者是理性的方向，是认识存在着"苦"的方向；后者是感觉的方向，品味幸福的方向。

所以说，陈文令的尝试实际上很难用作为中国现代美术主流的"流行口艺术"来概括。即使是选取社会方面的题材，他尝试的核心也仍然是他内心深处的"红色记忆"，他在不知不觉中被牵引向这里。这不同于地球引力，无论他走多远，都会被这种引力所牵引。不，可能走得越远反而越强烈。从童年时代带现在，他对艺术的感觉都来自于内心深处的"红色记忆"。

6　还是其他 – 歪曲的历史潮流、歪曲的自己

向自己的深处展开，作为一名日本人，我感到现代中国社会和中国现代美术界的状况是可能并不允许中国的美术家们单纯地向这个方向发展。现代的中国社会是由现代中国社会的历史和现状决定的，因此中国现代美术也是由中国现代美术的历史和现状决定的。它与美术发达地区美术的历史和现状肯定不同。在日本，近代美术的发展与他的地理位置无关，它位于美术发达地区的边缘，角落（也许不是），在这里出生长大的我能很清楚地判断出这一点。而在中国南部福建省安溪县金谷村长大的陈文令，也理应判断出这一点。美术与国际化是不投缘的。

尽管如此，美术的表现形式是非常有趣的，无论是在平面上绘画还是在物质上雕刻，从"文明"诞生以来，对人类来说表现形式都是共通的。不同的是所要表现的"内涵"。

虽说中国现代美术是由中国现代美术的历史和现状所决定的，"改革开放"以后，社会全体经历了"近代化（也就是西欧化）"的中国，也不可避免的受到西方美术发达地区的影响。比如现代中国人"消费行动"的内容以及质和量都发生了巨大的

、迅速的改观，这是过度"近代化（也就是西欧化）"的证据。生活在现代的中国人他们真正需要什么？毋庸置疑，陈文令的内心也抱有这些疑问。

7　原风景

但是，陈文令本质上是个感性的人。有一篇访谈的题目为《我也不知道自己是如何成长的》。在现在的中国，作为一个真挚的人从正面面对。但是他经常回到感觉的地平面。在那里，国家虽然还很贫穷，但是从某种意义上说没有限制自由自在的童年时光一直延续的地平面。它的外侧正蔓延着随着渐渐变得富足却抱有各种矛盾的现在的地平面。他被理所当然的撕裂，摇摆着。这种状况在美术表现上也被反映出来。即使这样，他选择积极地接受这些矛盾，在两极中游走。那时候支撑他的当然是幸福童年时代的记忆、描绘着村庄的建筑物、用各种材料创作出各种东西的孩提时代的记忆。人类就是被记忆塑造，在记忆中生存的生物。

　　可并不只是这些，因为年轻的时候陈文令学习过中国画，他能真正理解为了学习新的表现手法，必须要继承传统的表现形式的重要性。传统虽然意味着历史，但是在人的成长过程中毋庸置疑的成为人们记忆的"地"。这里我不由想起在前面略微提到的《人文山水》这部作品。它就像一幅画，一幅山水画。长4米，高1米，宽70厘米的一部立体作品。近看像是由《城市公牛》中牛那样的东西组成连在一起，稍微远观就如同都市的风景一般，在离得远些看上去就如同山水风景。

"人文山水"是应该指由代表自然界要素（山、水、树木等）的人间世界要素（人、生物、建筑物等）构成的风景（山水）吧。也就是指人间世界看上去就是这样一道风景（山水）。刚才提到的连在一起的各种要素，就像《城市公牛》、《瓢箪亭》一样，但是又是独立于这些作品的存在。他具有将人间世界看成风景（山水）那样的眼光。

把人间世界的各种东西分别创作成作品时，他把这些东西与自身分离开。所以，有时批判社会，有时表现得很幽默，有时是典型的"流行口艺术"。但是在《人文山水》中，却没有感受到这种抛开，从他自身分离的感觉。在这部作品中，他自身存在于作品之中，可以说作品与其创作者之间没有任何隔膜。

《人文山水》可能就是陈文令的原风景。是从小成长的故乡那山间的小村庄、是孩提时代的环境、是对美术充满憧憬立志用美术来表现的他的"原口美术"。与我前面提到的构成《红色记忆》的那些元素是相同的。他在这将近15年的时间，改变了形式，再次将《红色记忆》进行了进一步发展的作品呈现在我们面前。这样的"回归"不是简单地倒退，是螺旋的上升，这就是陈文令展开的方式。而这螺旋上升的轴心就是他的"原风景"。

　　我也不知道自己是如何成长的一没有问题，这样就好。他的感觉没有错。但是我希望，在螺旋楼梯上每上一个台阶，都不会离开自己的内心，甚至离内心深处更加接近。看着《人文山水》，我坚信这一点。

[2012]

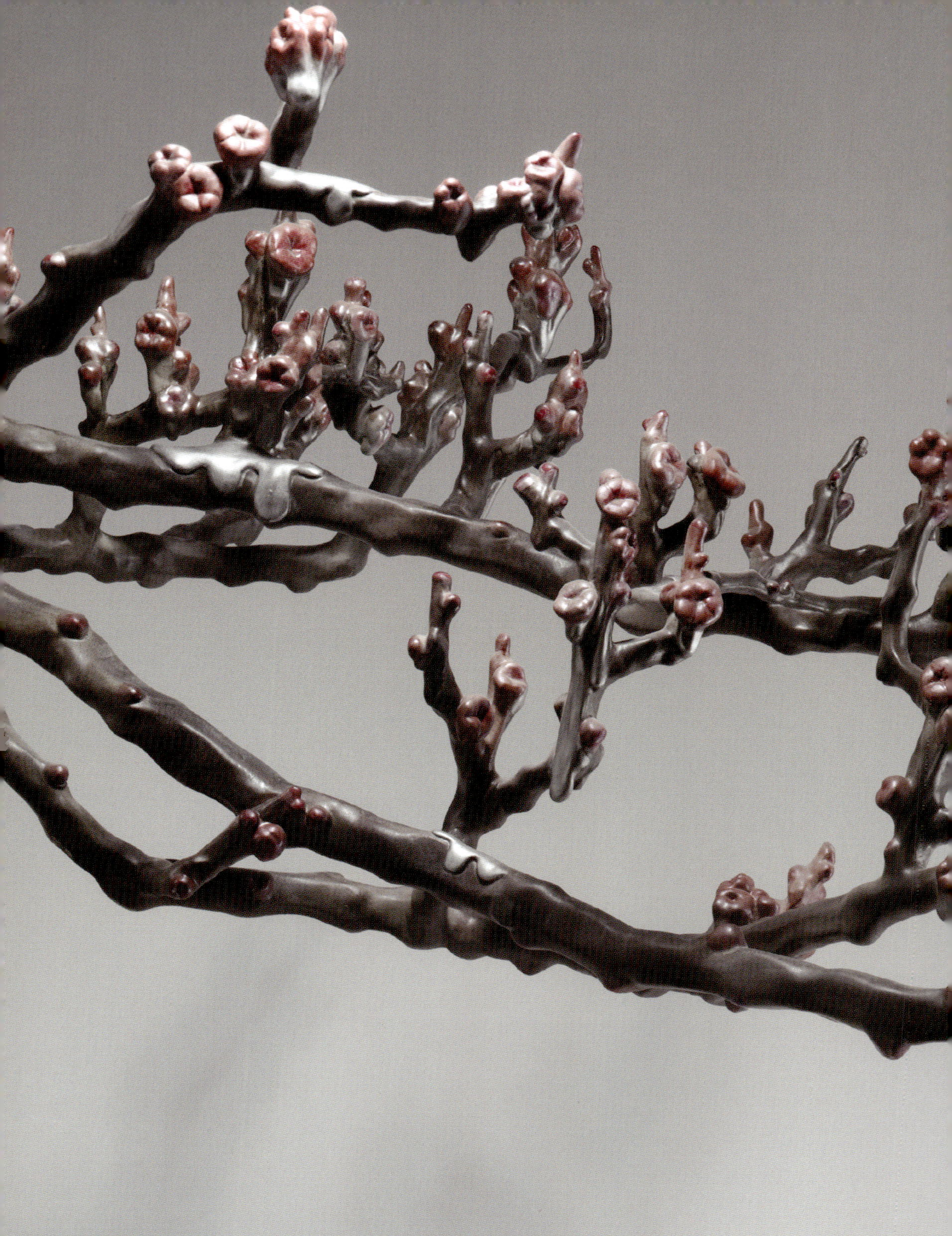

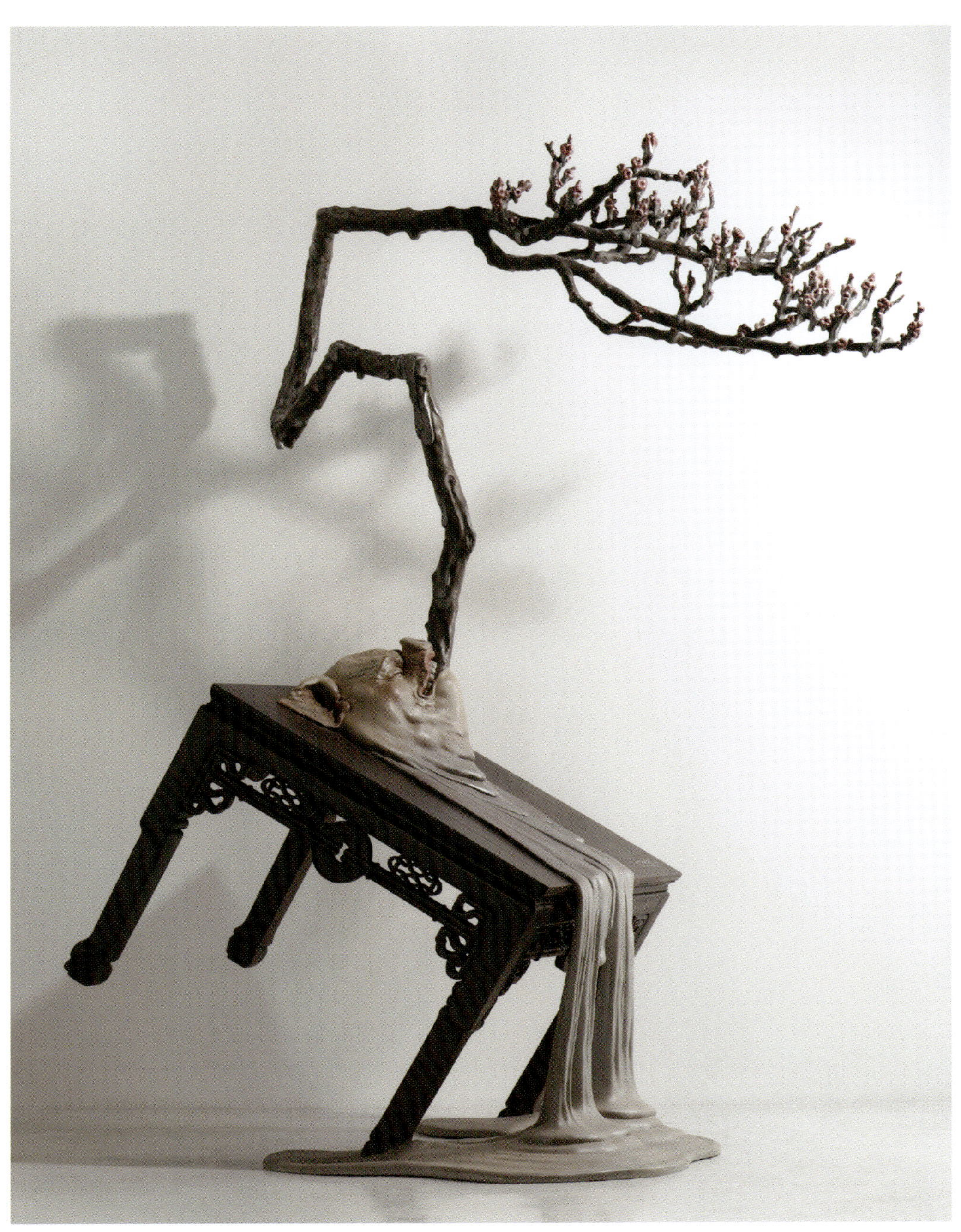

Mingled Scene / 混杂的风景, 2007

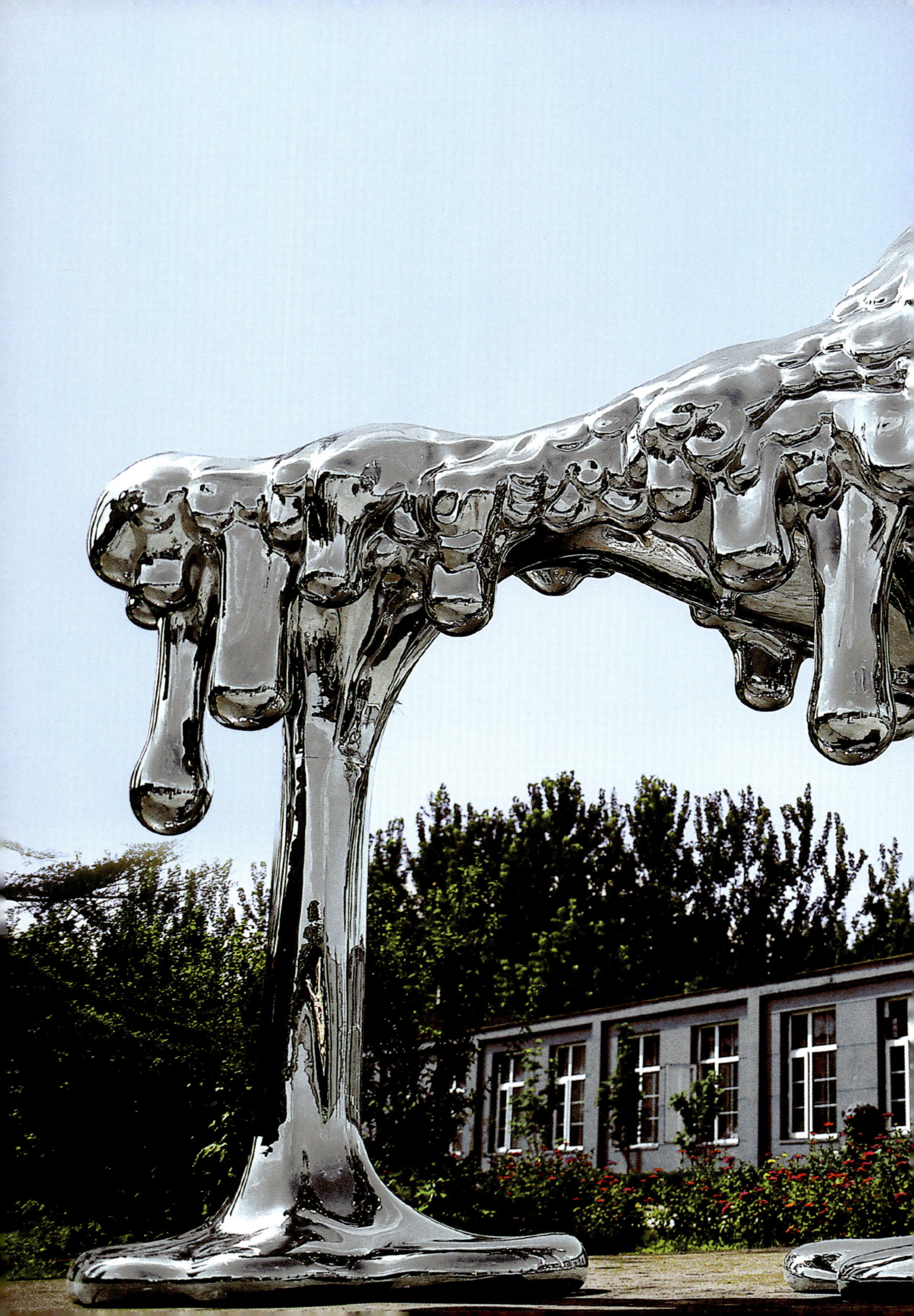

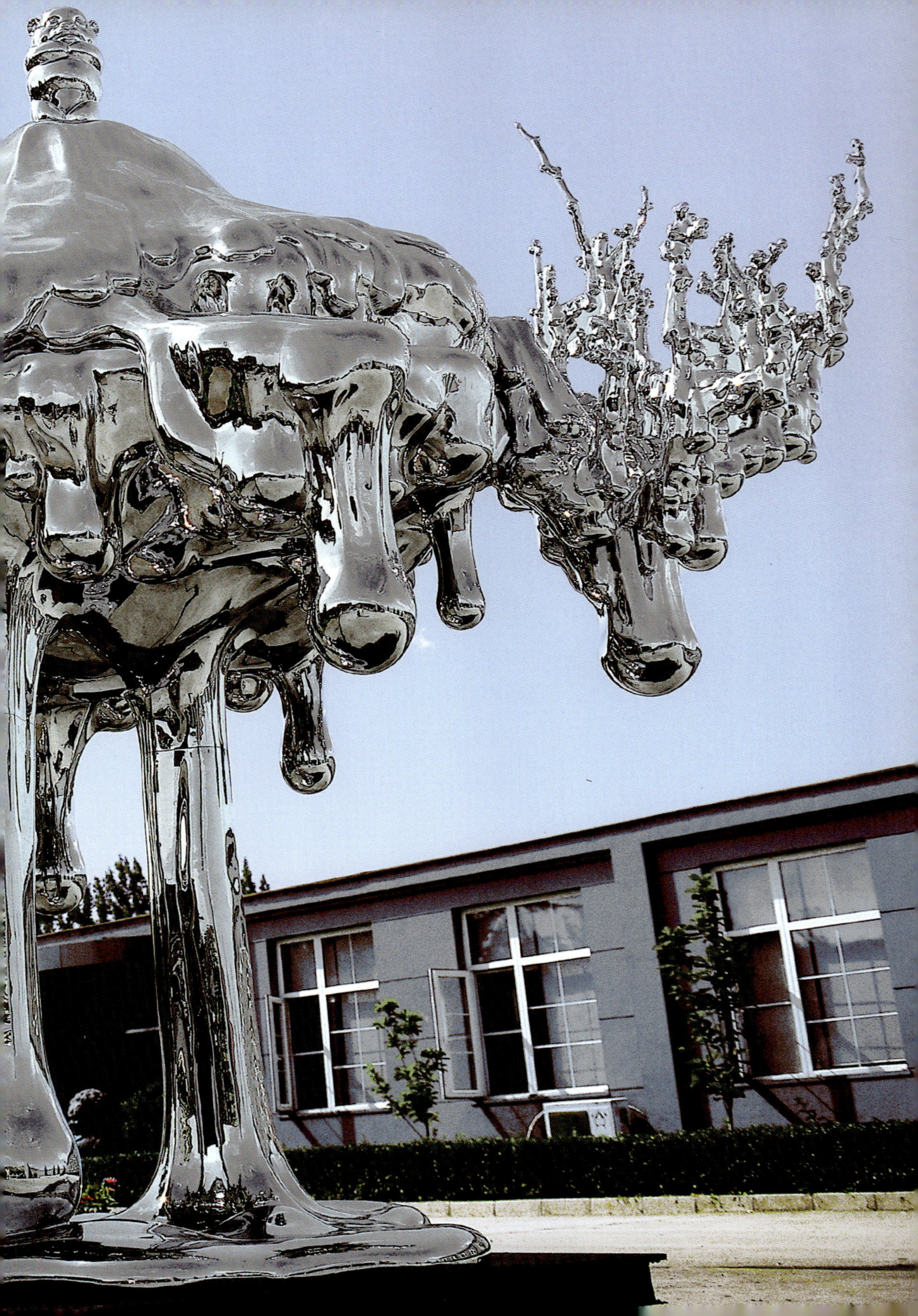

pp. 148-149
China Scene No. 1 / 中国风景NO.1, 2007

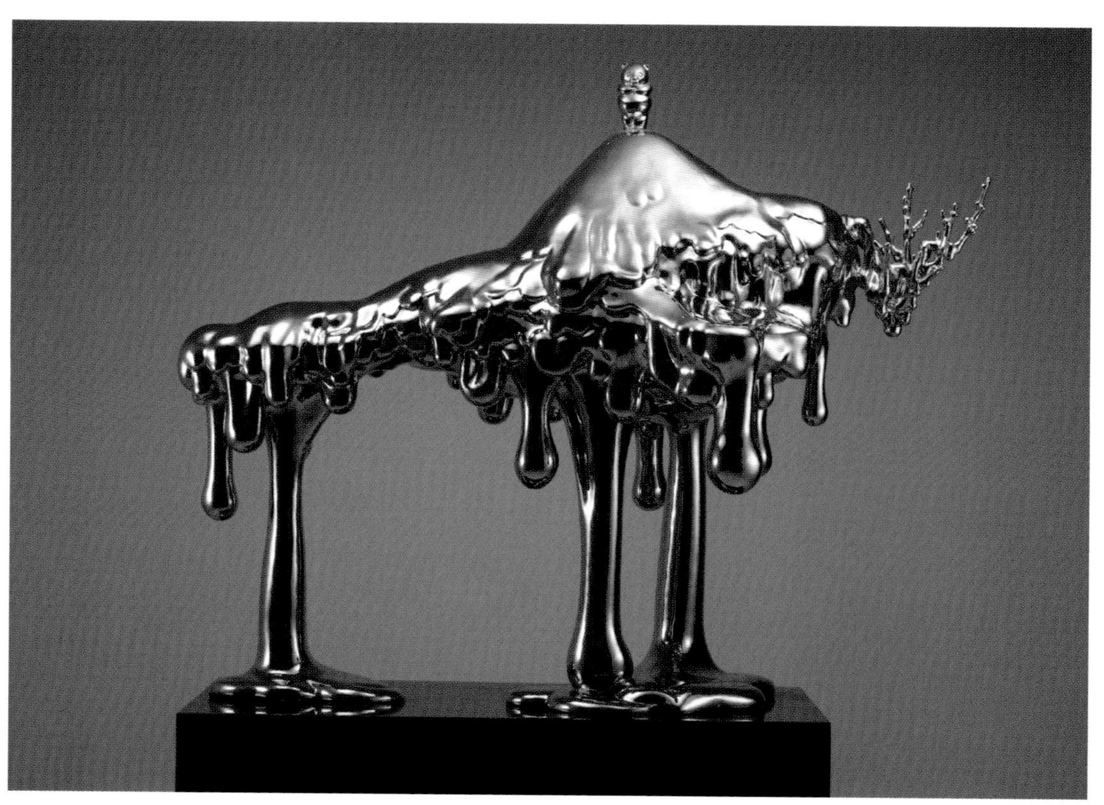

China Scene No. 1 / 中国风景 NO.1, 2007

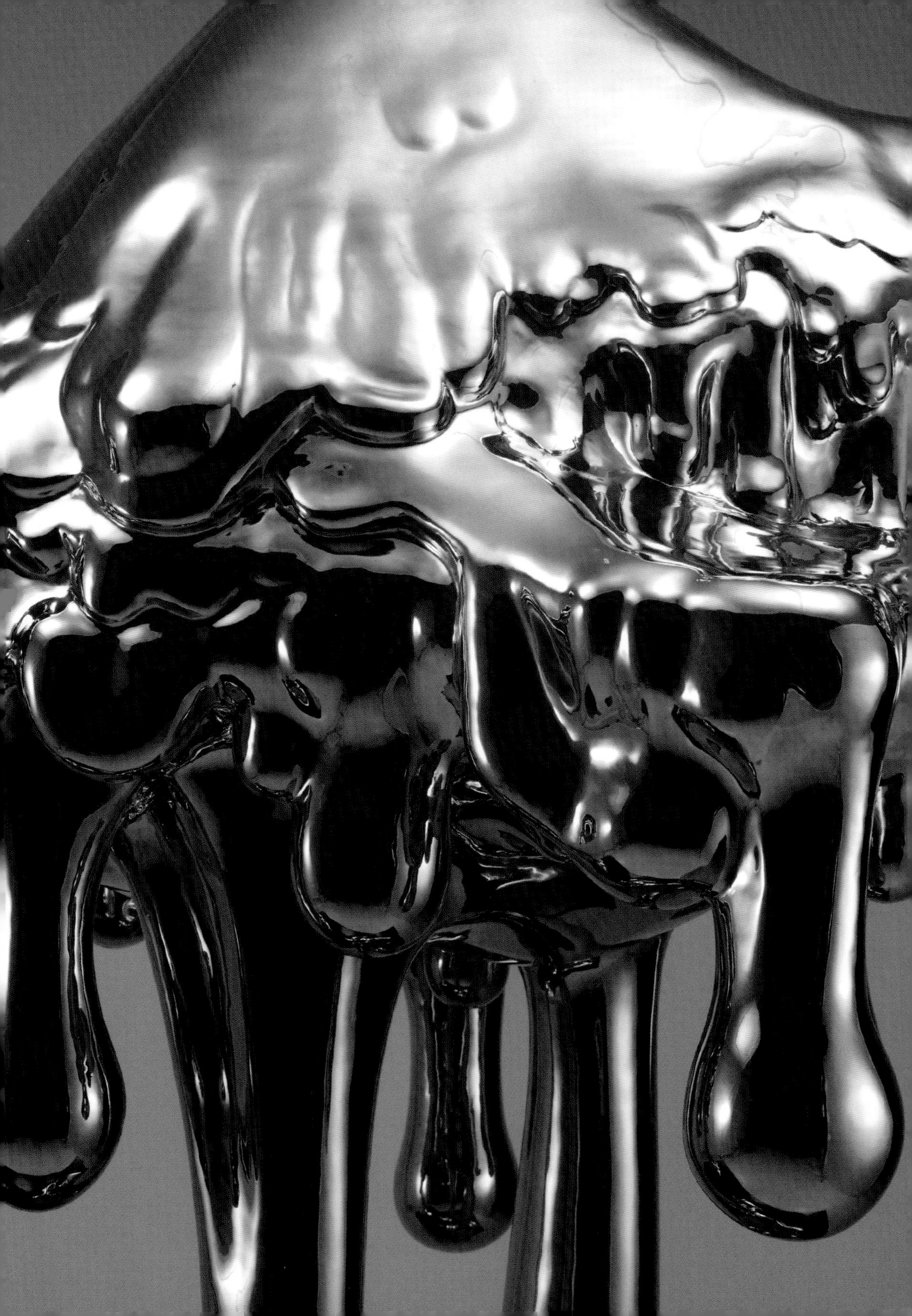

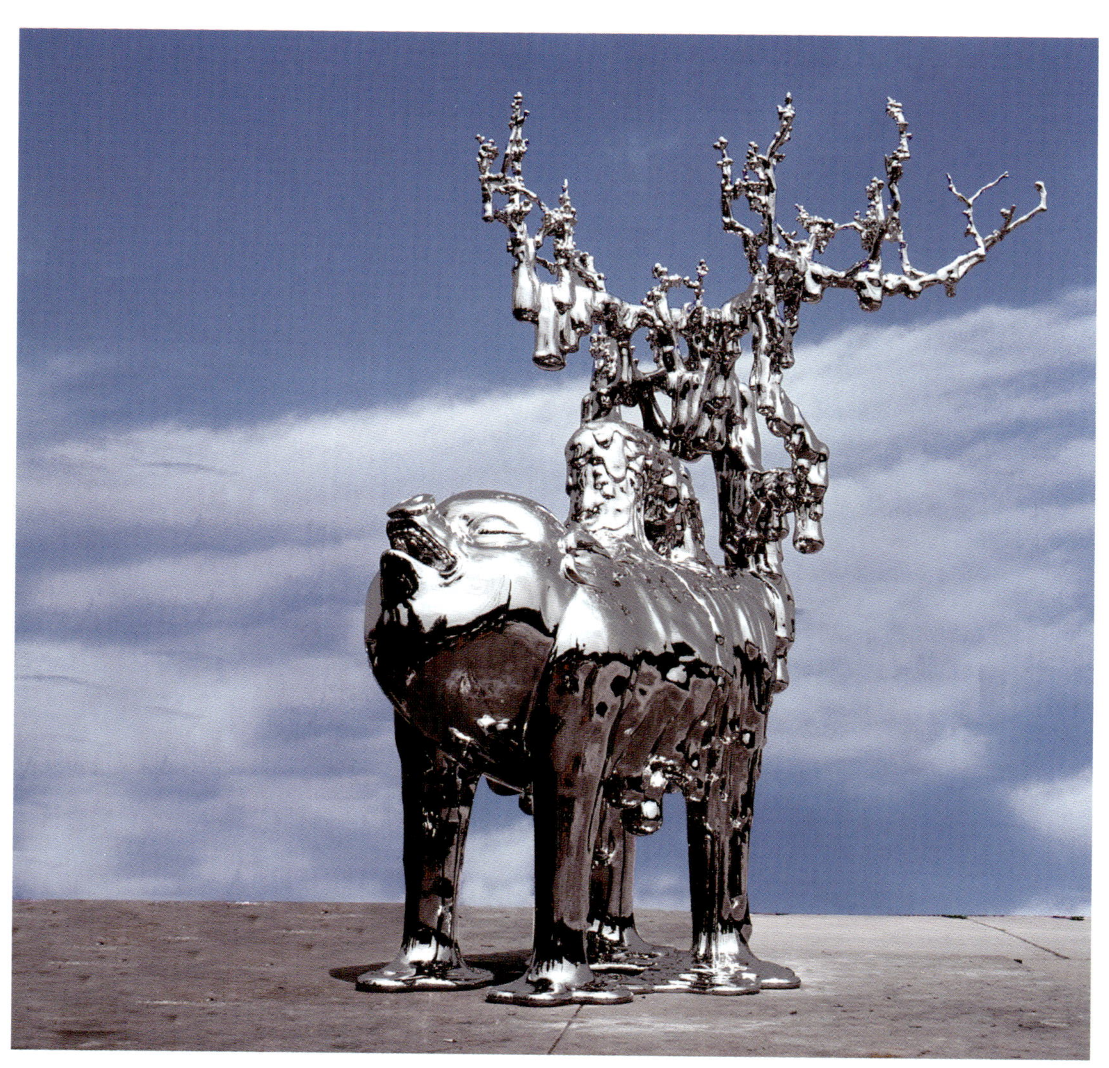

China Scene No. 3 / 中国风景NO.3, 2007   *China Scene No. 2* / 中国风景NO.2, 2007

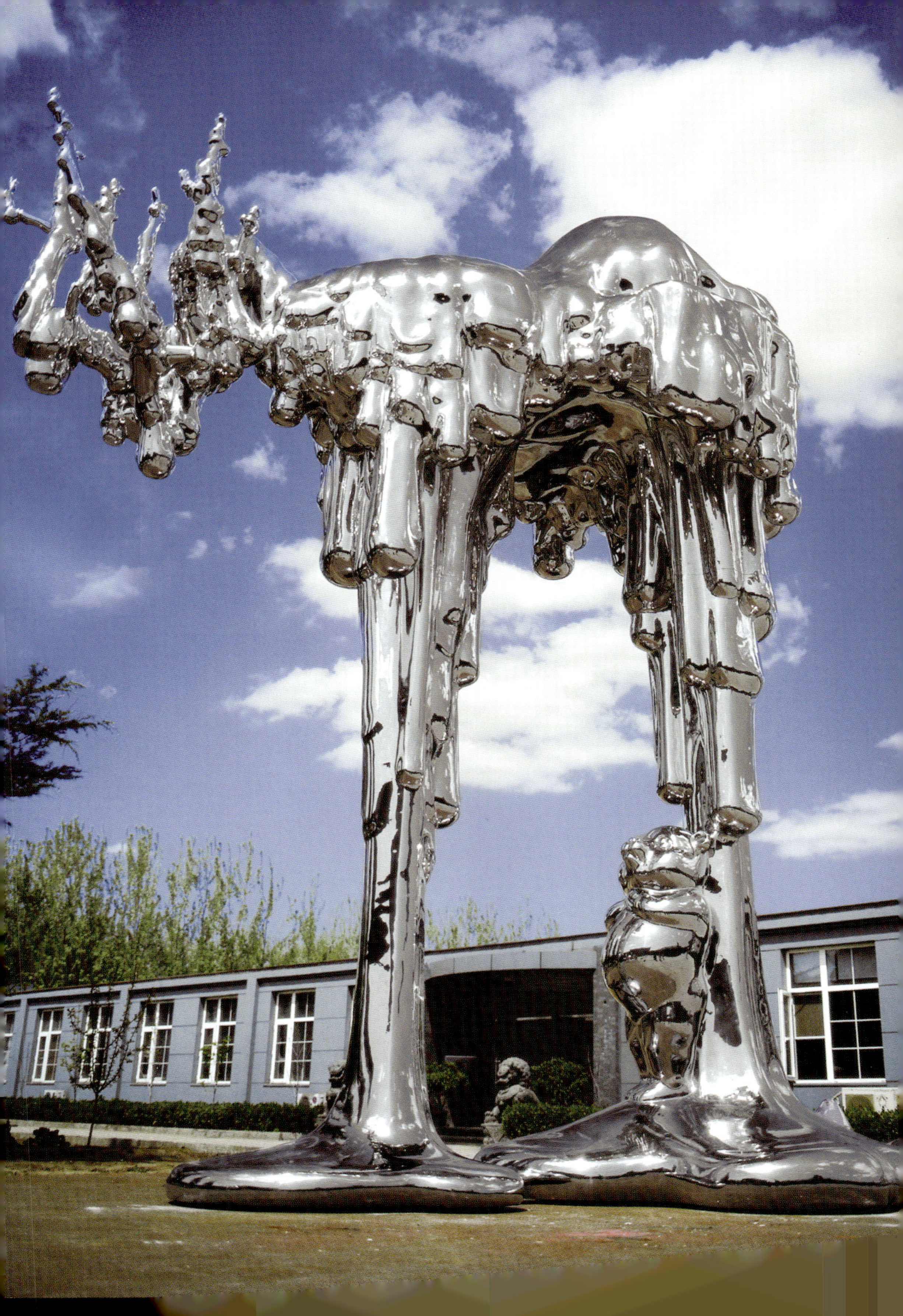

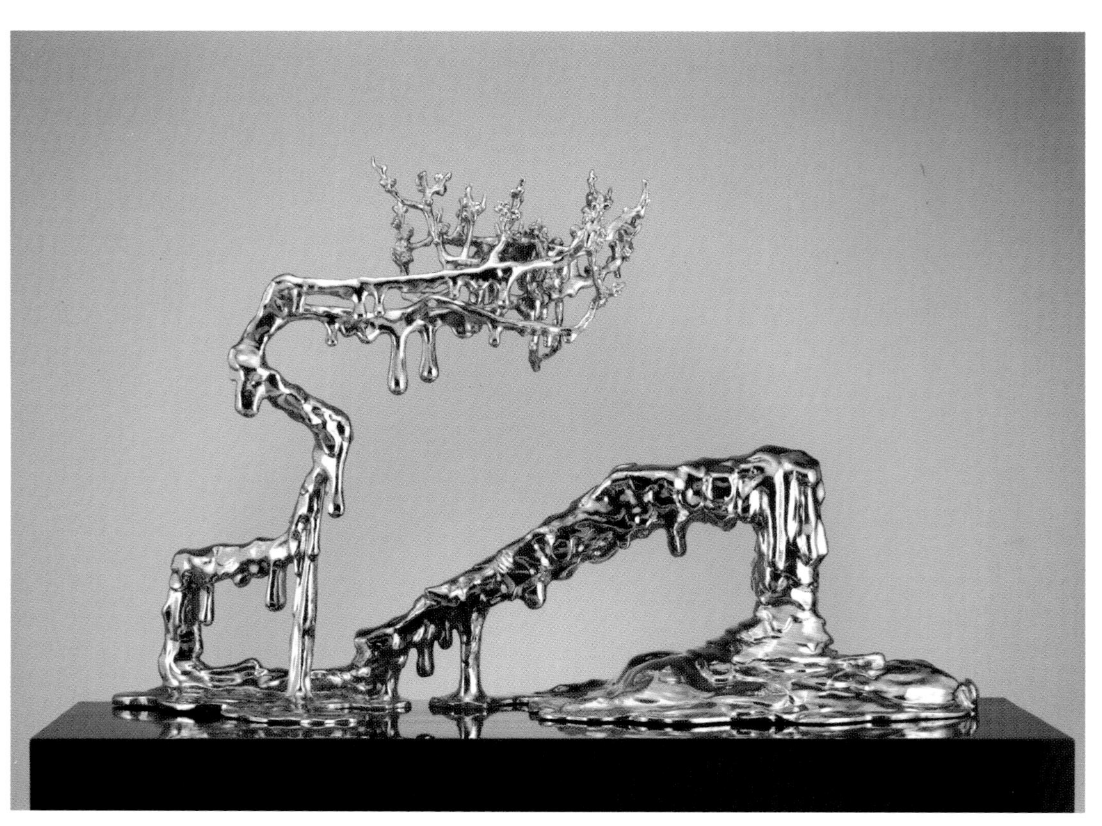

China Scene No. 4 / 中国风景NO.4, 2007

China Scene No. 4 Part / 中国风景NO.4局部, 2007

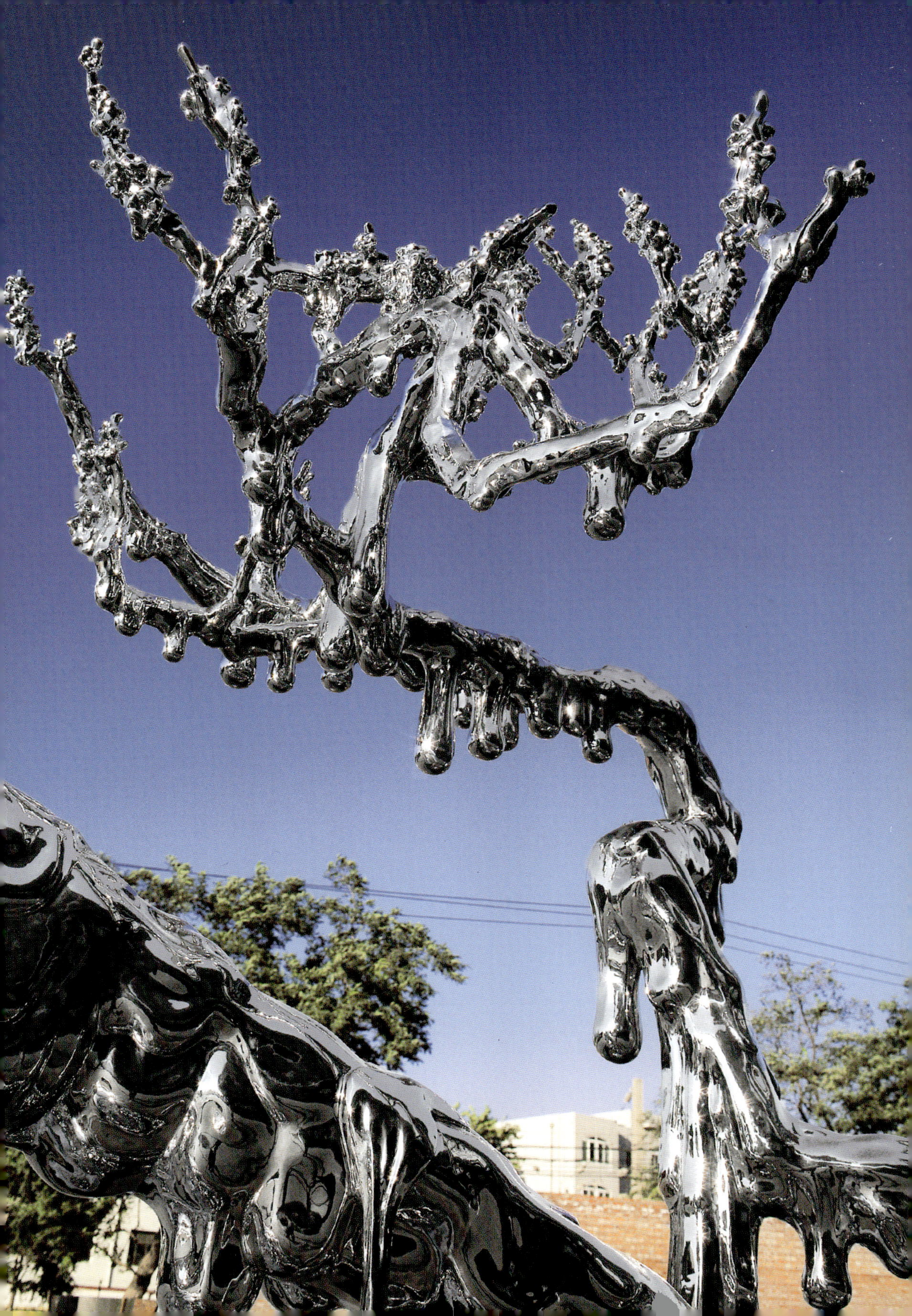

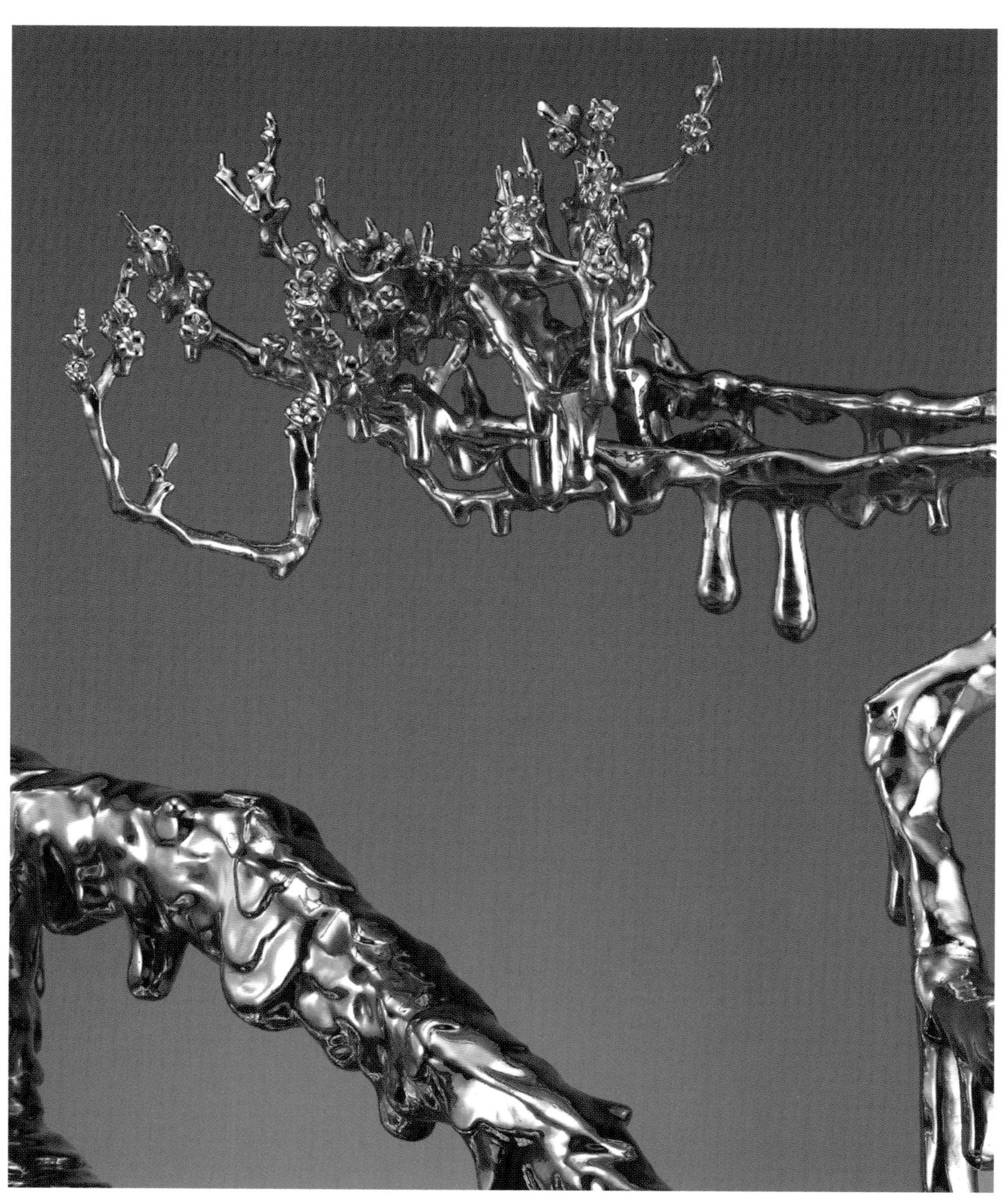

China Scene No. 4 / 中国风景NO.4, 2007

China Scene No. 4 Part / 中国风景NO.4局部,
2007

pp. 158-159
China Scene No. 6 / 中国风景NO.6, 2008

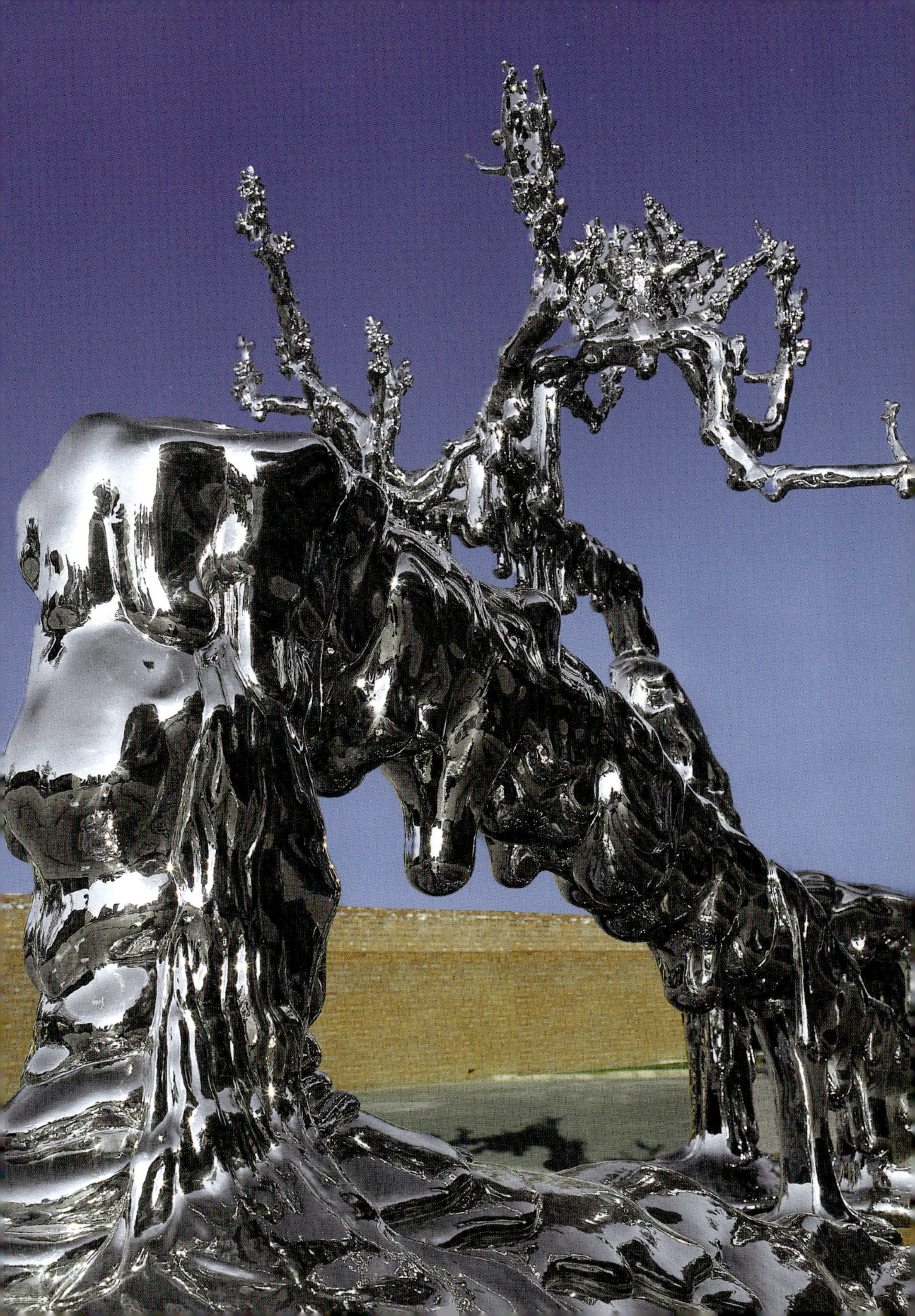

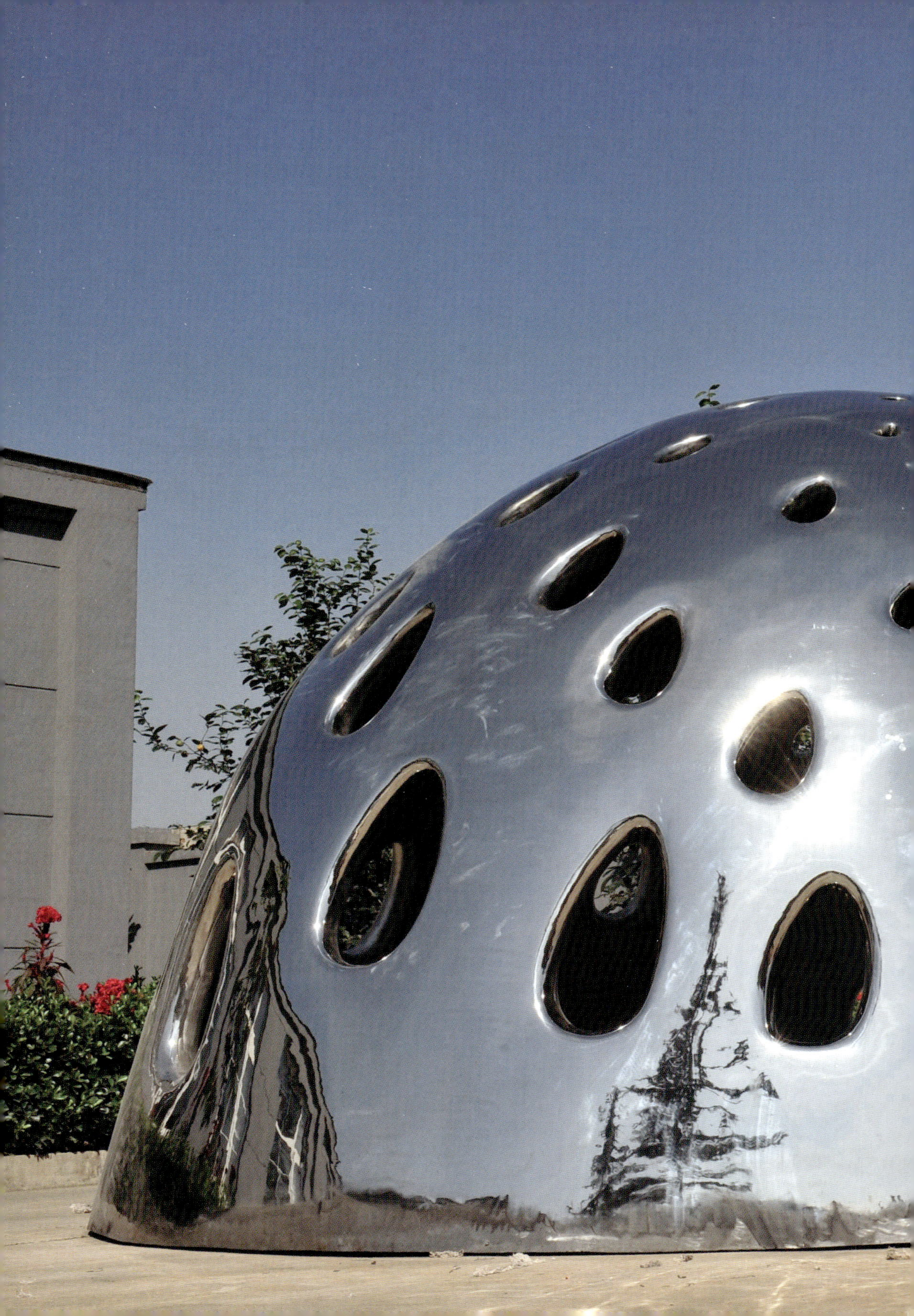

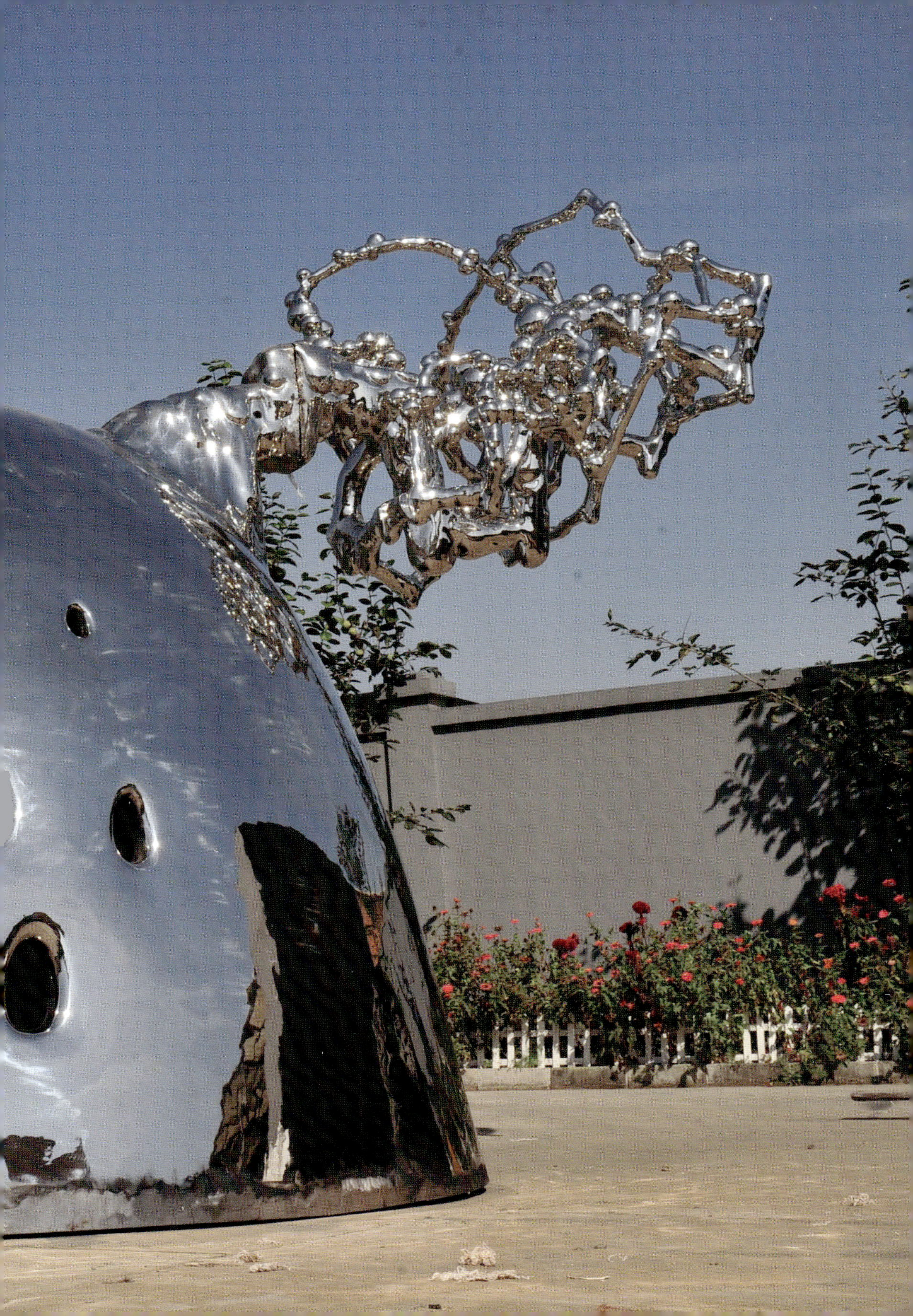

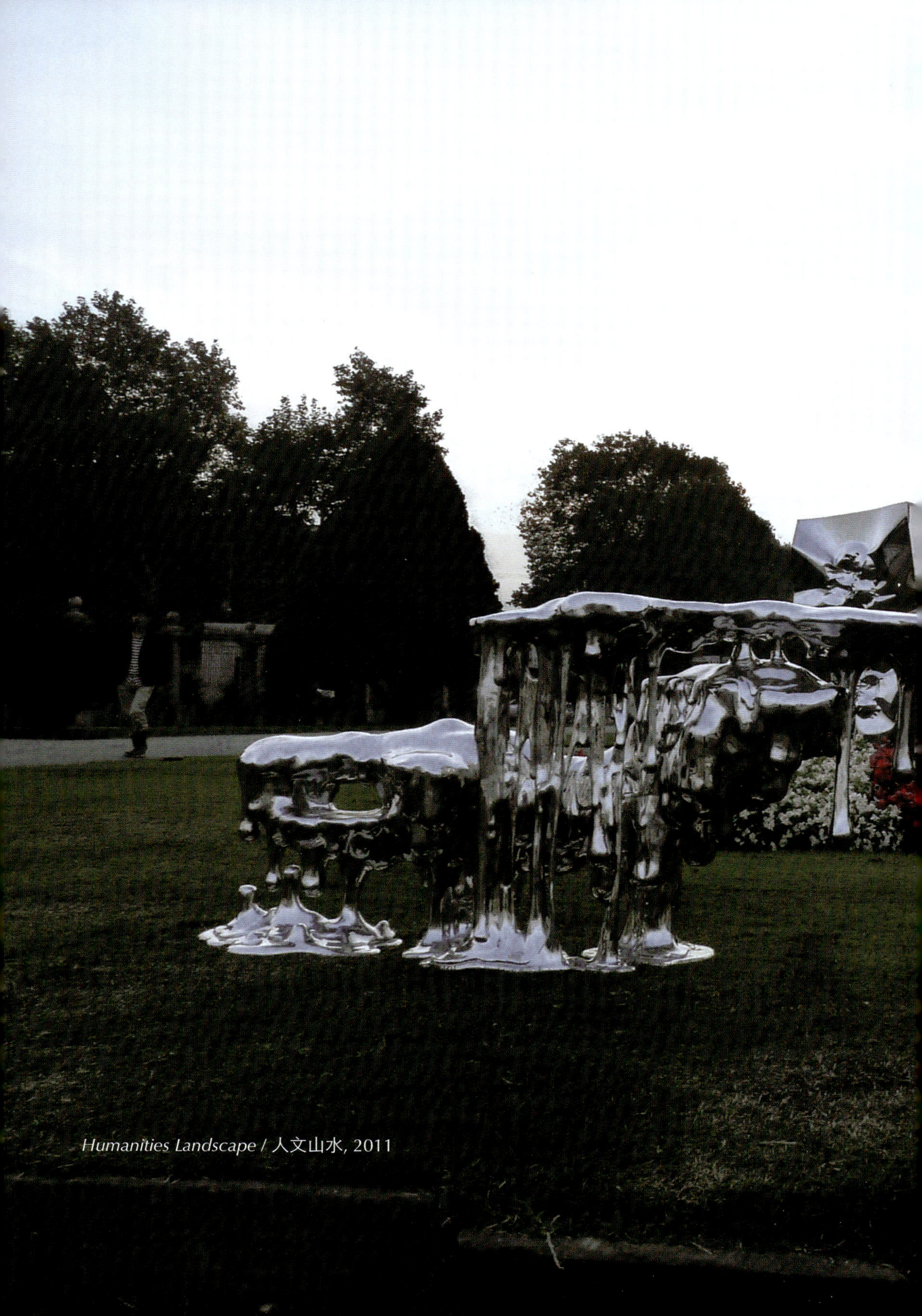

Humanities Landscape / 人文山水, 2011

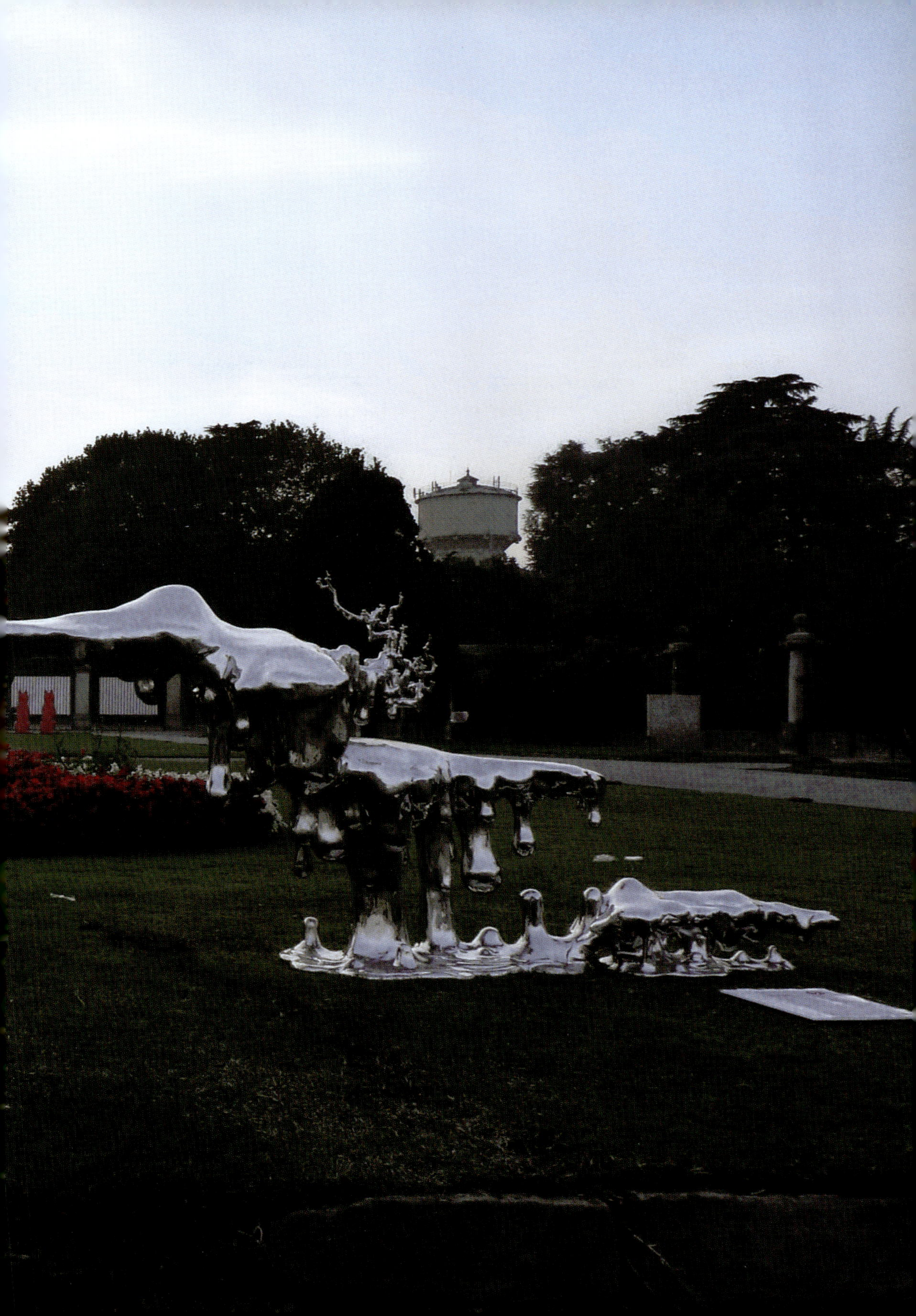

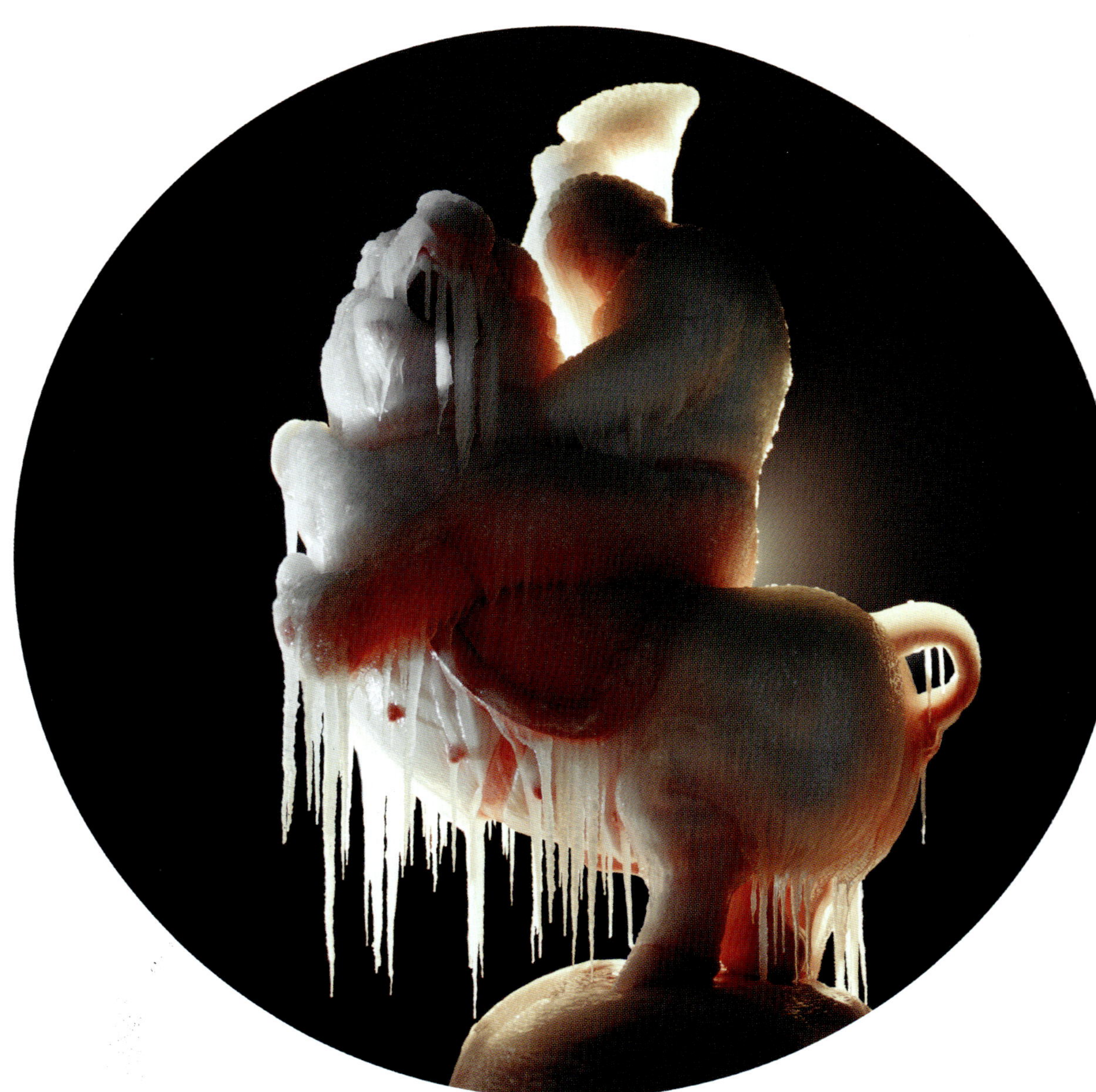

Freeze No. 2 / 凝固No.2, 2008

Biography

1969, born in Quanzhou, Fujian
  Province, China
Received Bachelor of Arts from the
  Sculpture Department of Xiamen
  Academy of Art and Design and
  Master of Fine Arts from the Central
  Academy of Fine Arts, Beijing
Now living and working in Beijing

Selected Solo Exhibitions

2012
*Exotic Landscapes – Chen Wenling's New
  Work*, PIN Gallery, Beijing, China
China Scene, Marina Bay Sands
  Conference Center, Singapore

2010
*The Suspense – Sculptures By Chen
  Wenling*, Today's Art Museum, Beijing,
  China
What You See Is Real, Odetoart, Singapore

2009
Emergency Exit, JoyArt, Beijing, China

2008
God of Materialism, Asia Art Center,
  Beijing, China

2007
Metamorphose, Makii Masaru Fine Arts,
  Japan
1999–2006, Vanessa Art Link, Jakarta,
  Indonesia

2006
Chen Wenling's Sculpture Solo Exhibition,
  Duolun Museum of Modern Art,
  Shanghai, China
Beneath Above, BANG-Beijing Art Now
  Gallery, Beijing, China

2004
Happy Life, Chinese European Art Centre,
  Macau, China

2002
Red Memory, Pearl Bay Beach, Macau,
  China

1991
Chen Wenling's Woodcarving Exhibition,
  Macau Art and Craft Academy,
  Macau, China

Selected Group Exhibitions

2013
55th International Art Exhibition of La
    Biennale di Venezia, Venice, Italy
Experiments in Chinese Contemporary Art,
    First Round "Conformation and
    Consciousness" Today Art Museum,
    Beijing, China

2012
*Chinese Contemporary Public Art
    Exhibition*, Kassel, Germany

2010
Living in Evolution, Busan Biennale, Busan
    Cultural Center, Busan, South Korea

2009
A Conversation with Chicago,
    Contemporary Sculpture from China,
    Millennium Park, Chicago, Illinois,
    U.S.A.

2008
*Third International Biennial of
    Contemporary Art*, Centro Andaluz de
    Arte Contemporáneo, Seville, Spain

2006
Hyper Design, Shanghai Biennale,
    Shanghai Art Museum, Shanghai,
    China

Awards and Honors

2012
Recipient of the 7th Annual AAC China
    Art Power Award for Excellence in
    Sculpture

2011
Awarded "Most Popular Exhibit" at the
    International Sculpture Exhibition in
    Aarhus, Denmark
Public Art Award at the *Sculpture by the
Sea* exhibition in Perth, Australia

2010
Annual "Good Announcement Bird" Art
    Award given by Alternative Space
Selected by *Art Value* magazine as one of
    the 2010 China's Top 100 Most
    Influential Artists

2008
Awarded the May Fourth Youth
    Outstanding Contribution in Art by
    Contemporary Art magazine

2003
Beijing Biennale, China Sculpture Special
    Exhibition, *Red Memory* was given
    the Most Popular Work Award

Public Collections

China Art Museum
Beijing Today Art Museum
National Gallery of Korea
Seoul Museum of Art
Doosan Art Center, Seoul
Houston Museum of Fine Arts
Denver Art Museum
Arox Art Museum
The White Rabbit Gallery, Sydney
Melbourne Museum
Guangdong Museum
Fujian Normal University
Nanjing University
Fujian Museum
Hubei Museum of Art
The Art Gallery of Western Australia

陈文令

1969年生于中国福建泉州
先后毕业于厦门工艺美术学院和中央美术
　　学院
现居中国北京，艺术家

重要个展

2012
"异度风景——陈文令新作展" 品画廊
　　北京 中国
" 中国风景"— 陈文令个展 金沙滨海会
　　议展览中心 新加坡

2010
"悬案"——陈文令新作展 今日美术馆
　　北京 中国
"你 看 到 的 是 真 实 的" 陈 文 令 个 展
　　ODETOART 画廊 新加坡

2009
"紧急出口"——陈文令新作展 卓越艺术
　　空间 北京 中国

2008
"物神"——陈文令新作展 亚洲艺术中
　　心 北京 中国

2007
"蜕变"——陈文令个展 井画廊 东京
　　日本
"1999-2006"——陈文令个展 华艺莎画
　　廊 雅加达 印度尼西亚

2006
"幸福生活"——陈文令个展 上海多伦
　　现代美术馆 上海 中国

2004
"幸福生活"——陈文令个展 厦门大学
　　中国欧洲艺术中心 厦门 中国

2002
"红色记忆"——陈文令雕塑展示行动
　　珍珠湾海滩 厦门 中国

1991
陈文令木雕艺术展 厦门工艺美术学院 厦
　　门 中国

重要群展

2013
第55届威尼斯双年展 威尼斯 意大利
中国当代艺术实验 第一回展 " 形态与意
　　识" 今日美术馆 北京 中国

2012
"大道之行---中国当代公共艺术展"卡塞
　　尔 德国

2010
"生存的进化" ——釜山双年展 釜山文
　　化中心 釜山 韩国

2009
对话芝加哥"——中国当代雕塑艺术 芝加
　　哥 美国

2008
第三届塞维利亚国际当代艺术双年展
　　CAAC 塞韦利亚 西班牙

2006
"超设计"——上海双年展 上海美术馆
　　上海 中国

曾获奖项

获2012年第七届AAC艺术中国年度影响
　　力雕塑类前三甲大奖
获2011年丹麦奥尔胡斯市国际雕塑展最受
　　欢迎大奖
获2011年 澳大利亚珀斯国际海岸雕塑展公
　　共艺术大奖
获2010年"报喜鸟"年度空间艺术大奖
2010 年入选"艺术财经"杂志, 中国百名
　　权力人物榜
获2008年 杂志"当代艺术", 五四青年艺
　　术杰出贡献奖
获2003年北京双年展中国雕塑特展, "红
　　色记忆"获最受欢迎作品奖

公共收藏

中国美术馆
北京今日美术馆
韩国国立美术馆
韩国首尔市美术馆
首尔斗山美术馆
美国休斯顿美术馆
美国丹佛美术馆
丹麦 Arox 美术馆
悉尼白兔美术馆
澳大利亚墨尔本雕塑美术馆
广东博物馆
福建师范大学
南京大学
福建省博物馆
湖北美术馆
西澳洲州立美术馆

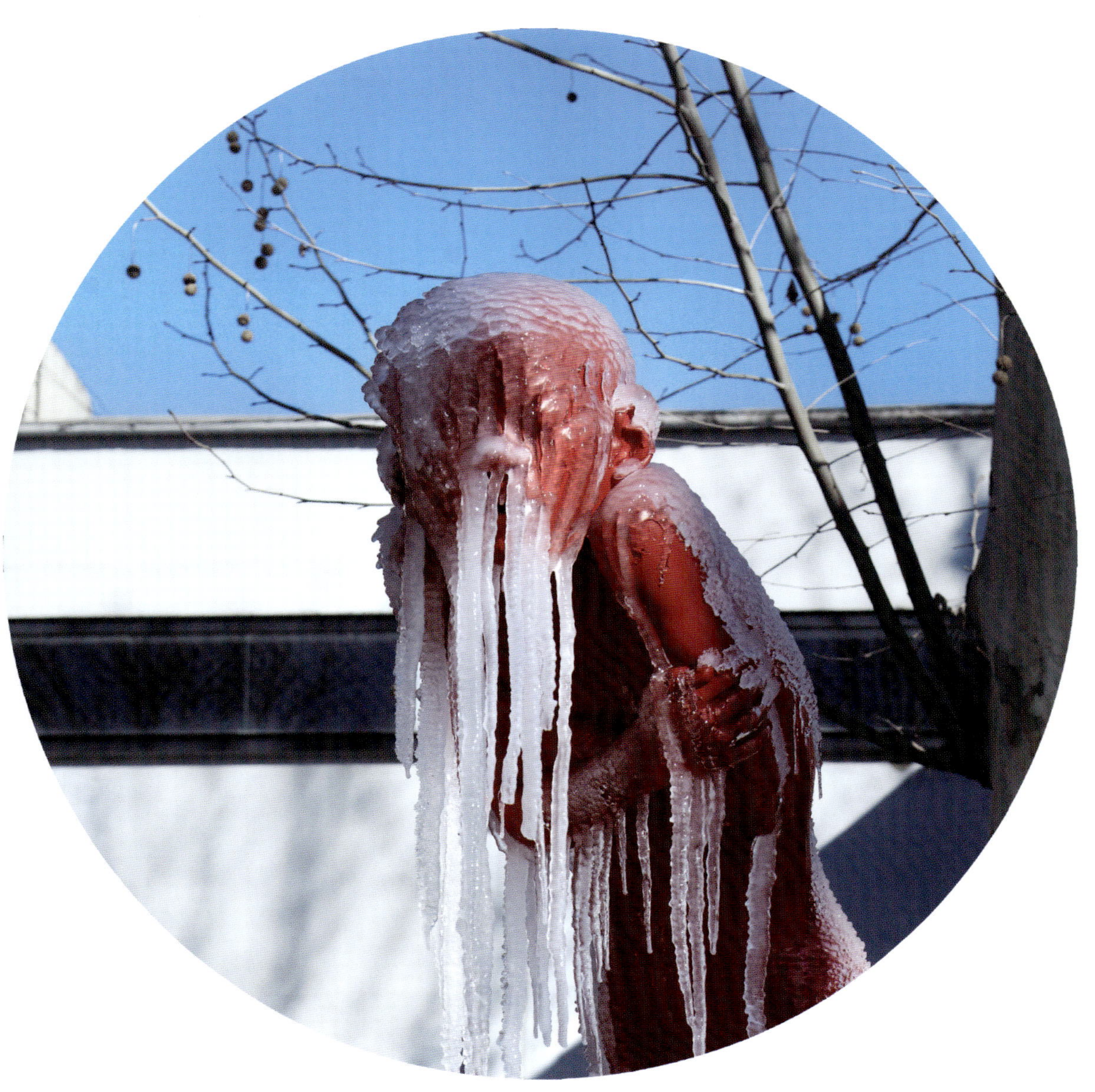

Freeze No. 8 / 凝固No.8, 2012

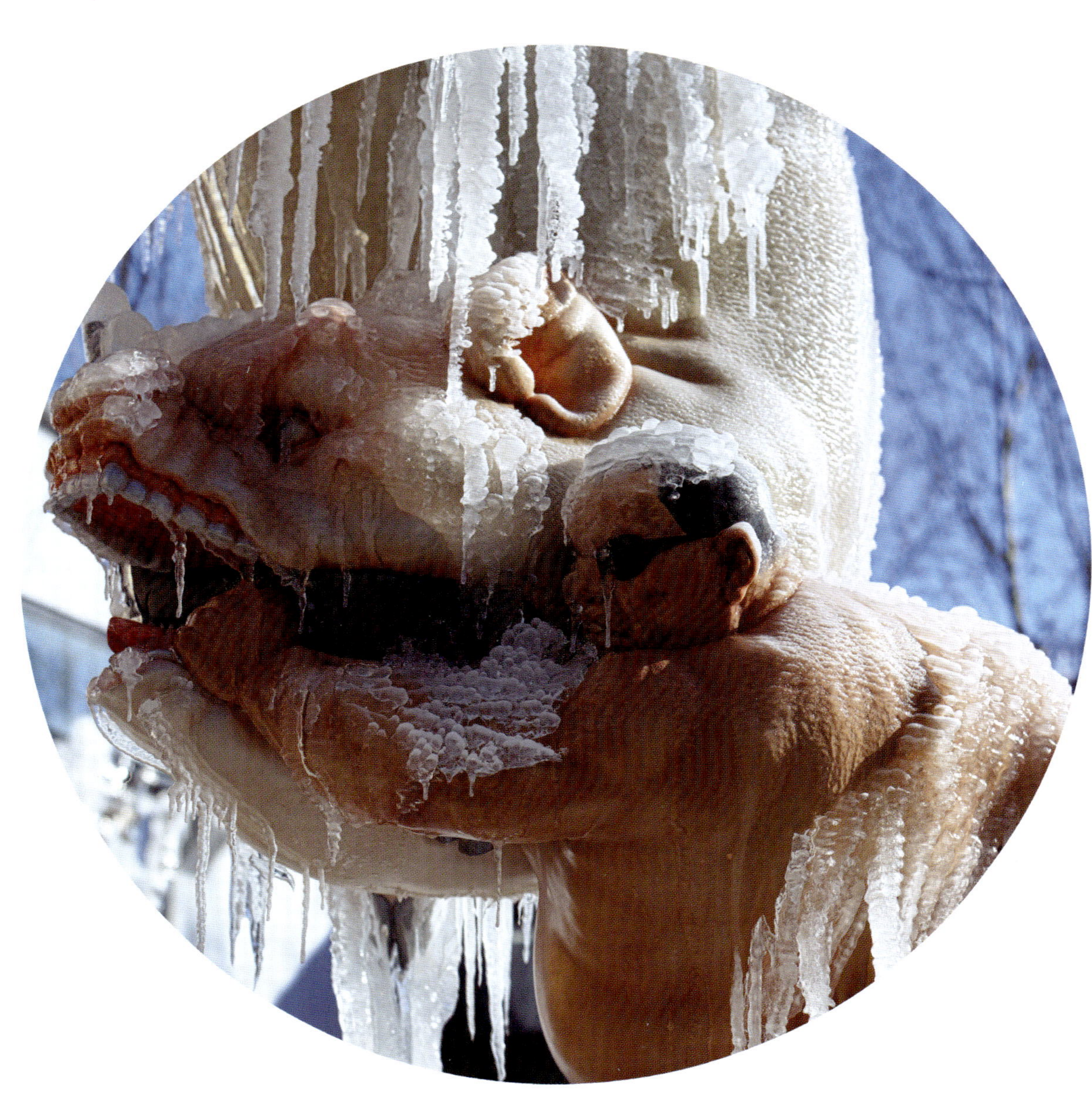

Freeze No. 4 / 凝固No.4, 2012

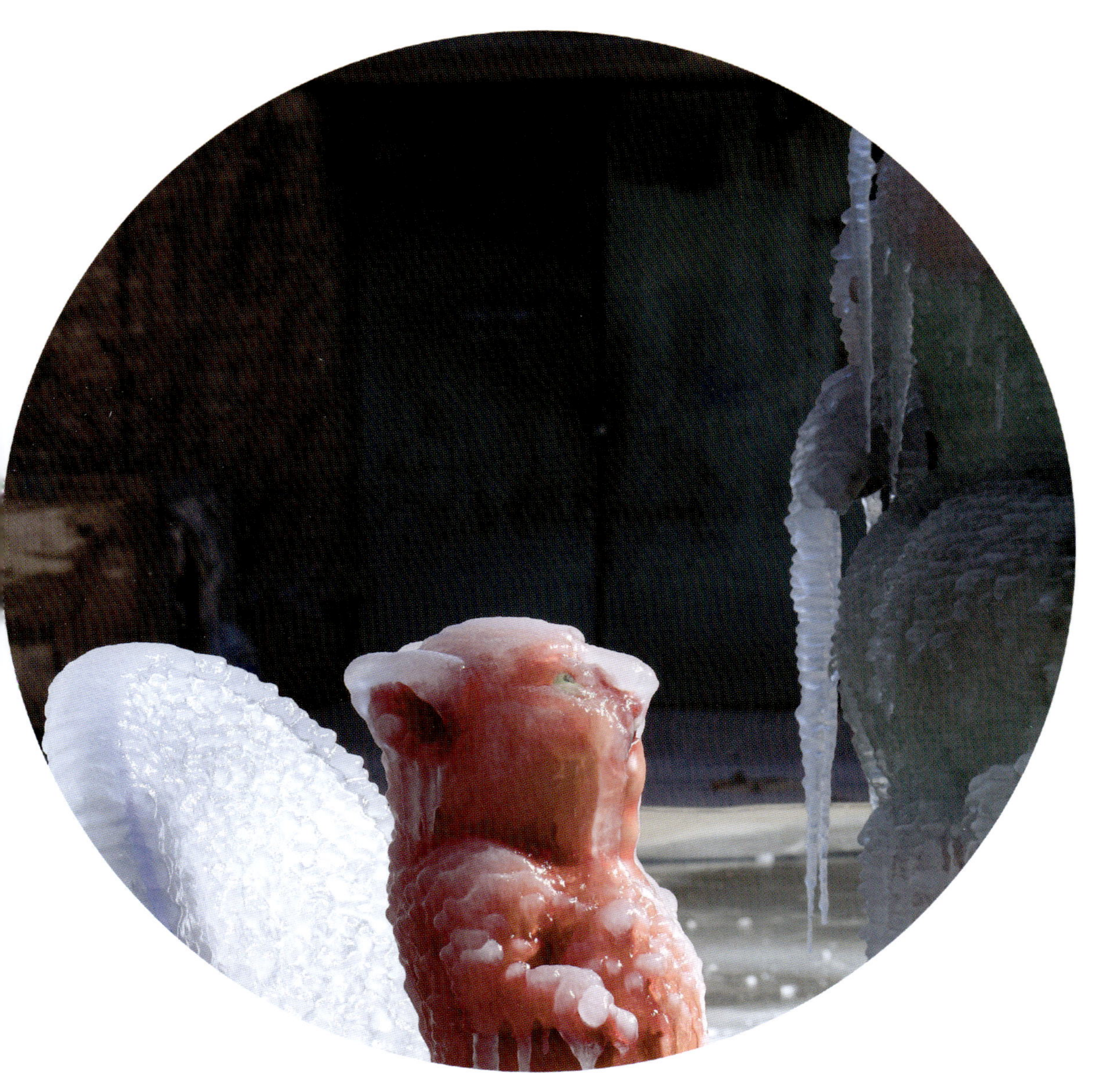

Freeze No. 5 / 凝固No.5, 2012

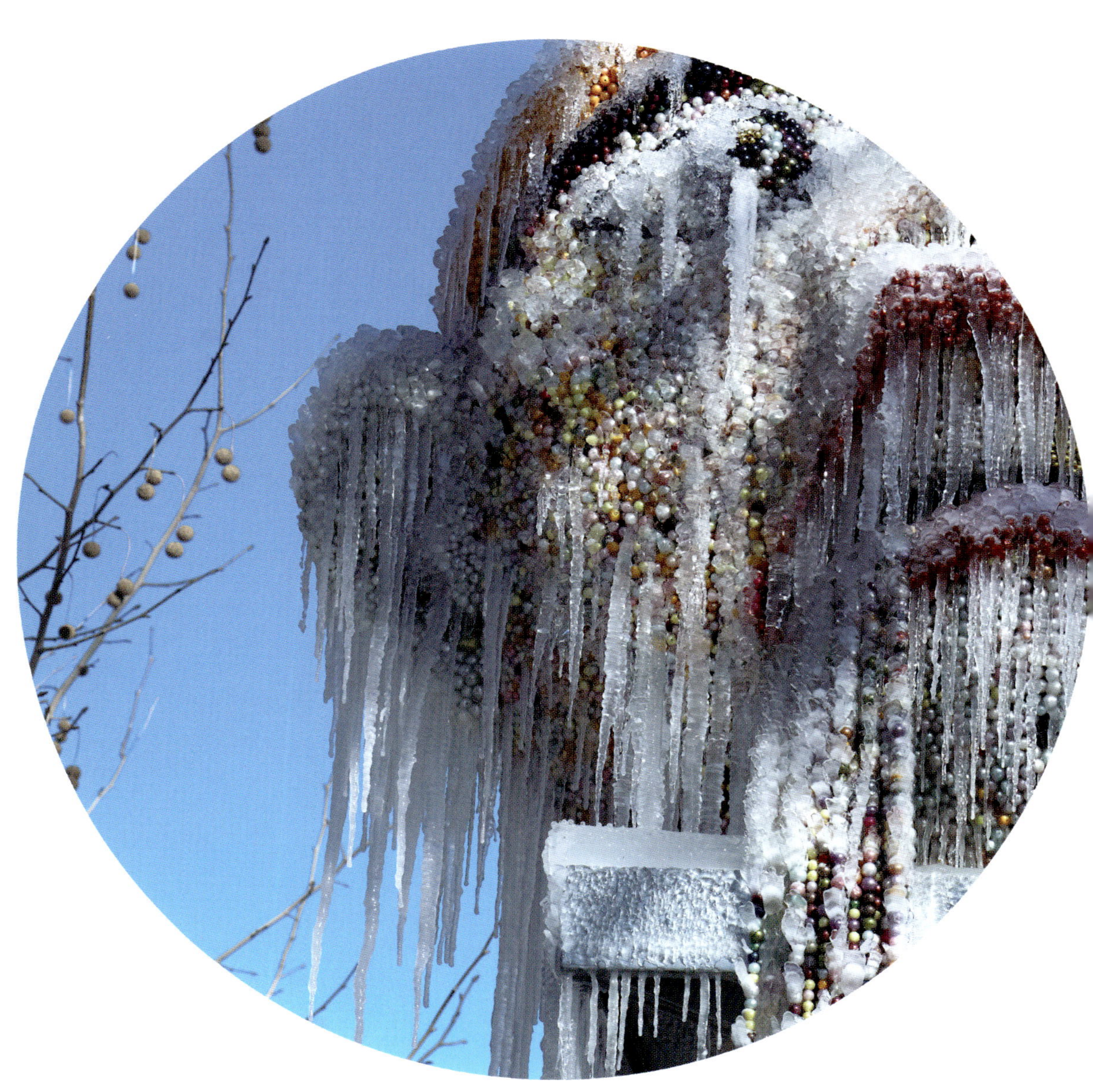

Freeze No. 6 / 凝固No.6, 2012

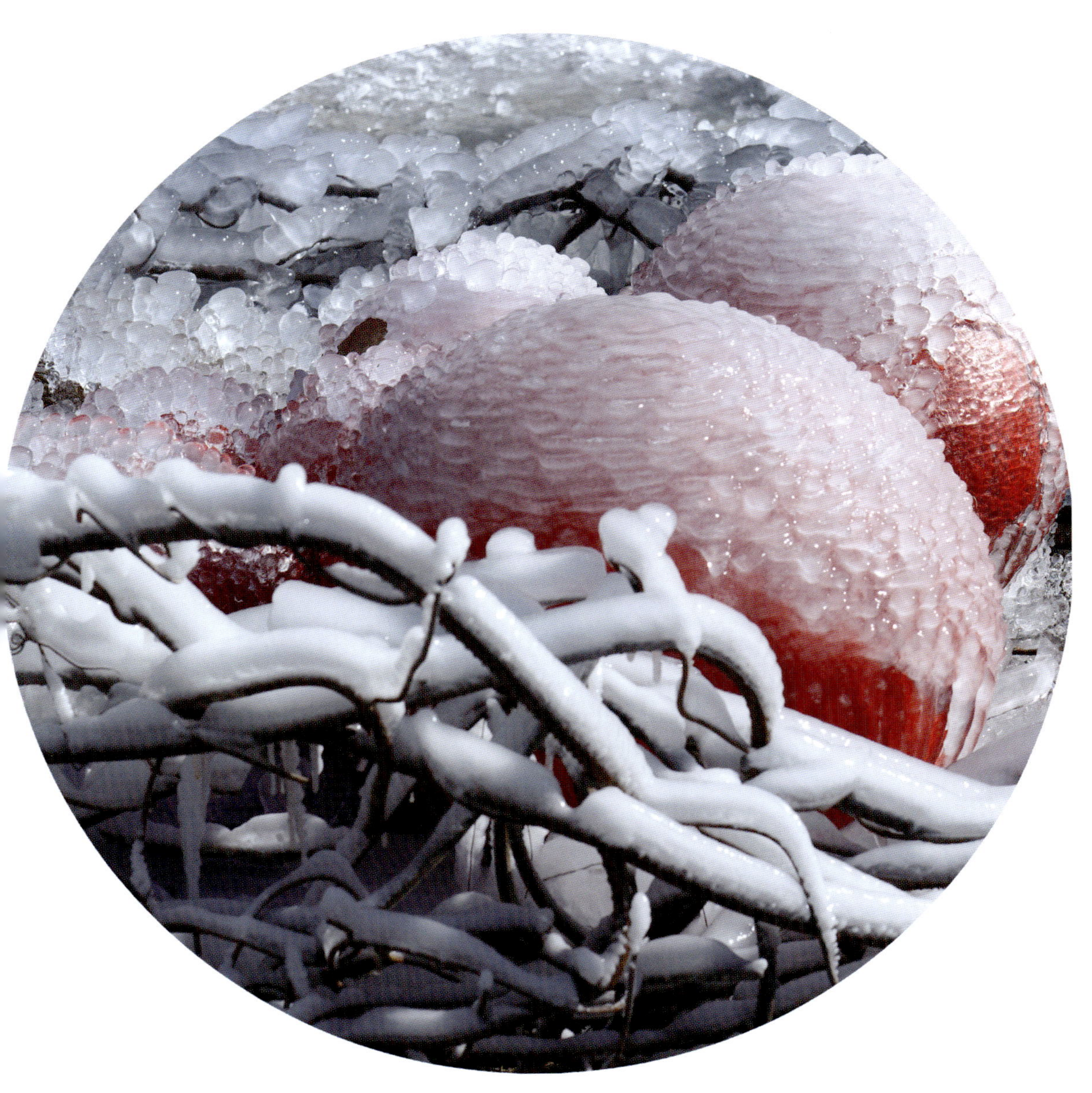

Freeze No. 7 / 凝固No.7, 2012

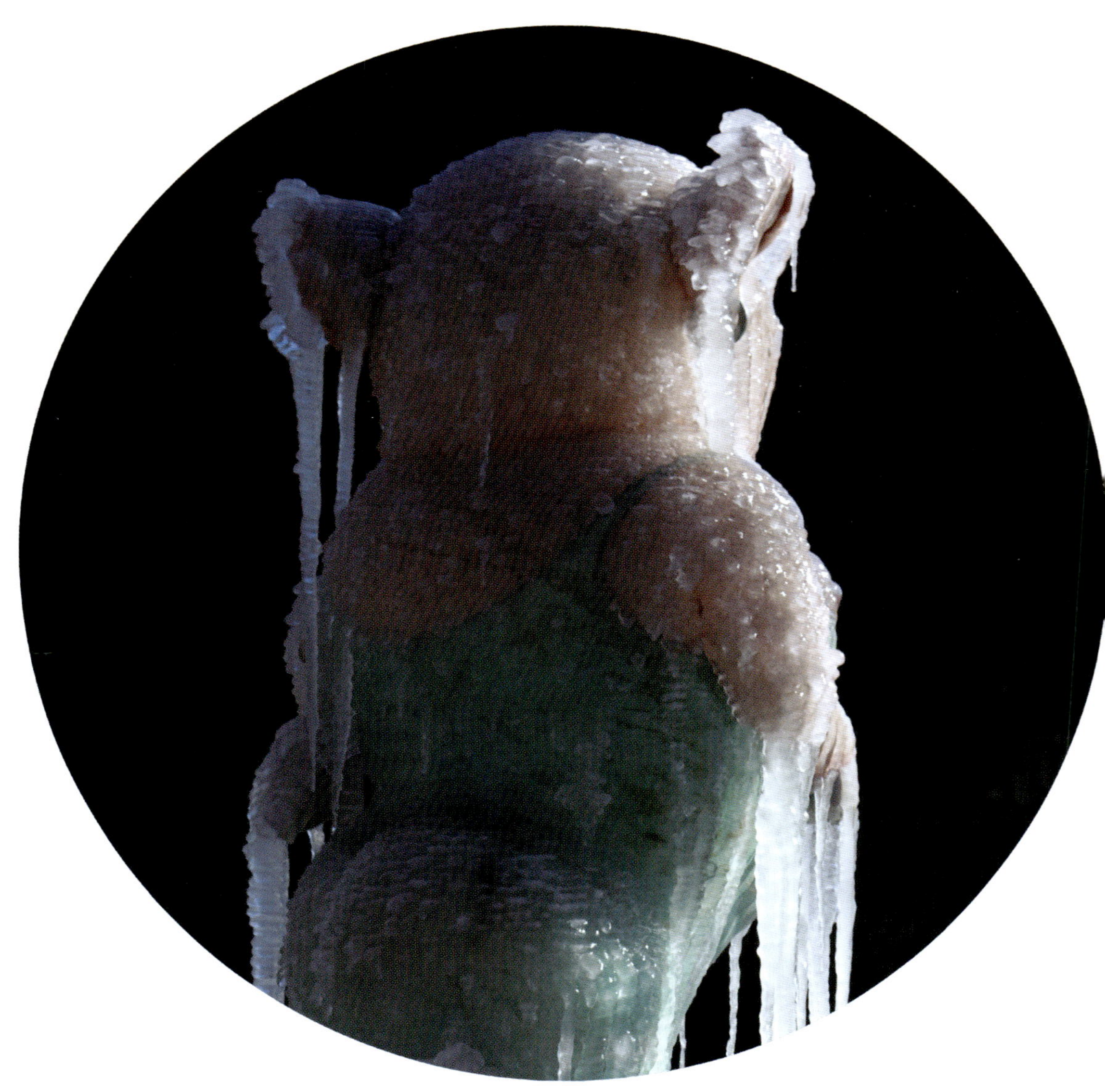

Freeze No. 9 / 凝固No.9, 2012

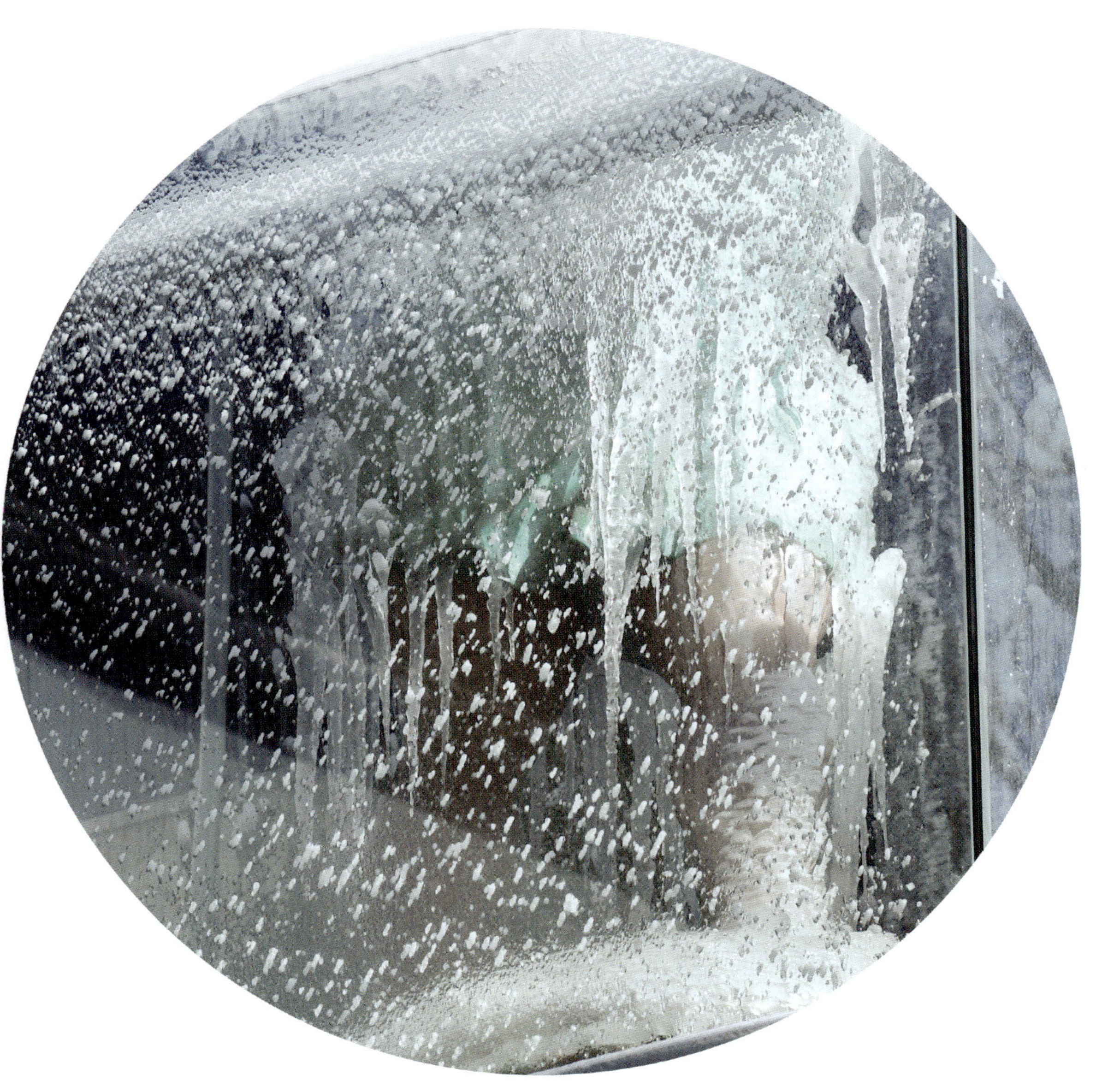

Freeze No. 10 / 凝固No.10, 2012

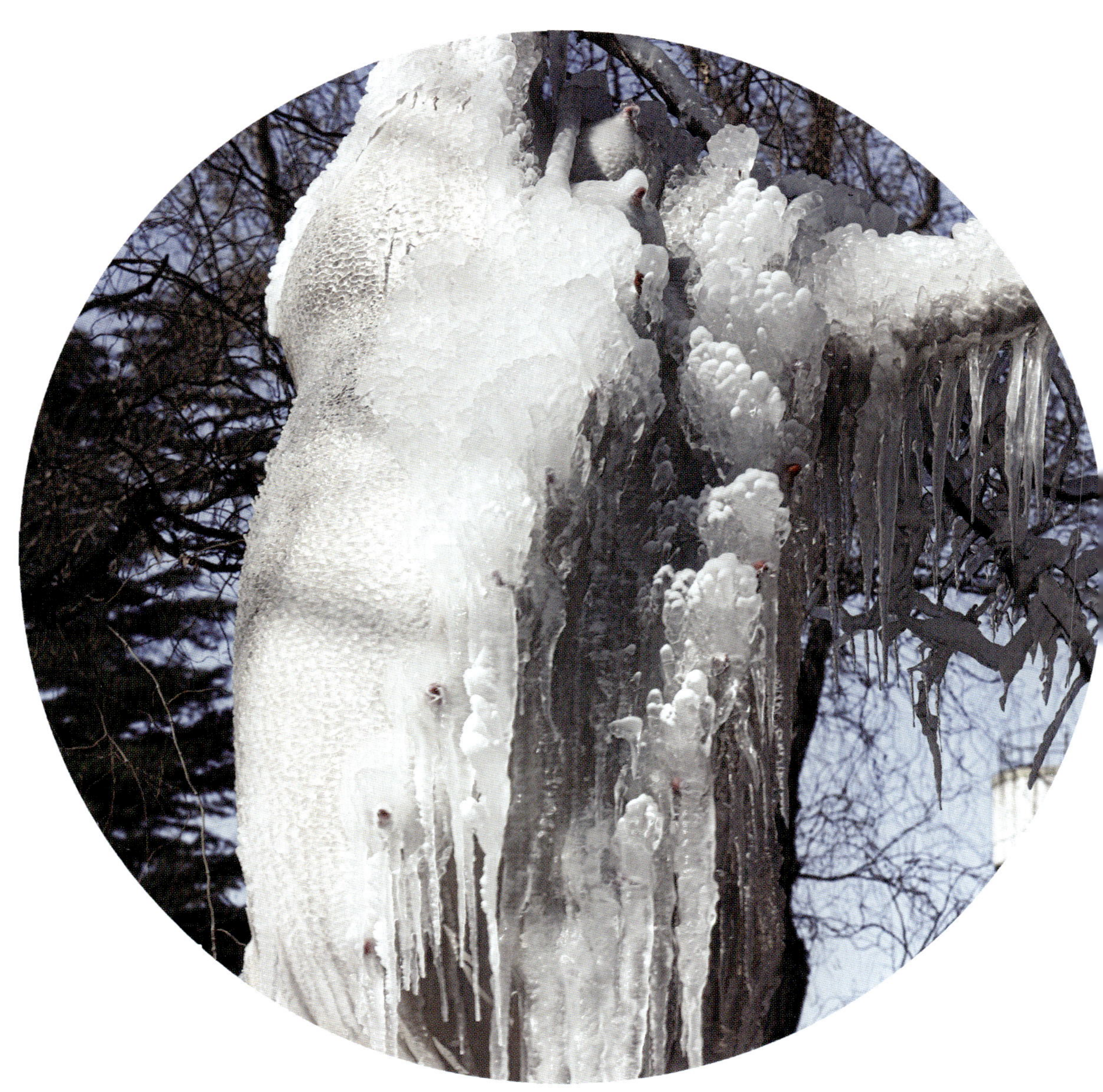

Freeze No. 11 / 凝固No.11, 2012

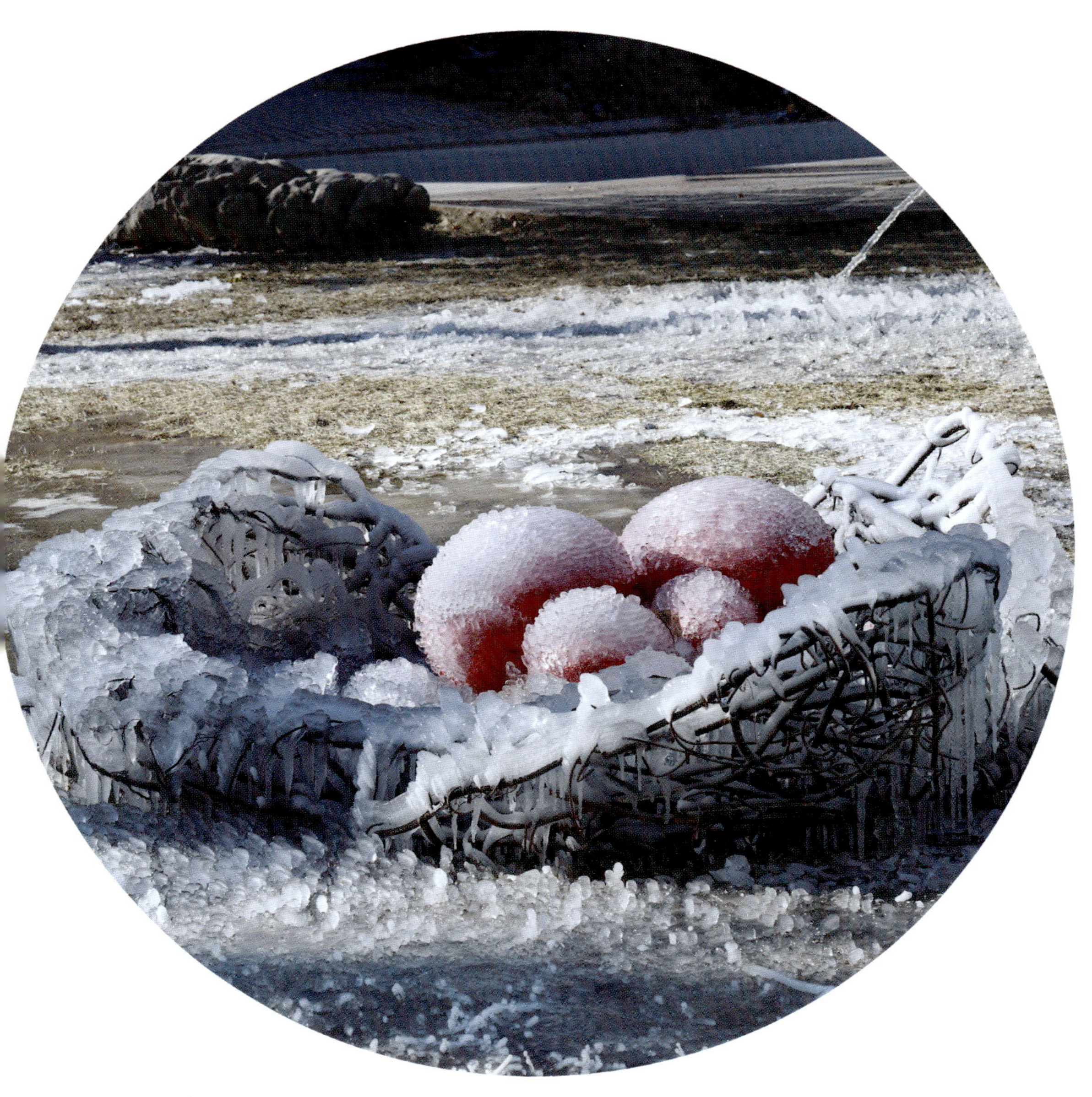

Freeze No. 25 / 凝固No.25, 2012

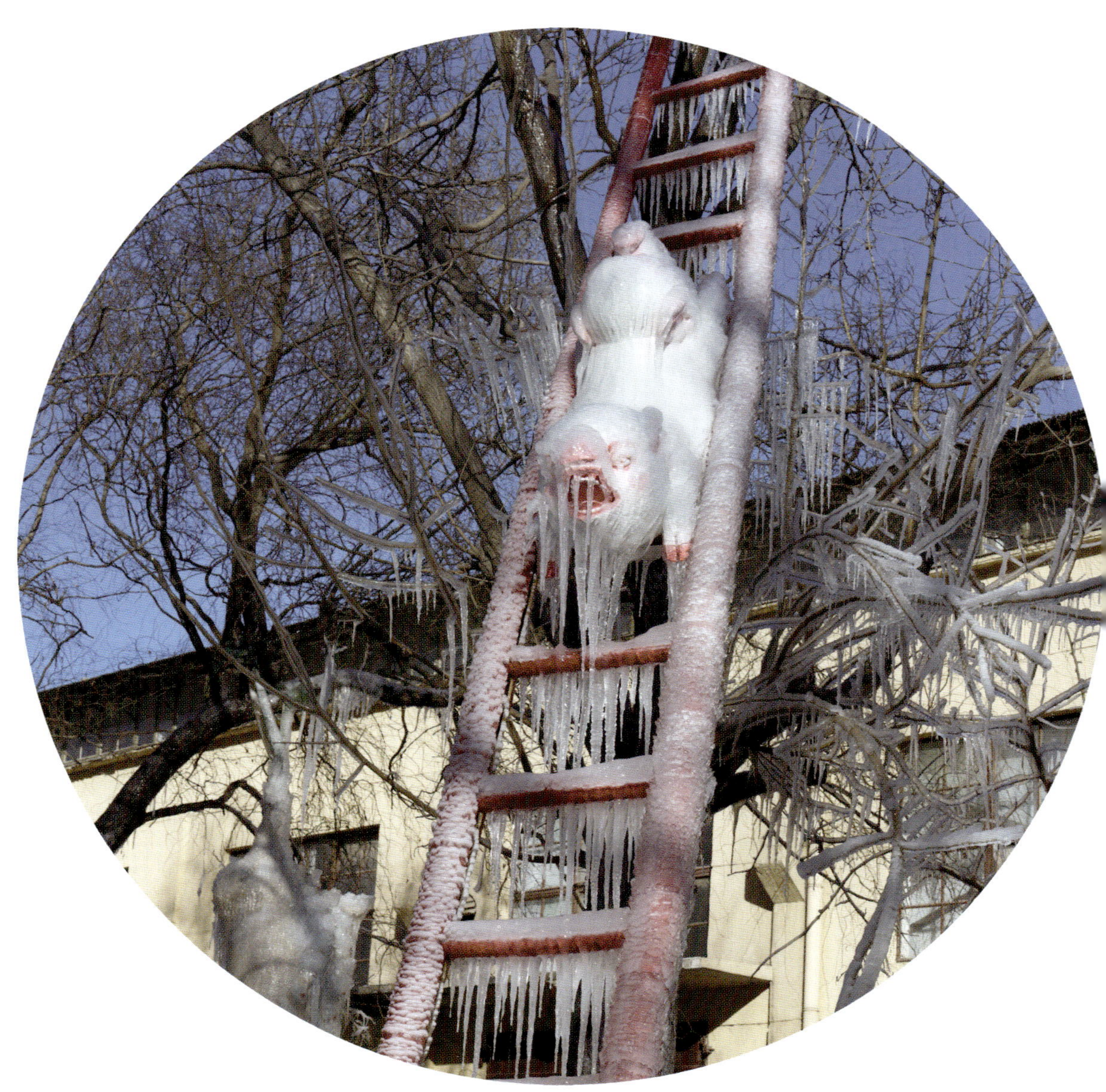

Freeze No. 13 / 凝固No.13, 2012

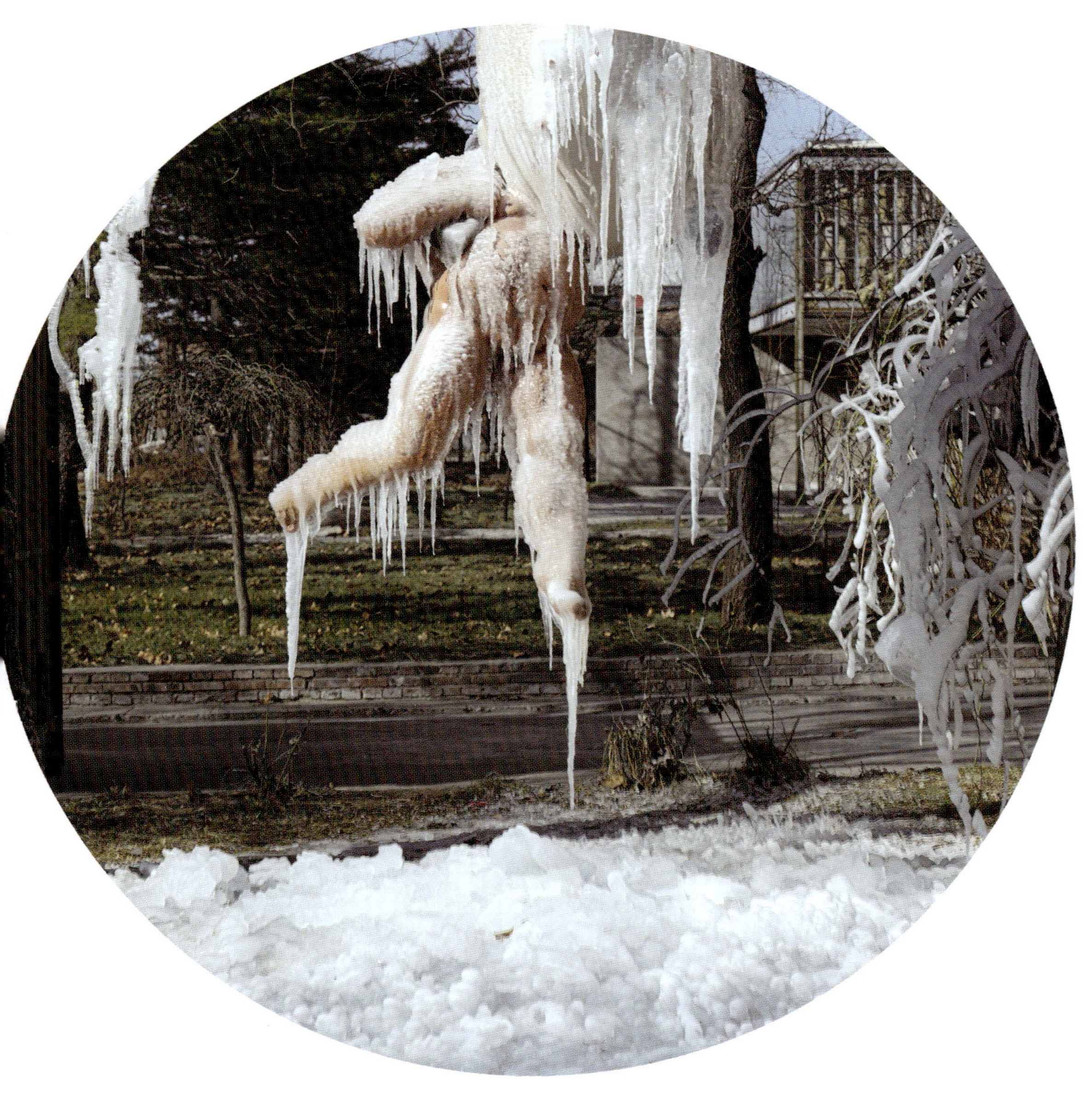

Freeze No. 14 / 凝固No.14, 2012

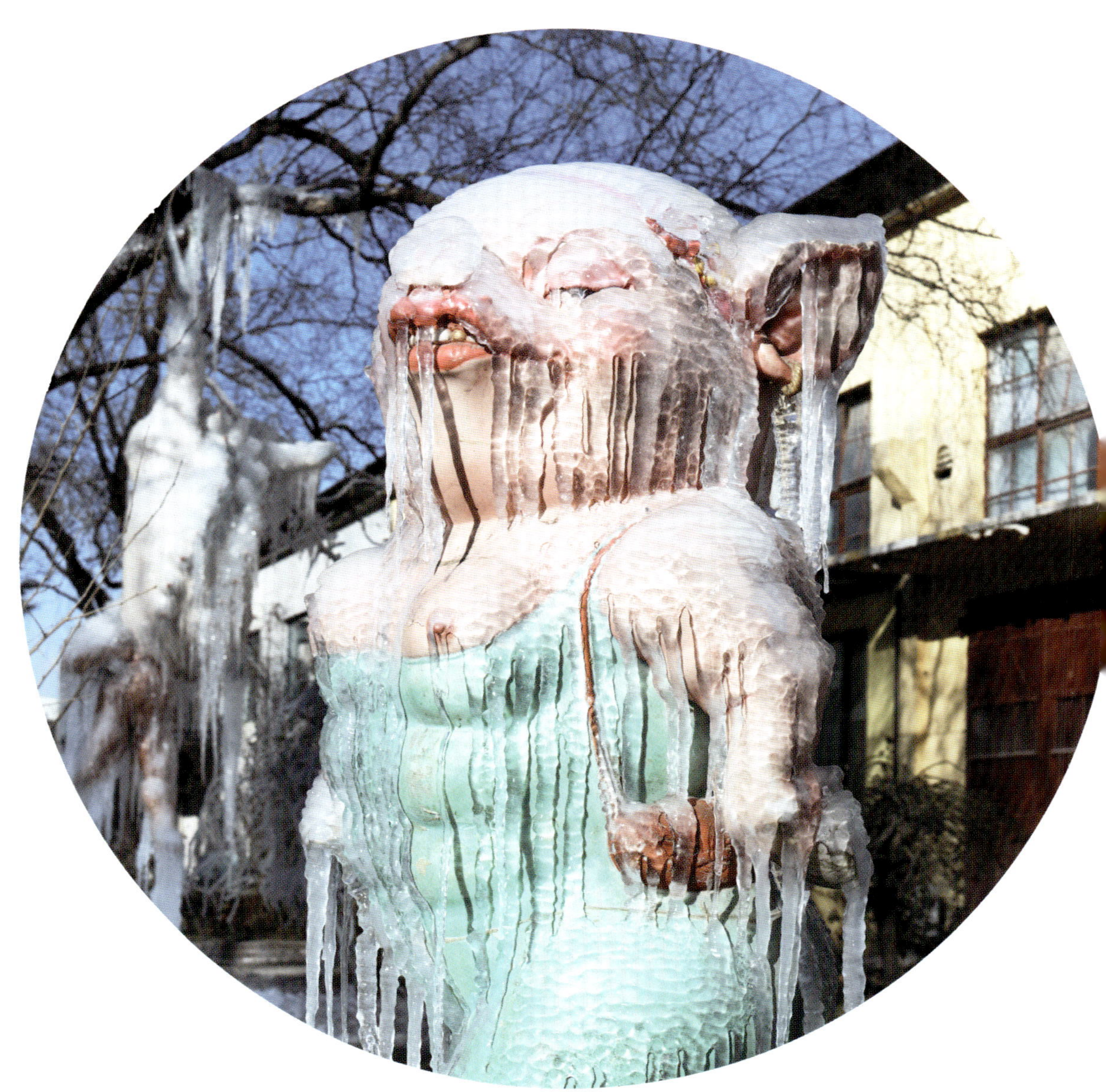

Freeze No. 16 / 凝固No.16, 2012

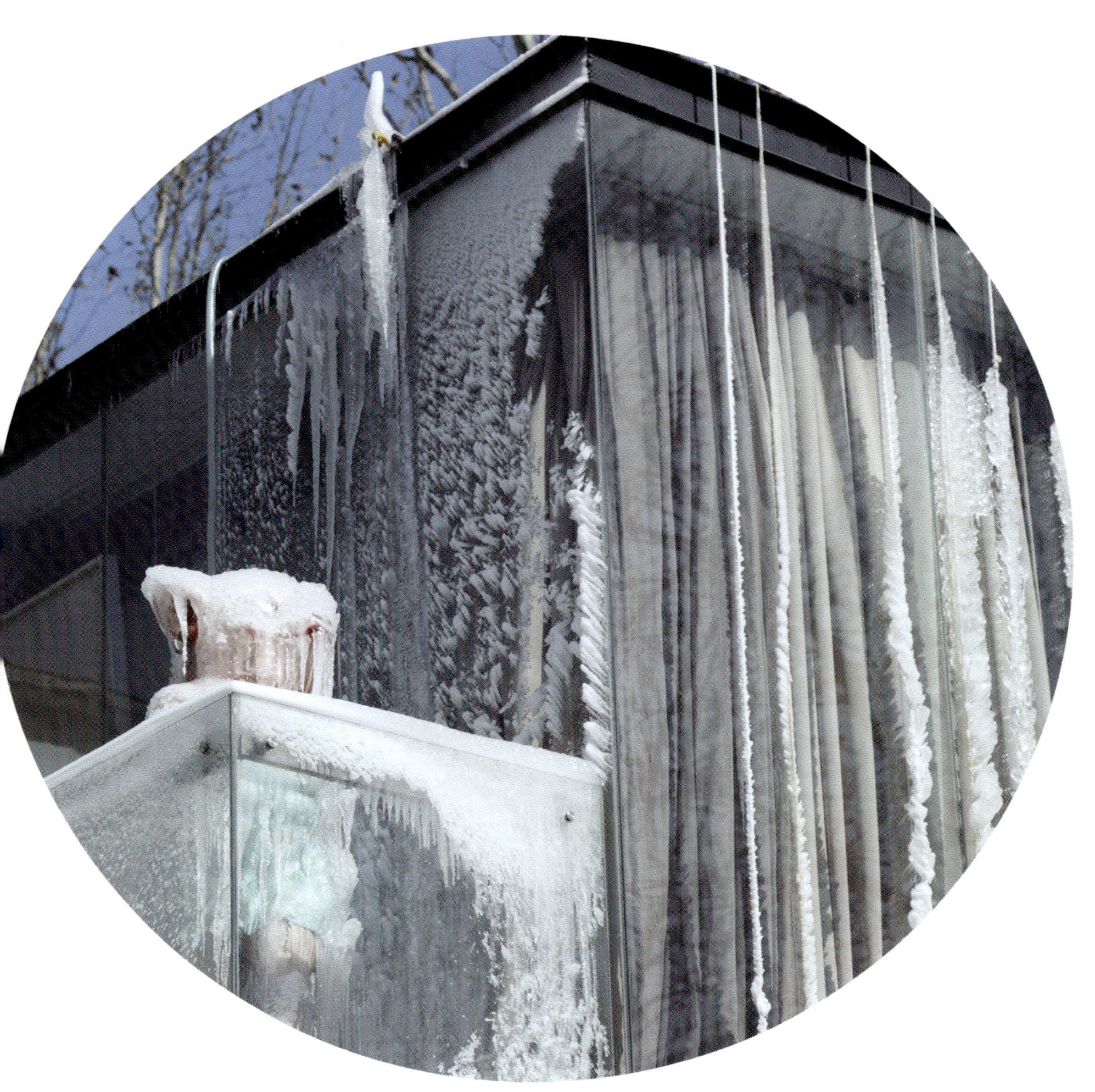

Freeze No. 19 / 凝固No.19, 2012

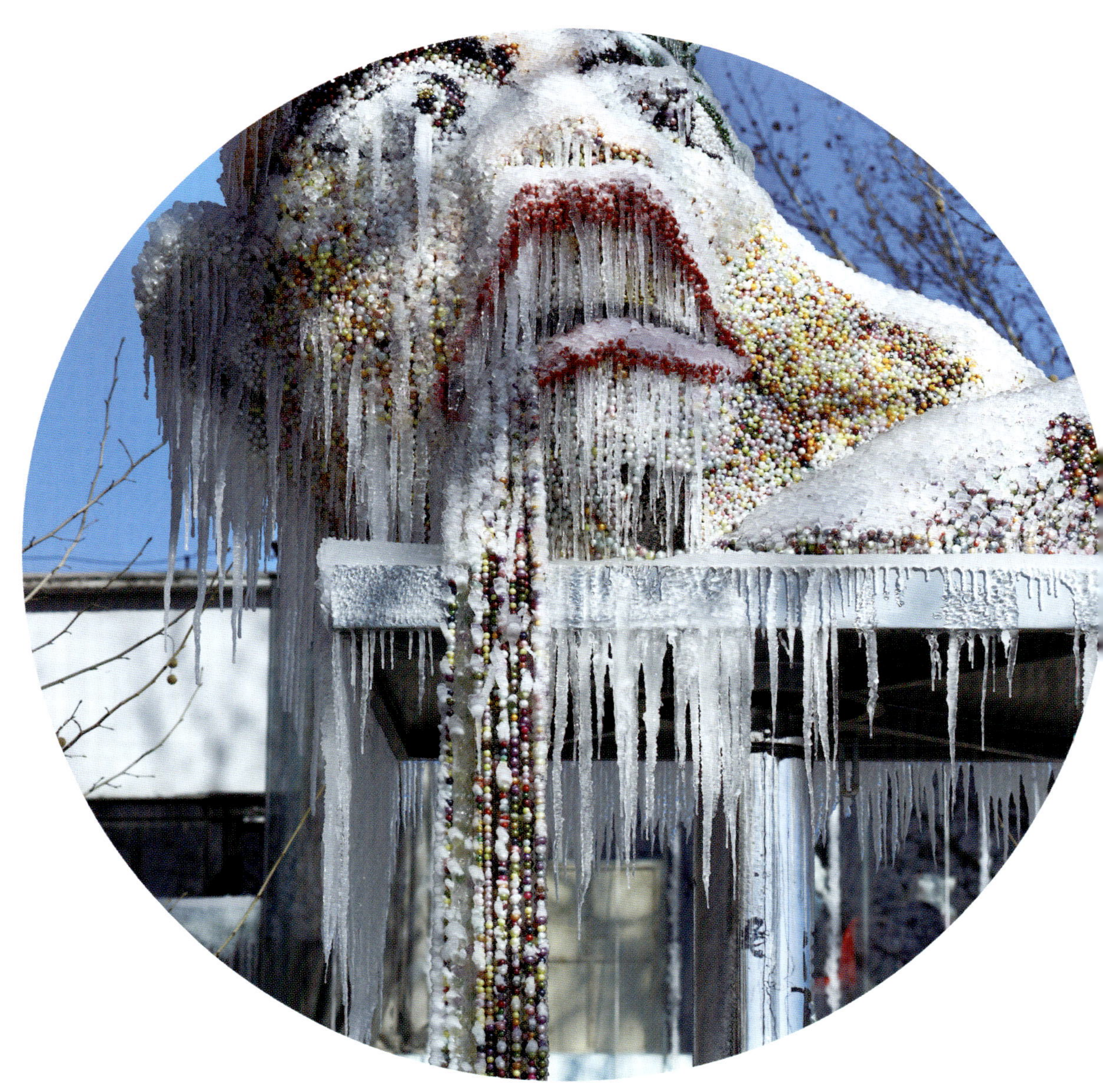

Freeze No. 20 / 凝固No.20, 2012

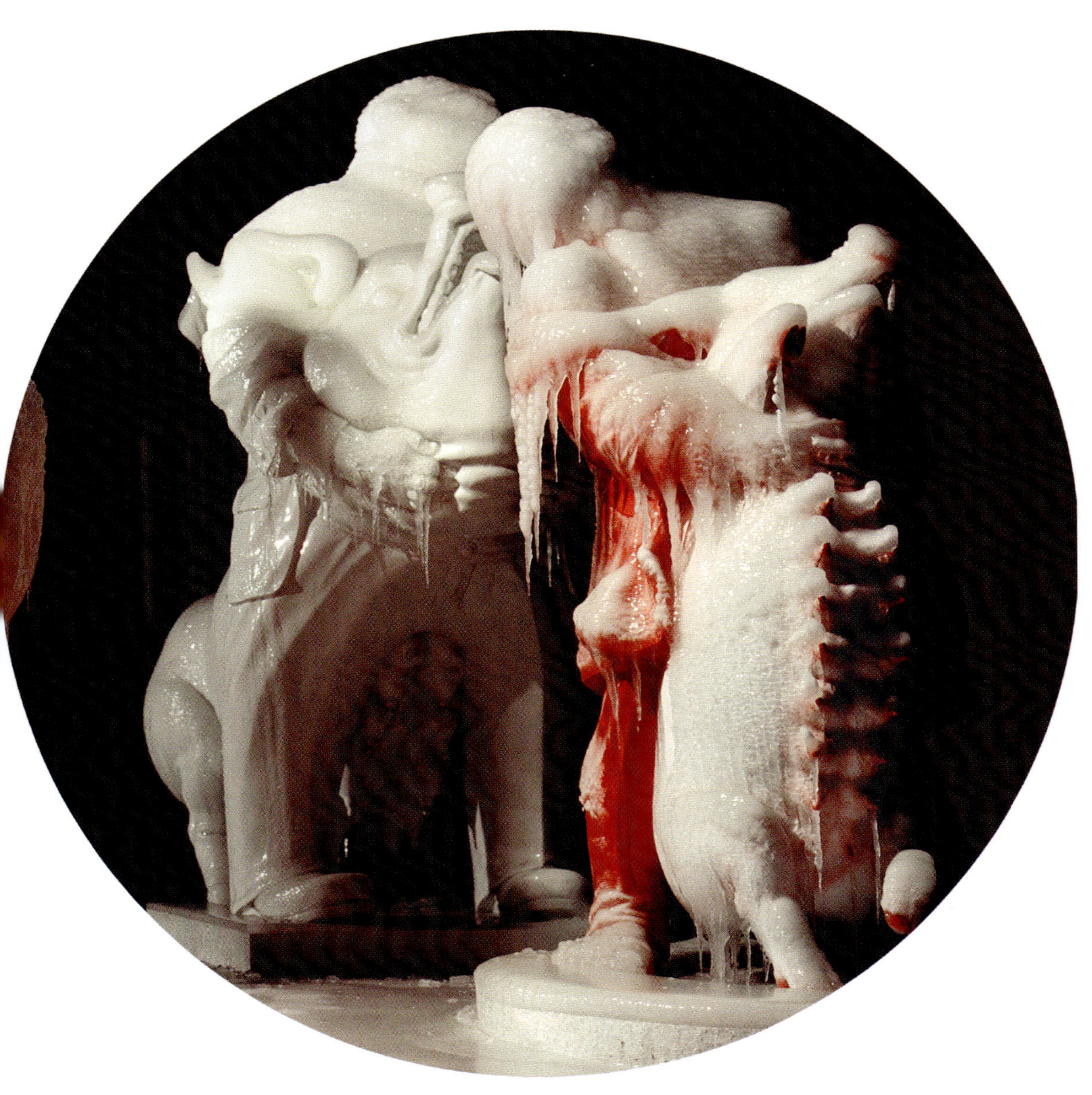

Freeze No. 22 / 凝固No.22, 2012

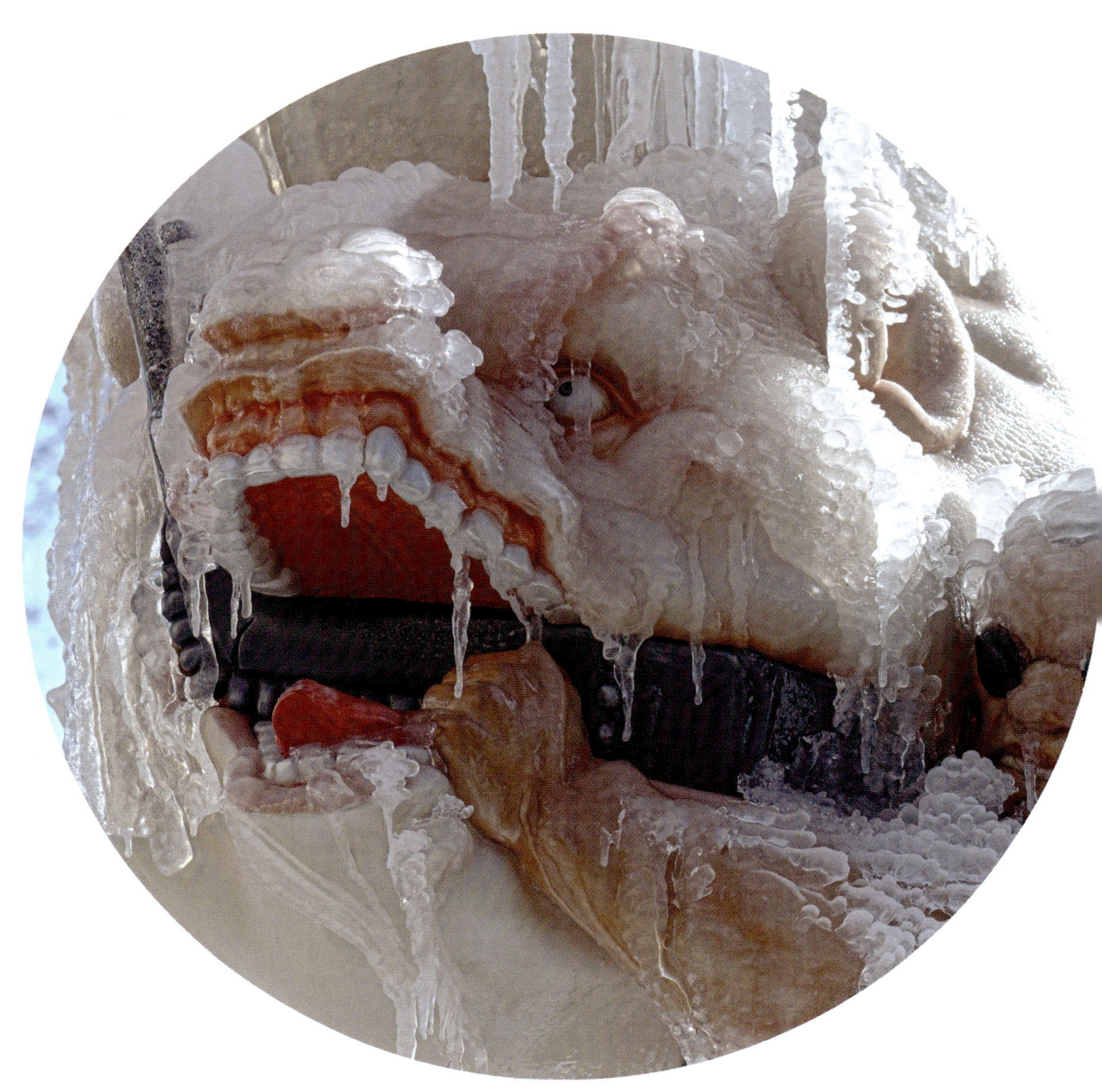

Freeze No. 24 / 凝固No.24, 2012

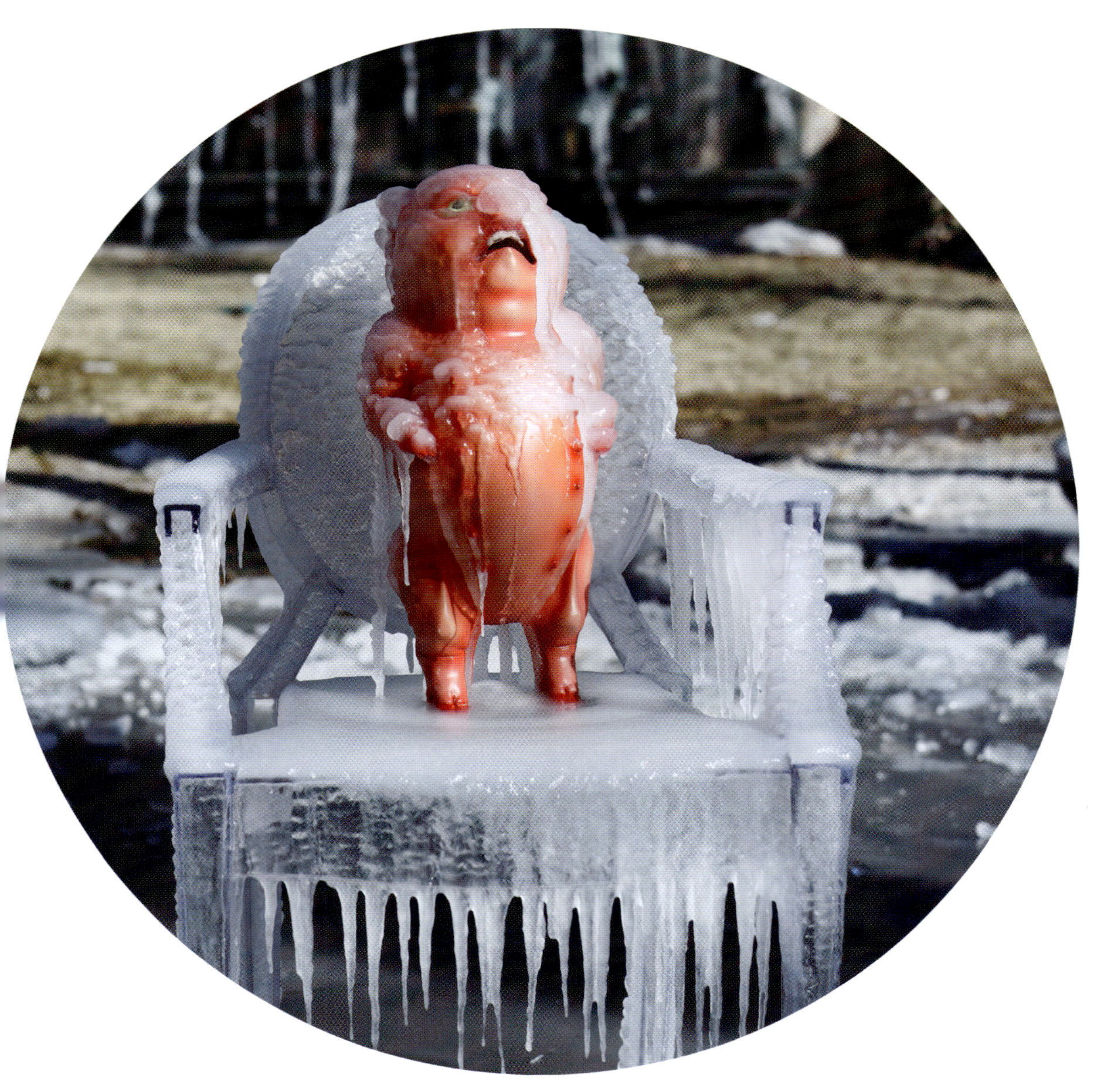

Freeze No. 26 / 凝固No.26,　　2012

List of Works / 作品列表

Page 42
The City Bull / 城市公牛, 2012
Stainless steel / 不锈钢
43 x 140 x 29 cm

Page 43
The City Bull Part / 城市公牛局部, 2012
Stainless steel / 不锈钢
43 x 140 x 29 cm

Page 44
The City Bull / 城市公牛, 2012
Stainless steel / 不锈钢
406 x 1305 x 258 cm

Page 46
The Illusor Part / 幻界局部, 2012
Stainless steel / 不锈钢
204 x 169 x 175 cm

Page 47
The Illusor / 幻界, 2012
Stainless steel / 不锈钢
204 x 169 x 175 cm

Page 48
Reincarnation of Mammoth in Kassel / 猛犸复活
在卡塞尔展出, 2012
Stainless steel / 不锈钢
600 x 920 x 282 cm

Page 50
Solo Exhibition, *Exotic Landscapes* exhibition
site / 异度风景个展现场, 2012
Stainless steel / 不锈钢

Pages 52, 66
God of Materialism / 物神, 2008
Painted fiberglass / 玻璃钢着色
200 x 365 x 252 cm

Page 60
Homunculus / 侏儒, 2005
Spray painted fiberglass / 玻璃钢烤漆
340 x 240 x 132 cm

Page 61
Homunculus Draft / 侏儒, 2005
Clay / 粘土
340 x 240 x 132 cm

Pages 62, 63
5.12 No. 1 12th May No. 1 , 2008
Mixed media / 综合材料
98 x 202 x 202 cm

Page 64
Uninvited Guest / 不速之客, 2008
Mixed media / 综合材料
400 x 255 x 235 cm

Page 103
Childhood-Horizon / 童年-海平线, 2010
Spray coated bronze / 铜烤漆
210 x 280 x 220 cm

Page 104
Red memory-Smile / 红色记忆-笑, 2007
Spray coated bronze / 铜烤漆
270 x 150 x 202 cm

Page 105
Childhood-Games / 童年-游戏, 2010
Spray coated bronze / 铜烤漆
201 x 60 x 50 cm

Pages 106–107
Childhood-Harbor / 童年-港湾, 2011
Spray coated bronze / 铜烤漆
205 x 215 x 660 cm

Page 108
Childhood-Horizon / 童年-海平线, 2010
Spray coated bronze / 铜烤漆
210 x 280 x 220 cm

Page 109
Childhood-Aubade / 童年-晨曲, 2011
Spray coated bronze / 铜烤漆
188 x 55 x 40 cm

Pages 110, 118
Happy Life No. 22 part / 幸福生活 NO.22局部, 2008
Painted bronze / 铜着色
185 x 87 x 87 cm

Page 116
Happy Life No. 6 / 幸福生活NO.6, 2003
Painted bronze / 铜着色
219 x 146 x 91 cm

Page 117
Happy Life No. 1 / 幸福生活NO.1, 2005
Spray painted fiberglass / 玻璃钢烤漆
220 x 140 x 130 cm

Page 119
Happy Life exhibition site / 幸福生活系列展出现场, 2005
Spray painted fiberglass / 玻璃钢烤漆

Page 119
Happy Life No. 2 / 幸福生活NO.2, 2005
Spray painted fiberglass / 玻璃钢烤漆
223 x 135 x 130 cm

Page 120
Happy Life No. 12 / 幸福生活NO.12, 2005
Painted bronze / 铜着色
48 x 60 x 24 cm

Page 121
Happy Life No. 21 / 幸福生活NO.21, 2008
Painted bronze / 铜着色
175 x 110 x 63 cm

Page 122
Valiant Struggle No. 1 / 英勇奋斗NO.1, 2006
Spray painted bronze / 铜烤漆
378 x 160 x 250 cm

Page 130
Valiant Struggle No. 11 / 英勇奋斗NO.11, 2006
Spray painted fiberglass / 玻璃钢烤漆
750 x 480 x 210 cm

Page 131
Valiant Struggle No. 10 / 英勇奋斗NO.10, 2006
Painted fiberglass   / 玻璃钢着色
310 x 150 x 130 cm

Page 132
China Scene No. 6 Part / 中国风景NO.6局部, 2008
Stainless steel / 不锈钢
290 x 480 x 380 cm

Pages 146, 147
Mingled Scene / 混杂的风景, 2007
Mixed media / 综合材料
274 x 215 x 120 cm

Pages 148-149
China Scene No. 1 / 中国风景NO.1, 2007
Stainless steel / 不锈钢
480 x 665 x 313 cm

Pages 150, 151
China Scene No. 1 / 中国风景 NO.1, 2007
Stainless steel / 不锈钢
155 x 182 x 100 cm

Page 152
China Scene No. 3 / 中国风景NO.3, 2007
Stainless steel / 不锈钢
520 x 330 x 310 cm

Page 153
China Scene No. 2 / 中国风景NO.2, 2007
Stainless steel / 不锈钢
505 x 486 x 230 cm

Pages 154, 156
China Scene No. 4 / 中国风景NO.4, 2007
Stainless steel / 不锈钢
97 x 147 x 67 cm

Pages 155, 157
China Scene No. 4 Part / 中国风景NO.4局部, 2007
Stainless steel / 不锈钢
405 x 608 x 265 cm

Pages 158–159
China Scene No. 6 / 中国风景NO.6, 2008
Stainless steel / 不锈钢
290 x 480 x 380 cm

Pages 160–161
Humanities Landscape / 人文山水, 2011
Stainless steel / 不锈钢
98 x 393 x 73 cm

Page 162
Freeze No. 2 / 凝固No.2, 2008
Photograph / 摄影
diameter / 直径 78.5 cm

Page 167
Freeze No. 8 / 凝固No.8, 2012
Photograph / 摄影
diameter / 直径 60 cm

Page 168
Freeze No. 4 / 凝固No.4, 2012
Photograph / 摄影
diameter / 直径 81 cm

Page 169
Freeze No. 5 / 凝固No.5, 2012
Photograph / 摄影
diameter / 直径 62 cm

Page 170
Freeze No. 6 / 凝固No.6, 2012
Photograph / 摄影
diameter / 直径 72 cm

Page 171
Freeze No. 7 / 凝固No.7, 2012
Photograph / 摄影
diameter / 直径 39.5 cm

Page 172
Freeze No. 9 / 凝固No.9, 2012
Photograph / 摄影
diameter / 直径 27.5 cm

Page 173
Freeze No. 10 / 凝固No.10, 2012
Photograph / 摄影
diameter / 直径 79 cm

Page 174
Freeze No. 11 / 凝固No.11, 2012
Photograph / 摄影
diameter / 直径 76.5 cm

Page 175
Freeze No. 25 / 凝固No.25, 2012
Photograph / 摄影
diameter / 直径 74 cm

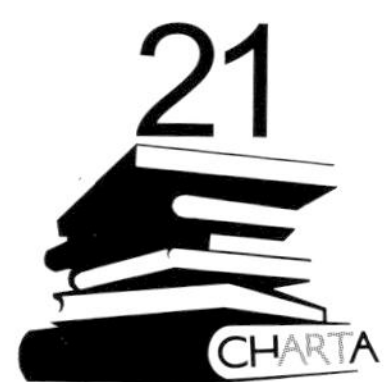